JOURNEYS IN SOCIOLOGY

D1521143

JOURNEYS in SOCIOLOGY

From First Encounters to Fulfilling Retirements

Edited by

ROSALYN BENJAMIN DARLING

and PETER J. STEIN

American Sociological Association
Opportunities in Retirement Network

TEMPLE UNIVERSITY PRESS
Philadelphia • *Rome* • *Tokyo*

TEMPLE UNIVERSITY PRESS
Philadelphia, Pennsylvania 19122
www.temple.edu/tempress

Copyright © 2017 by the American Sociological Association
All rights reserved
Published 2017

Library of Congress Cataloging-in-Publication Data

Names: Darling, Rosalyn Benjamin, editor. | Stein, Peter J., 1937– editor.
Title: Journeys in sociology : from first encounters to fulfilling retirements / edited by
    Rosalyn Benjamin Darling and Peter J. Stein.
Description: Philadelphia : Temple University Press, 2017. | Includes bibliographical
    references and index.
Identifiers: LCCN 2016042258 (print) | LCCN 2016057149 (ebook) | ISBN 9781439914748
    (cloth : alk. paper) | ISBN 9781439914755 (pbk. : alk. paper) | ISBN 9781439914762
    (E-Book)
Subjects: LCSH: Sociologists—United States. | Sociology—United States.
Classification: LCC HM478 .J68 2017 (print) | LCC HM478 (ebook) | DDC 301.0973—dc23
LC record available at https://lccn.loc.gov/2016042258

♾ The paper used in this publication meets the requirements of the American National
Standard for Information Sciences—Permanence of Paper for Printed Library Materials,
ANSI Z39.48-1992

Printed in the United States of America

9 8 7 6 5 4 3 2 1

To the memory of our mentors, Joseph F. Zygmunt, Wilbert Moore, and Suzanne Keller, and past coauthors Beth Hess and Liz Markson

Contents

Acknowledgments

This book is the result of the efforts of many individuals. We are especially grateful to Karen Gray Edwards of the American Sociological Association (ASA), who has been supportive of both the formation of the Opportunities in Retirement Network (ORN) and the concept for this book. She has served as our intermediary in proposing the book to the ASA and in working with Temple University Press to negotiate our publishing arrangements. We have continually relied on her good judgment and support. Thanks go, too, to Craig Schaar of the ASA for his clerical assistance.

We also owe a debt of gratitude to our volunteer peer reviewers, some of whom read more than their share of manuscripts and who were always willing to read "just one more" and to return their reviews in a timely manner. Our thanks go to Barbara Altman, Vern Bengtson, Jon Darling, the late Tuck Green, Debra Kaufman, John Kennedy, Corinne Kirchner, Scott McNall, Fred Pincus, Susan Prager, Mike Schutz, Natalie Sokoloff, Tom VanValey, and Joyce Williams. They provided insightful comments that enabled our authors to improve their work and to communicate their ideas in a more readable way.

We are, of course, indebted to our authors, who volunteered to share their stories and who graciously accepted our editing suggestions and those of our reviewers. Our primary concern in editing was to ensure the inclusion of all of the elements in our call for submissions. In general, we edited very lightly, allowing this group of distinguished sociologists to speak for themselves.

We also appreciate the efforts of Micah Kleit, our first editor at Temple University Press, who enthusiastically supported this book from the beginning and who shepherded it through the approval process. Aaron Javsicas, our second editor, was helpful in moving the manuscript from acceptance to publication, and we are grateful to Nikki Miller, editorial assistant and rights and contracts coordinator, whose pleasantness and efficiency have made the publication process as painless as possible. We also thank Rebecca Logan for her patience and assistance with the copyediting phase of our project and for her excellent suggestions. Finally, we thank Moira Johnson for creating the index.

Finally, as always, we appreciate the support of our families. Roz's husband, Jon, helped in many ways—and probably read more manuscripts as a peer reviewer than anyone else. Peter's wife, Michele Murdock, was supportive of our venture in many ways, including reading Peter's drafts. Both Jon and Michele were involved in many of our discussions, usually over dinner, about various aspects of the book.

JOURNEYS IN SOCIOLOGY

Introduction

ROSALYN BENJAMIN DARLING

This book grew out of my personal journey. In 2008, I made the decision to retire from a career in sociological practice and teaching and to relocate to a new community. However, like most major life decisions, mine was associated with anxiety about the correctness of my choices. After more than thirty years in Pennsylvania, my husband and I moved to what had been our vacation house on the western shore of the Chesapeake Bay in Maryland—an interim step in our eventual decision to relocate to Chapel Hill, North Carolina. Other than my husband, I knew of no other retired sociologists nearby and thought that knowing others at a similar life stage would be interesting and also supportive in alleviating the loss of a professional identity that comes with the transition to retirement.

That year, the Eastern Sociological Society (ESS) meetings were conveniently held in Baltimore. I contacted a friend and fellow sociologist, Natalie Sokoloff, who had not yet retired, and asked whether she would like to co-organize a session for sociologists who were retired or contemplating retirement. She enthusiastically agreed, and our session was well received. We had clearly struck a chord among colleagues at a similar career stage, and the ESS Opportunities in Retirement Network (ORN) was born. Although I am no longer directly involved, this group has continued to have an annual session at the ESS meetings.

In 2010, my husband, Jon, and I took the next step in our retirement journey, sold the house in Maryland, and moved to Fearrington Village (near Chapel Hill), a community consisting largely of retired professionals from many fields, including a few sociologists. Finding kindred spirits was not so difficult here, and Jon and I were able to get together with Peter Stein, a retired sociologist friend living in Chapel Hill, and Tuck Green, a retired sociologist also living in Fearrington Village. We talked about how the opportunity to participate in a group like ours was probably not an option for many retirees, and I proposed the possibility of a national ORN associated with the American Sociological Association (ASA).

Peter contacted ASA to set up a meeting, and in October 2013, Jon, Peter, and I met with Sally Hillsman and many members of her staff in Washington. They were very supportive of our idea and asked us to write a formal proposal for presentation to the ASA council. With the assistance of Jon, Peter, Tuck, and Karen Edwards, who had been assigned as our ASA liaison, I put together a proposal to create ORN as an official component of ASA, and the proposal was approved. Sadly, Tuck passed away before this book was published, but he did live to see the creation of both the national ORN and a retirement component that he initiated in the Midwest Sociological Society.

One of the first outcomes of the establishment of ORN was the creation of a Listserv for retired/emeritus members of ASA. The response was overwhelming! Numerous famous and not-so-famous retired sociologists posted messages about their activities in retirement. Many expressed their appreciation for a way to lessen their feelings of isolation from colleagues. I even connected with my first sociology professor at Harpur College (now SUNY's Binghamton University), Paul Eberts, whom I had never before thanked for introducing me to the field that would become my career.

Reading so many interesting stories of life in retirement gave me the idea for this book. I thought, "These could be expanded into chapters that would be fascinating to others at various career stages." I thought the book would be useful to sociologists and other professionals who were retired or contemplating retirement, as well as to students thinking about a career in sociology. A book of this nature also seemed to have potential value for courses on the sociology of aging, the life course, or occupations. So I asked Peter whether he would be interested in coediting such a book, and he agreed. We talked to Karen Edwards about publication under the auspices of ASA, and she got permission to publish our work as an e-book. Later in the process, we approached a number of university presses about the possibility of publishing a hard copy, and Temple University Press enthusiastically agreed to be a partner in the publication process.

Through the Listserv and a notice in *Footnotes*, ASA's newsletter, we issued a call for submissions, asking contributors to use a life-course perspective and to address the role of sociology in their lives. We eventually received manuscripts from twenty-two individuals, all of whom have had very productive careers. Each manuscript was sent to three peer reviewers, and most of the authors were asked to revise and resubmit their work. We accepted twenty of the revised manuscripts for publication in this book. Some of our later submissions came from our peer reviewers, who were inspired to write their own stories after reading the accounts of others. Because these essays are memoirs, we decided to minimize citations, which are generally found in more academic works.

Although the authors responded appropriately to our call for submissions, their approaches varied considerably. Some presented a more or less straightforward account of their lives from childhood through retirement, whereas others chose to focus on a particular time period. For example, Natalie Sokoloff discusses in depth the process involved in making the decision to retire. Janet Giele chose to include commonalities in the lives of other sociologists who grew up in the same Ohio county as she did. We think these diverse approaches add interest to the book.

Although I enjoyed writing and editing all of my academic articles and books in the past, this project turned out to be enjoyable in a different way, because these authors' accounts were so interesting to read. I was especially fascinated by the stories of working-class roots, like Bob Perrucci's, and stories of encounters with famous sociologists of the past, like Ed Tiryakian's. I was also struck by the parallels between the nonlinear careers of so many of the women and my own circuitous career path. Taken as a whole, these accounts are a fascinating microcosm of the twentieth century, including the Great Depression, World War II, the student protests and social movements of the 1960s and 1970s, and so much social change.

In his inaugural lecture in the ORN "A Life in Sociology" series, delivered at the ASA meetings in Chicago in 2015, Earl Babbie described his career as that of an "accidental sociologist." This description also fits the essays in this book. None of our authors grew up planning to become a sociologist; probably few children and adolescents do. Rather, these stories confirmed what I already knew as a symbolic interactionist—being in the right situation at the right time makes a difference. In virtually all of the essays, the author describes an encounter or series of encounters, typically with a mentor or significant other, that became a turning point leading to a career in sociology. Bob Perrucci's story of staying in college as a result of a chance encounter with an old friend is a great example.

In addition to accidental turning points, certain kinds of experiences seem to have occurred with relative frequency in this group of sociologists. Quite a few were involved in activism, often early in their lives. Several were involved in the well-known student protests at Berkeley. Many others had somewhat unconventional families of origin that differed in politics, ethnicity, or religion from those of others in their communities. Exposure to nonnormative ideas may have played a role in predisposing these individuals to choose sociology as a career.

Because so many of the essays include experiences in common, Peter and I discussed various ways of grouping them. The clearest difference was gender based. Most of the women's stories reflected the norm of male dominance that prevailed during much of the last century. I could easily identify with Debra Kaufman and Elinore Lurie, whose careers, like mine, took a backseat to those of their husbands for a time. Most of the men had more linear career paths, although military service intervened in some cases. Predictably, family life and child rearing also figured more prominently in the women's accounts.

We also considered separating those with more traditional, middle-class roots, like Janet Giele (and the fellow Ohio-born sociologists she discusses), Tuck Green, and Glen Elder, from the "outsiders," like Peter Hall, who grew up with a sense of differentness because his parents were Communists (in fact, two of our authors, Peter Hall and Fred Pincus, were "red diaper babies"), or Joyce Williams, who was negatively labeled because of her family's poverty. Art Shostak and David Simon both describe growing up Jewish in a non-Jewish community. Elizabeth Higginbotham describes her marginality as an African American woman in various settings.

Another small group of essays reveals the power of personal experience in determining a chosen field of study. Both Tom Scheff and Hank Fischer write movingly about how difficult life experiences led them to study sociology (Fischer) or to focus on a particular area within the field (Scheff). Both Tuck Green and Wendell Bell describe early experiences with low-wage laborers that made them more aware of social inequality and perhaps influenced their later decisions to become sociologists.

We eventually decided to simply group the essays chronologically, based on the year of the author's birth. For the first grouping, "Children of the Great Depression," we borrowed the title of one of our authors' (Glen Elder) books and include those born between 1924 and 1935. These writers' accounts truly reflect the sweep of history during the last century, and many were students of iconic American sociologists. The second grouping, "Coming of Age in the Postwar Years," includes authors born between 1937 and 1948, who generally have retired a little more recently. This division is rather arbitrary, and some of our older authors have more in common with our younger authors than they do with their agemates.

We asked each contributor to include a discussion of his or her activities in retirement. Clearly, these individuals are *busy*. Some continue to teach—in a variety of settings. Many continue to do research and write. For some, retirement is an opportunity to explore subjects of interest that were not pursued during the working years (Hank Fischer is probably the only sociologist to have published an article on the ebony jewelwing dragonfly). Still others are engaging in volunteer work and social and political activism, often making use of their sociological expertise, or finding new interests, such as genealogy or art. Retirement also offers more time for friends and family. In his nineties, Wendell Bell and his wife are still enjoying ballroom dancing; may their tango last for many more years!

Although we included only essays we received in response to our call for submissions, I continue to encounter wonderful stories of life in retirement. Just recently, I attended a talk by John Shelton Reed, a sociologist who retired from the University of North Carolina at Chapel Hill and who now travels in search of "true 'cue" (barbecue using a wood fire). He has just published his second book of recipes. We hope that you enjoy reading these stories as much as we did and find them useful in charting your own journeys.

PART I

Children of the Great Depression

1

Toward a Sociology of the Future

WENDELL BELL

The Trek West

I was born in Chicago in 1924 to a nineteen-year-old mother who had dropped out of high school and a nineteen-year-old father who was work- ing as a bricklayer for his contractor father. Home life was tumultuous, with occasional parties during which too much alcohol was consumed, often fol- lowed by arguments, shouting, and slamming of doors. My mother was not happy.

Nearby, my maternal grandmother was not happy either, because my grandfather, a traveling salesman for Marshall Field's department store, had affairs with other women, drank too much, and often responded to her con- cerns with an angry rant.

My mother and her mother both left their husbands at the same time. In 1929 they took me by train to Fresno, California, because that was where my great-grandfather, A. D. Robinson, had settled. For a time he had been in charge of the farmers' market that formed twice a week next to Courthouse Park. Later, he became city license clerk, a job he held for many years before he died in his late nineties.

This chapter draws from Wendell Bell, "From Fresno to the Future," in *Intellectual Trajectories*, vol. 1, ed. David E. Apter and Patricia Dallai (New Haven, CT: Yale University Koerner Center, 2009), 37–55. I thank the Koerner Center for permission to use this work. For photos illustrating this chapter, see http://www.wendellbell.com/gallery.

Growing Up

Fresno is where I grew up. I took for granted, as most of us kids did, the beautiful blue skies, the sunshine, and the views of the snow-capped peaks of the Sierra Nevadas. My grandmother stayed home and took care of me while my mother went out to work. Although times were tough, my mother quickly found a job as a clerk for the Sun-Maid raisin company. Soon, she became a bookkeeper at a Kut Price Drugstore. Barely, we managed to survive the Depression years.

I was oblivious of the worries and struggles these two women faced. I was having a great time, going to school and playing with my friends. During childhood and adolescence, family, friends, and teachers dominated my life. But two other things also affected me greatly. The first was reading. It began with my grandmother reading aloud to me. She started with children's books, but before long she simply picked the books she liked and read to me from those. As I got older, I read more and more on my own. I devoured everything I could lay my hands on, especially stories about World War I flying, such as the pulp-fiction periodicals *G8 and His Battle Aces* and *Daredevil Aces*.

The second thing that influenced me was working. My mother didn't like to see me sitting around "doing nothing." She often would see me reading and scornfully say, "Why are you wasting your time reading a book?" Yet she tolerated reading. But she did not tolerate just lazing around. Thus, I was prodded and nagged to get after-school and summer jobs. Looking back, I see my work experiences as important in making me sensitive to the inequalities and injustices of race, class, gender, and power in the everyday lives of people and motivating me to understand the world through the eyes of others.

When I started working, at about the age of ten, I sold magazines such as *Collier's* and the *Saturday Evening Post* door to door. Then I got an after-school job with a candy distributor. I worked in his garage filling small plastic bags with various candies and putting on labels.

The hard physical labor started later, when I got a job one summer digging Johnson grass out of vineyards. In summer the temperatures hover in the nineties and can rise above one hundred degrees. Tending the fields and crops is hot, hard work.

In the vineyards, I had a workmate, "Delipah," an immigrant from India, a Sikh who wore a turban even in the terrible heat. The boss would get us started in the morning and then leave us to do the work. Delipah and I would each pick a row of vines and dig out the Johnson grass. Delipah would often come help me keep up with him by working some on my rows.

I worked another summer in orchards picking peaches, more slowly despite my efforts, than most of my Mexican coworkers. I had some relatively easy jobs too: working as a clerk and fountain server at the College Pharmacy, working as a salesman in Harry Coffee's upscale men's clothing store, and cleaning and repairing cash registers for the National Cash Register Company.

Then came more physical labor—working on a bull gang at a warehouse of United Grocers, next to the Santa Fe railroad yard. I had this job just after graduating from high school, mostly while I was waiting to get into the navy. I emptied freight cars and trucks, moving the contents (from boxes filled with cans of Campbell's soup, olives, carrots, or green beans, etc., to 100-pound sacks of sugar and 150-pound sacks of salt), and stacking them in the warehouse, often almost to the ceiling. Eventually, I was promoted to loading the trucks that took deliveries to grocery stores.

Generally, we worked in "gangs" of two, three, or four. The other workers were mostly Italian Americans, who seemed to have a near monopoly on the warehouse jobs. In the course of working all day—or part of the night while loading trucks—our minds were free and we could talk. So I learned the life stories of most of the people with whom I worked and found them fascinating, if sometimes heartbreaking.

I am indebted to them for telling me their stories and revealing to me the common humanity we share. But some of them already seemed totally burned out and defeated in their early or mid-thirties. Thus, they taught me that I did not want to do that type of work for the rest of my life.

Men of Raenford

Earlier, when I was about thirteen, a friend of mine went off to be a cadet at the Raenford Military Academy, located in the San Fernando Valley at the edge of the Santa Monica Mountains. When he showed me the brochure, I started nagging my mother to send me there. She finally investigated Raenford and decided to let me go.

I spent a storybook two and a half years at Raenford. I learned close-order drill, became a cadet officer, had mandatory study hall five nights a week, took eight solid courses each term, was active in sports (swimming, basketball, fencing, and football), and went to dances at a local girls' school.

Raenford was where some members of the motion-picture industry sent their children. Most of the students were from the nearby area and went home on weekends. Film stars like Barbara Stanwyck, Robert Taylor, Constance Bennett, and Chester Morris came to pick them up. Darryl F. Zanuck, then head of Twentieth Century Fox, had a polo field within walking distance of the school on which we practiced football. Miss Horton, who ran the dining hall at Raenford, was the sister of actor Edward Everett Horton, whom we saw frequently. For our school plays we went to a major-studio costume department to be outfitted.

Although I found it thrilling to routinely see and live among so many Hollywood celebrities, for me what was more significant about Raenford was its library. The few students, like myself, who didn't live in the local area, spent their weekends at Raenford. We went for hikes, swam in the large pool, and played basketball. Occasionally, we hitchhiked to Hollywood and saw a movie on Saturday afternoon. But most of all we read, curled up in one of the big leather chairs in the library. I read hundreds of books at Raenford and skimmed many more. I read everything, from T. E. Lawrence's *Seven Pillars of Wisdom* to all of Edgar Rice Burroughs's Tarzan series, as well as his books of science fiction. I wanted to read every book in the library, and the range was great.

Return to Public School

I decided to return to public school in Fresno for my last year and a half of high school. Roosevelt High School was conveniently located just a block from where my mother and her new husband then lived.

Then came December 7, 1941, and the Japanese attack on Pearl Harbor. Young men from all over Fresno lined up to enlist for military service, including many Roosevelt seniors set to graduate in January 1942. Since I already had enough credits to graduate, I chose to graduate with them, instead of waiting until my scheduled graduation in June.

But when I tried to sign up for the V-5 Naval Aviation Cadet Program, they told me that I was too young and to come back when I was eighteen. My dream was to be a naval aviator, so I decided to wait until my birthday. By then, however, there was a backlog of young men like myself in the Navy Reserve. Thus, I had a waiting period before being called to active duty. I was frustrated by the delay. Looking back, I realize that the delay may have saved my life. I was called to begin training May 12, 1943.

Flying during and after World War II

I spent three full years on active duty in the navy. On October 18, 1944, I received my wings of gold and became an officer and a naval aviator. Then I began operational training. I traveled throughout the United States, the Bahamas, Cuba, Hawaii, and finally across the Pacific, ending up in the Philippines.

I have many flying stories, but I won't tell them here. Yet several things about my navy experience definitely helped shape my future. The first and most important was that I qualified for the GI Bill, which, after the war, would help pay for both my college and graduate school educations.

Second, for a period of about ten months, I served as copilot for a senior officer who was a task unit commander. Working for him gave me insight into the decisions that defined our world in the navy. Sometimes these decisions were mistakes and had to be corrected. It was a constant process of monitoring the results of decisions and actions, rethinking, and, if necessary, making changes in beliefs, tactics, and strategies.

Third, I learned that the success of a mission often depended on the ingenuity of the lower-ranking officers and enlisted men who carried out the orders. If going by the book meant we weren't achieving our objectives, we often threw out the book and improvised. One way or another, in our group we got three squadrons of planes and their crews into the air every day.

Fourth, when I was a member of a squadron stationed on the Philippine island of Samar, one of our duties was to fly into typhoons, gathering weather information and tracking the eye of the storm. Where was the typhoon going? Both navy and other officials acted on this information—for example, to order ships and planes moved out of the typhoon's predicted path and to alert military personnel and civilians. This experience helped make me a future-oriented sociologist later in my life because I had witnessed the importance of foresight—in this case, to prevent damage and loss of life by knowing some small aspect of the probable future.

Fifth, my navy flying experiences gave me a sense of confidence in my abilities to learn and to function among very capable and talented people. For example, in my first assignment at Flight Training School, I became the cadet battalion commander.

Sixth, if you'll excuse the apparent contradiction, flying is a down-to-earth activity. When on a collision course with a mountain, you don't pause for a philosophical discussion on parallel universes, the postmodern meaning of truth, or whether or not a mountain is really real. Hit it and splat, you're injured or dead!

Seventh was the devastation of war. Although the fighting had ended by the time I reached the Philippines, its effects were everywhere: the sunken and partially sunken ships in Manila Bay; the destruction still visible in Manila, with occasional piles of rubble and bullet holes in the walls of buildings; displaced people whose homes had been destroyed; Filipinos struggling to find work at the American military bases; families living in caves near our base on Samar.

For a few glorious months after the war, I earned my living as a commercial pilot, qualifying for my flight instructor's license within a few days. In addition to teaching local businessmen and others to fly, I worked as a charter pilot, flying passengers and ferrying aircraft to various destinations. On weekends, I sometimes did stunt flying at air shows.

College and Graduate School

In the latter part of 1946, I enrolled at Fresno State University and loaded up with courses. As college demanded more and more of my time, I gradually stopped flying. In 1947–1948, I served as student president, campaigning with the slogan "Student government is like a kiss; you have to share it to enjoy it," which at the time I thought was pretty clever.

In a political science class, I met a gorgeous young woman named Lora-Lee Edwards, and within a year we were married. (Today, as I write, Lora-Lee and I are looking forward to our seventieth wedding anniversary.)

I was very busy at Fresno State, making up for lost time and learning a lot from some dedicated teachers, including Professor Earl Lyon in the English Department.

How did I end up in sociology? At Fresno State, I majored in social science, thinking that I wanted to go on to law school. Before graduation, however, I changed my mind and told Professor Lyon that I wanted to do graduate work in English, hoping to become a professor and maybe, eventually, a writer. "My field is bankrupt," he said. "Try sociology, a developing field with a future!"

He recommended the University of California, Los Angeles (UCLA), where a former roommate from his graduate school days at UC Berkeley, Walter Goldschmidt, was on the faculty of the Department of Anthropology and Sociology. Probably not fully understanding the difference, Lyon had said "sociology," even though Goldschmidt was an anthropologist. As a result, I applied to the program in sociology instead of anthropology. Chance and error, of course, may enter into the best-laid plans, as they obviously did here.

In January 1949, Lora-Lee and I put everything we owned into our old, gold DeSoto and drove to Los Angeles, where I had been accepted for graduate work in sociology at UCLA. We lived in subsidized veterans housing, popularly known as "Fertile Valley," and paid our bills mostly with money from the GI Bill and my teaching assistantship.

Thanks to Professor Leonard Broom I got involved in studying the social areas of Los Angeles and San Francisco, building on the work of Eshref Shevky, who was also one of my professors at UCLA. Among other things, I was able to demonstrate that three major variables (socioeconomic status, familism, and ethnicity) accurately summarized the many social variations among city dwellers and that neighborhoods could be usefully classified into different social areas according to these variables. After Shevky and I published our book *Social Area Analysis*, many other researchers carried out the construction of social areas not only in American cities but also in a comparative framework in many cities throughout the world.

People of the City

When I went to my first full-time faculty job at Stanford University in 1952, I was put in charge of directing a new survey research center. Although this took a good portion of my time, I was able to pursue my own work on social areas as well. I wanted to go out into the neighborhoods and study the residents. Thus, I conducted sample surveys in selected social areas in San Francisco, interviewing hundreds of people about their beliefs, attitudes, and behaviors.

My research showed that many of the generalizations of the time about the lonely, anomic, socially isolated city dweller were oversimplifications. In fact, only a few social areas typically contained such people. Many social areas, to the contrary, were characterized by frequent participation with neighbors, relatives, coworkers, or other friends, often supplemented by attendance at meetings and events of a variety of formal social organizations, as well as a well-developed sense of community.

Following Shevky, I worked with a theory of social choice, focusing on how people decided to seek certain lifestyles as evidenced by the types of social areas in which they chose to live. In viewing the cityscape as a product of individual and collective decision making and deliberate action, I went beyond the theory of city development based on impersonal, unconscious, natural forces then associated with the Chicago school of "human ecology."

After moving to Northwestern University in 1954, I continued my urban research. In the 1950s the United States was undergoing a migration to the suburbs. The standard view at the time was generally negative. Much was being written about "cracks in the picture window," "split-level headaches," and "the suburban sadness." I did studies in Chicago city neighborhoods focused on what people liked or did not like about their neighborhoods and why people had moved to the suburbs.

As people were deciding to make a move from the city to a suburb, they knew their present situation in the city and what their past experience had been. They also had an *image of the future* of what life would be like after moving to the suburbs. What I found, contrary to much of the condemnation of the suburbs, was that most people who moved there were satisfied. They moved to the suburbs seeking a better place for their children, a sense of community, and larger and better housing—and that was what they found.

The Decisions of Nationhood in the Caribbean

In 1956, Lora-Lee and I spent the summer in Jamaica, where I intended to construct the social areas of Kingston. On arriving, however, we found ourselves in the middle of Jamaica's political transition from a British colony to independent state. Everyone from sugarcane workers to the merchant elite, and from market women to university professors, seemed to be interested only in what would happen to Jamaica (and to themselves) when the island became politically independent. I confess to becoming totally caught up in their excitement, their hopes, and their fears for the future. So I switched my research to study the transition to political independence.

During the next twenty-five or so years, with the help of both American and West Indian graduate students, I investigated how the decisions of nationhood were being made in former British colonies as they went through the processes of becoming politically independent states—from Jamaica in the north through Antigua, Barbados, Dominica, Grenada, and other territories to Trinidad and Tobago and Guyana in the south. Descendants of African slaves or East Indian indentured laborers numerically dominated the populations of these emergent states.

At UCLA, where I had moved in 1957, we studied the new nationalist leaders in these territories as they set about constructing their new states' futures. In addition to writing constitutions, the leaders chose national mottoes, flags, heroes, flowers, birds, and other symbols that would signify the character and meaning of their new states.

More important, the former subjects and their leaders decided what geographic boundaries their new state would have; what kind of government it would have; what role the government should play in regulating the economy; what kind of social structure the state should have (e.g., how could it put an end to racial inequality and create more equal opportunity?); what national character of the people should be encouraged (e.g., should it be an egalitarian and inclusive character freed from the heritages of slavery, indentured labor, and an authoritarian social system?); what new national cultural traditions to foster (e.g., should the African and East Indian origins of the majority of the people be celebrated, and should a new national history be written that emphasized the long struggle for freedom against oppression?); and what global alliances the new state should make as it stepped onto the international stage.

With the help of graduate students from Yale, where I had moved in 1963, we did follow-up studies to evaluate the performance of the new national leaders after they came to power. We wanted to find out how successful they had been in realizing their preindependence goals and their earlier positive, idealistic images of their new states' futures. To find answers, we looked at changes in the leaders' rhetoric and beliefs, the social legislation they had enacted, and other relevant economic and social indicators.

Over the years, we conducted many studies focusing on different issues throughout the Caribbean. Although much of our research centered on leaders, we also studied students, slum dwellers, and sugar-factory workers.

Becoming a Futurist

Starting about the mid-1960s, I began to explore the principles of futures thinking and the role of images of the future in decision making and social action. A major focus was on how choices, decisions, and social action shaped and reshaped social institutions and structures, not simply on how social order shaped human action. With the publication of *The Sociology of the Future*, jointly edited with James A. Mau, I started devoting most of my research and teaching to the new field of futures studies.

Everywhere, people produce some part of the coming future by their acts, whether they are aware of it or not. Everywhere, the images of the future some people hold may clash with images held by others. Everywhere, the past is finished and cannot be altered, although *ideas* about the past can be changed. And everywhere the future offers possibilities of new and better lives, as well as possibilities of disaster. Often, the realization of these possibilities is contingent on the choices humans make and the actions they take.

This is not to say that the future always turns out as people hope and plan. There may be unintended, unanticipated, or unrecognized consequences of human action. People don't always know what they are doing. Also, there are natural forces beyond human control. Constant monitoring is necessary, as is a willingness to change one's methods and policies when they are not working as planned.

As I approached retirement age, I was committed to trying to understand the role of futures thinking in social change—on the one hand, to discover how images of the future are born and shaped and, on the other hand, to learn how images of the future interact with individual and collective beliefs, values, decision making, and actions to shape the futures of individuals, societies, and cultures. I kept asking, what constitutes a better world, and how can we humans help to bring such a better world into reality?

In a world dominated by corporations, government bureaucracies, and other social institutions and organizations, the individual person may seem unimportant, without power or influence. Yet that view is an incomplete understanding of social realities. In fact, each of us human beings is in most situations a more or less conscious and controlling agent of our own actions as we move through the routines of everyday life. Thus, a full and complete social analysis requires bringing individual people into the equation as active, purposeful, future-oriented, and creative actors. Each day by their actions they contribute to the creation of our experienced social realities, often reinforcing but sometimes reshaping social and cultural patterns.

Retirement

By 1990, I had become deeply involved in trying to produce a work of synthesis that would contribute to establishing the study of the future as an accepted organized body of knowledge and to help create a professional community of futurists. But at my then-rate of writing I might never get it finished in my lifetime. Thus, I arranged with Yale to start phased retirement (working for Yale only about one-quarter of the time) for four years beginning in 1991, after which (in 1995 at age seventy) I would retire fully.

Thus, I began my retirement by significantly *increasing* my work on what would be become the two-volume *Foundations of Futures Studies*. Volume 1, *History, Purposes, and Knowledge*, is focused on possible and probable futures and how we can make grounded, reliable, and valid assertions about them. Volume 2, *Values, Objectivity, and the Good Society*, deals with preferable futures and how we can justify, both theoretically and empirically, assertions about what is good.

Also, I increased my participation in sociology and futures conferences. Focusing on the study of the future, I gave keynote addresses, delivered papers, published more articles, gave lectures and workshops, and so on in, among other places, Canada, Finland, Iceland, Japan, Mexico, Spain, Taiwan, Wales, and in the United States (Maxwell Air Force Base in Alabama; Boston; Chicago; Greensboro, North Carolina; New York; San Diego; San Francisco; Seattle; and Washington, D.C.).

Thus, I retired from Yale so I could spend more time working on the development of futures studies. I was able to continue to do so until I reached my late eighties, at which point for health reasons I had to start cutting back on both travel and new commitments for speaking or writing. I used the extra time, though, to write a memoir, *Memories of the Future*.

Conclusion: A Future Is Coming

Looking back, I was surprised to learn how important my early years were in setting the course for the rest of my life. In the simple, everyday experiences of childhood, I can see the beginning of interests that shaped my later years. They included early influences from my mother and grandmother and later from my calm and tolerant stepfather; classmates who helped me experiment with life; teachers to whom I am forever grateful for their teachings and encouragement; and my friends and colleagues.

I was surprised, too, to see how influential my early periods of reading had been. Stepping into a new world by opening the pages of a book was a life-changing act for me. In books, I vicariously experienced events, identifications, emotions, and moral judgments over a wide range of diverse human behaviors.

Working with a variety of people continued my lessons. From these real-life encounters, I learned that nearly anyone could commit a cruel act. Yet I also learned that nearly anyone is capable of kindness and helping others: my fellow vineyard worker, Delipah, who helped me; the Mexican peach pickers who accepted me; the Italian American warehousemen who shared their life stories with me; the capable navy pilots, who stressed competence and performance; the West Indian nationalist leaders, who had hopeful dreams for the future of their new states and worked to make them come true; and many others.

Teaching—helping young people move toward their desired futures, just as others have helped me—has given me some of my greatest pleasure, especially learning of accomplishments of former students. This is particularly true of graduate students, many of whom have become friends and professional colleagues and achieved far more in their lives than I have. By any objective assessment, I have learned as much from them as they have learned from me.

I must at least mention three other things that were important in sustaining me throughout my life. One was the twenty-three years Lora-Lee and I devoted to keeping horses and training in horse care and riding (dressage, cross-country, and stadium jumping). For Lora-Lee, it became a profession, and she taught riding to many students. We spent several occasions living in England and France, continuing our training in horsemanship, usually combined with my sociological work. Lora-Lee and I are convinced that caring for and riding horses over the years kept us much healthier and physically capable than we would have been otherwise. The second thing was ballroom dancing, which we took up after we felt we could no longer physically keep up all the work required to care for the horses. The dancing, like the horses, demanded physical activity and mental focus, which provided balance in our lives. And third was that Lora-Lee is an artist and taught art for more than forty years. Through her work she expanded our understandings and appreciation of life.

Although I have often failed, throughout much of my adult life I have tried to contribute, even in a small way, to a better future: to a sustainable world in which all people would coexist in peace; would enjoy freedom, fairness, and respect; and would live long, self-directed, socially beneficial, loving, and satisfying lives. And I have tried to work toward what Menno Boldt in his 2011 book, *A Quest for Humanity: The Good Society in a Global World*, calls "transcendent humanity":[1] no slamming of doors in the faces of other people. Rather, opening one's heart to others with empathy and understanding, recognizing the dignity of every human being, and showing respect for friend and stranger alike—and yes, also foe.

Most important of all has been the love and support given to me by my wife, Lora-Lee, and by our family. Now, at age ninety-two, I should probably stop working and instead spend time with Lora-Lee, enjoying together what's left of our lives—including getting back to our ballroom dancing. (Argentina and the tango still seductively beckon.)

---

1. Menno Boldt, *A Quest for Humanity: The Good Society in a Global World* (Toronto: University of Toronto Press, 2011), 204.

2

Semper Sociology

Edward A. Tiryakian

n 2004 I officially became "emeritus" but since then have remained active
in the profession. I welcome this opportunity to make a progress report of
my long career.

Preprofessional Period

Shortly after my birth on American soil, the great economic crash of 1929 severely affected our family and led to my mother taking me to France, where
her family lived. For the next nine years, I went to school in Nice and lived as
a young Frenchman, learning history though a French perspective (including that trouble frequently comes from across the Rhine). My self-identity
was jarred in the summer of 1941, when the American consul sent notice to
American citizens to consider returning home in the face of gathering war
clouds in Europe. My mother immediately responded by getting tickets on
an Italian ship leaving from Genoa, and we boarded the ship on September 1,
1941. I found it exciting that we were followed up to Gibraltar by a menacing
German submarine.

Once in the States, I found becoming an American relatively painless,
through the excellent public schools of Mount Vernon, New York, and participating in the available popular culture of sandlot games. A rare treat on
Sundays was walking with my father on Manhattan's East Side, past ethnic neighborhoods—perhaps a foundation for a future sociologist! In any
case the peak experience of my adolescence was giving the valedictorian

address on great contributors to science: Albert Einstein, Louis Pasteur, and Booker T. Washington.

My mainly halcyon college years were spent at Princeton (1948–1952). I was attracted to it perhaps because of its Wilsonian legacy of idealism in foreign affairs. In my sophomore year, I renounced a medical career but found a welcome major in sociology. I enjoyed special relationships with Mel Tumin, Marion Levy, and a young instructor, Harold Garfinkel, whose courses were exciting ventures into what he later termed "ethnomethodology." I thought of a career in public international law, to the dismay of my sociology advisers. As graduation approached, I naively thought of getting a J.D. and a Ph.D. as suitable preparation for a career in foreign affairs. I consequently applied to Yale and Harvard law schools, and, at the recommendation of Levy and Garfinkel, to Harvard's graduate sociology program. Accepted by Harvard on both counts, I ambitiously thought of two years of sociology in arts and science, two years of law, and a fifth doing a thesis on conflict resolution in the sociology of international law. However, I was to complete only the first part.

Becoming a Sociologist

The first weeks as a graduate student at Harvard in September 1952 were eventful, to say the least. My first appointment was a meeting with the director of graduate studies, Gordon Allport, a benign gentleman, delighted to see I had taken a course at Princeton with one of his best students of social psychology, Hadley Cantril. I immediately signed up for Allport's seminar in discrimination and prejudice. Shortly after, I had a brief meeting with my major adviser, Talcott Parsons, more reserved than Allport but kindly disposed to my interest in theory. Finding out that I had command of French, he recommended that I invest time reading Émile Durkheim in the original—advice that has served me well.

I went at lunchtime to the Graduate Center cafeteria and sat down next to a young man. We struck up a conversation, and he told me he had come to Harvard to specialize in political science. Noticing his accent, I asked him where he was from. "Poland," he replied, "but I have a difficult name." I smiled and said, "I have a difficult one myself. What's yours?" Smilingly, he responded slowly and carefully, "Zbigniew Brzezinski." Just then, at the other end of the cafeteria I saw a very attractive young woman at a table with four other men. On an impulse, I excused myself, walked across the cafeteria, and sat down at the one vacant chair. I listened intently to the ongoing philosophical conversation between the woman and the male students until the latter all left for classes, and I had the pleasure of walking out with her, though not knowing her name. Two weeks later we again met at the cafeteria, after which I told a surprised friend that she was the person that I wanted to marry. It took me a year of pursuing and persuasion, but we did marry a year later just before classes started, as I found my lifelong companion, well worth leaving behind a possible long-term friendship with the Polish political scientist destined to become Jimmy Carter's national security adviser.

My initial intellectual excitement was sustained throughout the year of being a student during the department's golden period of high productivity by the entire senior faculty, especially by Talcott Parsons. A particular attraction was the sociology interdisciplinary seminar in Emerson Hall (the department home until 1963), with Parsons at the head of a long table. To his left sat cigarette-stomping Samuel Stouffer, who had made his mark with quantitative empirical research in the American Soldier series; and to his left, Florence Kluckhohn, an energetic enthusiast of field research on Native American value systems. To the right of Parsons were the most advanced students, seated in hierarchical order all the way back to where I, as the most junior student, sat facing Parsons, feeling initially like a junior guest watching the deities on Mount Olympus. From being an observer to being an ongoing participant was a rewarding gradual socialization process, culminating in my presenting a theoretical analysis of role differentiation as a function of birth order, which the senior faculty encouraged me to give at the spring meeting of the Eastern Sociological Society.

In my second year, I was awarded a coveted Teaching Fellowship, assigned in the fall to Pitirim Sorokin's undergraduate survey of the history of social thought. The secretary of the department, knowing that Sorokin had been shunned by graduate students as a superannuated figure of the past, told me not to worry, that I would be assigned to George Homans in the spring. After a few weeks, however, I found Sorokin to be a very exciting, thought-provoking authority on great figures of the past and major social patterns. One day he arrived before his lecture and asked me to distribute dittoed sheets with passages from Parsons's *Social System*, which curiously duplicated (!) passages from Sorokin's earlier textbook. Being Sorokin's teaching assistant and having Parsons as my intellectual mentor put me in an unenviable position. The document circulated sotto voce in the department but also reached others outside. Using diplomacy, I became good friends with both and despaired of their publicized mutual antipathy. In retrospect, I hypothesize academic resentment stemming from the 1930s, when Parsons as a younger faculty member had a more democratic, inclusive approach and success with graduate students, like Robert Merton and Bernard Barber, than did hierarchical, European-trained Sorokin. You could become an active contributor to Parsons's theorizing but not to an encyclopedic mind. Losing his best students to a junior faculty member must have been galling.

In any event, I was relieved years later when Parsons graciously responded to my invitation for a contribution to a *festschrift* honoring Sorokin with an excellent original piece of theorizing ("Christianity and Modern Industrial Society"); teaching at Princeton, I had thought such a volume might show Sorokin that the profession still acknowledged him as a leading light, despite past controversies. Reconciliation certainly did occur when a distinguished group organized a write-in campaign that elected him president of the American Sociological Association (ASA), for which I then served as program chairman, and welcomed him at the 1965 meeting. A year after his death in 1968, in a time of great social conflict, the 1969 ASA meetings saw radical students displaying a new collective identity, expressed in a badge proclaiming, "Sorokin Lives!": he had become a symbolic figure of antiwar and antiestablishment protest. I also had the pleasure of seeing Sorokin's spirit make a return to postcommunist Russia, when in 1999 I participated in a conference in his memory held in bitter-cold Moscow and St. Petersburg.

Besides gaining valuable teaching experience, I spent the second year meeting all course requirements and planning a doctoral dissertation. My comparative interests led me to apply to the Fulbright program for research stemming from my work with Allport on South Africa's racial policy. The United States and South Africa shared much in common as Protestant settler societies, with a common nineteenth-century exodus trek in Conestoga wagons, gold mining, and a divergent twentieth-century racial policy. This seemed quite adequate for a comparative analysis. My wife, training as a historian, planned research on the history of the Indian immigration to South Africa.

The Fulbright Commission notified us that they liked our academic credentials but had no exchange programs for South Africa. However, if we could submit individual proposals before Thanksgiving, we would have an excellent chance for each receiving an award for the Philippines. Although nobody at Harvard had worked on the Philippines, I could not resist the opportunity of doing field research and discussed this with Parsons, Alex Inkeles, and Peter Rossi. By Thanksgiving I had read enough to formulate an original empirical study of occupational stratification in a "developing society" eighty-five hundred miles away (while my Spanish-speaking wife proposed doing an archival study of Spanish colonial policy in the nineteenth-century Philippines). As a Christmas present, we were informed that we had received Fulbright research fellowships.

Consequently, at the start of our third year of marriage, Josefina and I left the States and found a modest apartment in Manila in proximity to San Juan del Monte, the semiurban site for my study in the metropolitan area. Doing field interviews on occupational rankings, including mainly curious but illiterate agricultural workers, was a methodological challenge, matched by going farther into the interior of Central Luzon to a no-man's land with security problems from an insurgent agrarian movement known as the Huk Rebellion. Enriched with a variety of field experiences and raw data, and with my giving a weekly university course on social movements, my pregnant wife and I left the Philippines and, after a stopover in Tokyo, returned to Harvard.

A year later, on April 1, 1956, I turned in my dissertation, having completed all requirements in four years. My last activity had also been very rewarding, as a Teaching Fellow in a year-long course taught by Henry Murray and Clyde Kluckhohn, "Ideas of Human Nature from the Greeks to the Present," during which they invited me to give a lecture, "Modern Existential Thinking," that apparently went over very well. The student phase of my career was over. I had internalized a professional identity of being active in teaching and research, molded by a highly productive faculty and in the general spirit of camaraderie in social relations.

On My Own: Back Home at Princeton

Two weeks before commencement, I received an unexpected phone call from Wilbert Moore at Princeton asking if I could teach a core graduate course in methodology and a large undergraduate course in social disorganization. I had not prepared for either, but the chance to return to my alma mater as a faculty member was compelling: I immediately accepted and spent the summer avidly reading the literature in each field.

Returning to the joint Department of Economics and Social Institutions, I found a congenial interdisciplinary environment with easy interaction between myself and younger economists. I offered new courses, published parts of my dissertation, and made an extensive trip to sub-Saharan Africa to gauge social change in advanced colonial African society, from Senegal and Nigeria to Southern Africa and Zanzibar. I also took the opportunity to spend a junior sabbatical in Paris, working on French ideology of colonialism and its connection with existential social philosophy.

Returning to Princeton, I found my situation drastically changed, as the department had split into two, economics and sociology, with a new sociology chair playing the part of the grim reaper with the nontenured faculty. Informed there would be no tenure for me made me experience the painful condition of alienation that I had lectured about. But deep despondency changed to elation a few weeks later after receiving an invitation from Harvard to be a lecturer in social relations. In effect, a catastrophe turned into a three-year advanced postdoctoral fellowship, and I returned to my graduate home in 1962. For my wife, Josefina, who had spent years raising our two sons, Cambridge provided the opportunity of returning to a professional career. One of the first scholars at the Radcliffe Institute for Independent Study, she renewed her dormant graduate work in Latin American history, eventually earning a Ph.D. from Harvard in 1969.

Making the most of what I knew would be a limited time, I published theoretical pieces on Durkheim and existential phenomenology and made enduring friendships with new colleagues such as David Riesman and S. N. Eisenstadt. The latter participated in a faculty seminar organized by Parsons and Robert Bellah on evolution and social change, a major academic issue reflecting what the world was witnessing as "the winds of change." A university travel grant allowed me to visit parts of francophone Central and Eastern Africa. Avoiding jail after violating the curfew in a contested zone in the Cameroons and meeting there a World War I German-speaking tribal chief are unexpected moments I still remember. In Kenya I tried unsuccessfully to meet anthropologist Jomo Kenyatta, then in jail for being an instigator of the Mau Mau Rebellion but who years later became Kenya's first president. The materials I gathered on the closing period of colonial society in the new era of African independence were useful for a course I taught at Harvard on African modernization and for links in Boston with a faculty group following events in sub-Saharan Africa.

One of the Boston scholars I met was Phillip Bosserman, who had visited Albert Schweitzer and his famous hospital in Lambaréné. Delighted to find I had been to Gabon and spoke French, Phil told me he had just returned from preparing a dissertation on Georges Gurvitch, with whom I had communicated in doing the Sorokin *festschrift*. Gurvitch was a founder and president of the professional organization Association Internationale des Sociologues de Langue Française (AISLF). Phil suggested I join, and undoubtedly my becoming a life member was to provide long, sustaining career enrichment. It is worth more than a brief mention.

An Important French Connection

AISLF was founded in the late 1950s as an alternative to American quantitative survey methods and draws on French cultural, empirical, and analytical traditions. I enjoyed its humanistic approach at my first meeting in Royaumont, France, in 1965 and noted the *gemeinschaftliche*, or communitarian, ambience, more like a regional meeting in the States than the national ASA setting. At its congress in 1971 in Hammamet, Tunisia, during an antiestablishment upheaval at the business meeting, I found myself unexpectedly elected to the executive committee as part of a new slate representing the "Third World" (a residual category since council seats were reserved for France, Belgium, Switzerland, and Canada). I continued as an American anomaly on the executive committee and was elected president in Geneva in 1988; the vice president, Renaud Sainsaulieu, arranged for me to have a visiting appointment at the elite Sciences Po in the spring of 1992 to prepare my presidential address (presented in Lyon in June 1992). Sainsaulieu was one of several close friends I made at AISLF, as was Georges Balandier, a remarkable Africanist and theorist of modernity, and Fernand Dumont, the leading sociologist of Quebec.

My long association with AISLF has provided me with opportunities to publish original pieces in French and to travel widely to congresses and colloquia (most recently in 2012 in Morocco), and through contacts with the ex-Soviet world, to various places in Eastern Europe. One prized experience occurred in Skopje, Macedonia, in 1999. I hired an Albanian taxi to drive me and a Macedonian sociologist without official laissez-passer documents to Pristina, capital of Kosovo province, days after the Serbian withdrawal in the face of American bombing. Having a beer in the only place open and facing victorious Albanians and dejected, angry Serbs was a unique field experience.

Duke: A Permanent Home

While at Harvard, I received a tenured offer to join the joint Department of Sociology and Anthropology at Duke University. My interest in sociological theory was shared by the chair, John McKinney, and the university was also expanding in international studies, where I had done relevant work. Before settling down, I flew to Nigeria to interview African entrepreneurs regarding Max Weber's insight on the origins of capitalism. Unfortunately, I arrived at the outset of a military coup d'état that completely isolated Lagos from the rest of the country. After four days in an "anomic situation," I managed to leave Lagos for Abidjan, Ivory Coast, but this experience ended seeking to do comparative field research in Africa. Two new ventures were to follow.

At Duke in my third year, McKinney, who had modernized the department, suddenly left for higher administration. I accepted an unexpected interim appointment as chair and went to the ASA meetings where new chairs were briefed on how to handle growing student protest. I returned to Duke and had an open meeting with graduate students, who appreciated my democratic overture. Consequently, while other sociology departments were in disarray, we kept to our routine work. More challenging for me was my senior colleagues charging me with informing four junior colleagues (two sociologists, two anthropologists) they would not get tenure for lack of adequate publication. I found that a very stressing situation but managed to handle the matter and was relieved after the first accepted the decision without rancor. Unfortunately, I was unable to make my vision for a new integrated Department of Social Relations take hold among senior sociology and anthropology colleagues.

I left after a term and returned to Paris for a sabbatical. There I chanced to attend a public meeting of dissident groups protesting cultural oppression of their homelands, which were culturally distinct regions *within* established Western nation-states (such as Wales, Basque Area, Corsica). Thus began a radical extension of work I had done on African nationalism: the study of modern ethnic nationalism, of the periphery against the dominance of the center. What causes a group to reject a state identity and seek much greater autonomy, even independence? Stemming from this were a set of activities I undertook for three decades: conducting courses and a faculty seminar on nationalism and modernity, carrying out research in several countries, and directing a faculty exchange program in Quebec studies to supplement Anglophone prominence in Duke's Canadian studies.

In the midst of these activities, I was invited by a new provost to head Duke's Center for International Studies in 1988. I accepted, making a careful study of how such centers operate elsewhere and finding particularly congenial the one at Pittsburgh, headed by the late Burkart Holzner, on whose board I served for ten years. Putting intellectual ideas ahead of financial resources was a cardinal error on my part, though my core vision of the center as the magnet for internationalizing the university did eventually become a university priority after I left the position (and as the provost left Duke).

Returning to Duke after a year's research in Palo Alto at the Center for Advanced Study in the Behavioral Sciences, I was preparing for retirement when the Fulbright Commission invited me to become director in 2002–2003 in the New Century Scholars Program. A team of thirty scholars, selected from countries as varied as Belgium, Sri Lanka, Nepal, Israel, Tibet, and Australia, each pursuing an individual project on the central theme of sectarian ethnic and cultural conflict, would be linked to one another electronically and meet together at the start and end of the year. Coordination was challenging, but my experience directing previous interdisciplinary seminars was very helpful. A boon to group solidarity was spending a week together in a previous hot spot, Belfast, Northern Ireland, which gave us an opportunity for field interviews with key individuals in the peace process.

Postretirement: Old and New Ventures

I became emeritus in 2004 and have sought to stay active. The hardest adjustment has been not teaching my regular departmental courses, but my department has generously provided me an office. I have also found an academic program at Duke providing me the opportunity of giving yearly graduate-level seminars on themes not usually part of a standard sociology curriculum (such as comparative study of natural and man-made disasters, and philanthropy and altruism).

Keeping professionally active also means attending and presenting papers at various organizations such as ASA, the International Institute of Sociology (IIS), and the International Sociological Association (ISA). I have two networks of particular interest. One is a group of scholars seeking to promote the study of Sorokin in a new ASA section, Altruism, Morality, and Solidarity. The second is a multinational network of scholars centered at Oxford who publish the bilingual *Durkheimian Studies*. Meeting with other—and often much younger—scholars who share my passion for Durkheim and his relevance for major contemporary questions has meant much to me. A treasured moment was being the keynote speaker in October 2012 at the University of Porto Alegre, Brazil, at an international conference organized by a young Durkheimian, Raquel Weiss, and where I met a young French scholar, Matthieu Béra. Matthieu and I were amazed to find in Porto Alegre an Auguste Comte religious temple, with a congregation of about fifty meeting Sundays—a fit setting for a country that has adopted Comtean positivism as its national motto!

While it is a rejuvenating pleasure to become friends with new and junior colleagues, like Weiss and Béra, it is also a great sadness, with increasing frequency in recent years, to lose great friends like Bob Merton, Bob Bellah, Fernand Dumont, Shmuel Eisenstadt, Raymond Boudon, and Phil Bosserman. Perhaps being an only child has made me see close friendships as a family extension.

There is a last postretirement zone that needs mention, combining past and future. Though Armenian on both sides, I have never lived in an Armenian community; nor do I speak Armenian, a complex Indo-European language. Present Armenia is a small country, living in an "unhealthy neighborhood" as Prime Minister Netanyahu has said about Israel's situation. It had lost much of its territory and one-third of its population in terrible massacres by the successor state of the Ottoman Empire at the time of World War I. With 2015 looming ahead on the horizon as the one hundredth anniversary of the start of the terrible genocide in Anatolia, I took my son on our first visit, beginning in Istanbul (which had been Constantinople from 1453 to 1924), the family home until they emigrated in 1896, and then on to Yerevan, where Russian is more a lingua franca. My son remembered enough Russian from college days that we could proceed without getting lost.

Returning home with materials and contacts made with sociologists interested in collaborative research on topics other than genocide in the two countries, I started to plan major themes for a graduate seminar in 2015 on extreme violence. In July 2014 I participated in the ISA congress in Yokohama and took the occasion to make a side visit to Hiroshima. As any visitor, I was struck at the Peace Memorial Park as much by remains of the utter desolation created on August 6, 1945, by the first atomic bomb as by the yearly public ceremony at the park in favor of world peace and renunciation of weapons of mass destruction. Not recrimination or revenge but reconciliation.

I returned to Duke and added to my courses sections on what I had seen, supplementing comparative aspects of genocide with comparative aspects of the process of reconciliation. I gave the seminar in 2015 and will repeat it again as a new avenue for my sociological undertaking in keeping with semper sociology.

3

Three Lives in Two Americas

ROBERT PERRUCCI

I have always thought of myself as having been three different persons because I believe that I have lived three distinctly different lives. This is not simply a matter of change over the life course, from childhood, to youth, to early adult, to mature adult, and so on. This is a matter of having lived three discontinuous lives, meaning that one would not predict one life from the other. It is probably true that most lives have elements of predictable transitions and discontinuities that are shaped by unexpected events. From a life-course perspective these critical incidents are what Anselm Strauss called "turning points," which create the circuitous pathways that shape a life. To add to the complexity of three lives, I had the benefit of living in two very different Americas. This knowledge of two Americas is based on my research as a sociologist and reported in several of my publications, including my book *The New Class Society*. I believe that during my lifetime there has occurred a great divide in the way people live and that my three lives have been interrelated with the two Americas—not in any cause-and-effect fashion but nonetheless interrelated.

My first life was in New York City, beginning with my birth in 1931 and ending in 1954, soon after my discharge from the Marine Corps on October 31, 1953. My second life was transformative, as I entered the world of ideas, beginning with my college years at Cortland State and my postgraduate years at Purdue University. The transformation continued into my third life as I became an assistant professor of sociology in 1962. The two Americas involved, first, a period where my life at the bottom end of the class structure provided few material resources or incentives to think beyond where I was headed, if I was lucky—a job in construction or in a low-skilled blue-collar job. In the second America, I came to believe that I could achieve more because I had the GI Bill, which made it possible for me to have the financial means to try to do something different, such as finish high school and go to college.

First Life: 1931–1954

Born on the Table

I was born on a kitchen table on the second floor of 144-29 105th Avenue in Jamaica, Queens, New York City, on November 11, 1931. I was never told why I had a midwife delivery. Was it culture or finances? My childhood years were spent with my mother when she was home; she worked as a domestic and often lived in. When my mother was gone, I lived with my paternal grandmother (Camille) and grandfather (Roberto). Roberto and Camille came to the United States from Bari, Italy, in 1910 with their son, Dominic (my father), who was four years old. Roberto and Camille would have nine additional children who became my five aunts (Laura, Mary, Ann, Annette, and Florence) and four uncles (Vito, Mike, Jack, and Pete). We all lived in the same up-down apartment with one bathroom upstairs and one bathroom downstairs. I have very little early memory of my father, who left for work in Washington, D.C., in the mid-1930s (and never returned). He went to D.C. for construction work. My best memory of him was during my visits with him in the 1940s when he drove for Yellow Cab Company in D.C. (which he did for about thirty-five years). I rode with him in the cab, and my job was to enter all fares in a record book (time and location of pickup and drop-off), and collected fares. When I rode in the cab with my father, he liked to work the cab stand at the Mayflower Hotel. Ironically, many years later, I gave my acceptance address as the incoming president of the Society for the Study of Social Problems (SSSP) at the same Mayflower Hotel.

Early Street Life

Elementary school at P.S. 50 is pretty much a blank. My father, his nine siblings, and I all went to P.S. 50. My father left school (or was asked to leave) in the sixth grade. Only one aunt and one uncle finished high school. I spent a lot of time with Olga, a family friend, who taught me to appreciate music, such as that of Fats Waller, Pinetop Smith, and Django. I remember being an avid listener of the late-night jazz radio program *Robbins Nest*, emceed by Fred Robbins. Robbins was the ultimate "cool" persona; at that time in my life being cool or hip was the desire of all young men. I think that I listened to *Robbins Nest* mostly during my high school years. This early love of jazz continues to this day.

Most of my after-school hours were spent hanging out in front of Al's corner candy store, a couple of blocks from my house, with five or six of my friends. We pitched pennies, played cards, and got into mischief. We played a lot of stickball in the P.S. 50 school yard and softball at a nearby vacant lot. My daily family responsibilities involved collecting the bread order from the bakery and picking up the daily newspaper for my grandfather (*Il Progresso*—he could read; my grandmother could not), along with his Italian-style crooked cigars (De Nobili), which he usually crushed and stuffed in a corncob pipe. He smoked on the stoop because my grandmother did not permit him to smoke in the house. She was in charge long before the feminist movement. When I lived with my grandparents, I had the typical immigrant family experience of living with two languages; they spoke to me in Italian, and I answered in English.

When I was thirteen to fifteen years old, I was into bike racing. My uncle Vito, a longtime bike racer, introduced me to the sport and helped me join the Long Island Wheelman's Association and the Italian Sport Club. In the summer we raced early every Sunday morning: sprint races (two and five miles) and road races (twenty to fifty miles). I was the junior road champion in 1946 or 1947. When I wasn't racing, I biked everywhere. My street bike had a fixed gear and no brakes, so I braked with my legs and leather gloves applied to the front wheel, which was just as effective as braking in modern bikes. My love of biking has continued, as I have biked to work for more than forty years.

Day Trips out of the Neighborhood: High School, 1945–1948

I went to Brooklyn Technical High School by mistake. I was sitting in Shimer Junior High when the teacher asked, "Who wants to take the test for Brooklyn Tech?" What's that? It's a two-day test, so you get out of school to take the test. Out of school for two days—that's for me! I took the test, and several months later I learned that I had been admitted to Brooklyn Tech. So I went, mainly because Olga, the family friend, said it was a good school and she talked me into going. I was not happy with that decision. Every day, I had to take the bus to the subway. Get on the E train to Queens Plaza. Transfer to the GG local train to Fulton Street. Walk two blocks to Tech, across the street from Fort Greene Park. Tech was a thirteen-story factory. I didn't like Tech, but I learned a lot of math, science, and industrial arts (strength of materials, foundry, design, etc.). In my senior year I was going "on the hook" a lot, without telling my mother. Sociologists may have discovered the importance of the peer group, but I lived it. My mother was called to school several times to explain my truancy. Near the end of my senior year, knowing I was in grade trouble in most of my classes, I quit. I simply stopped going, and no one ever said anything about it. My mother invented the "don't ask, don't tell" policy long before Bill Clinton. And it worked. She could focus on her job as store manager working with Louie Goldman at Crown Cleaners, and I moved on to look for a job.

One of the more important accidents in my life that resulted in gain by indirection—that is, realizing a positive outcome that I did not pursue intentionally—was my registering for the draft a year early.[1] The law required registration for the draft at age eighteen. I registered when I was seventeen, stating that my birthday was November 11, 1930, rather than 1931. I did this so I could use my draft card to get into bars and drink. The result was that I did get into bars and also that I probably got drafted into the marines earlier than I would have. In fact, if I had registered when I turned eighteen, I might never have been drafted. If I had never been drafted, I would not have received Korean GI Bill benefits and would never have finished high school or gone on to college.

Manhood à la the Albert Viscuse Association: 1948–1951

The Albert Viscuse Association (AVA) was a store-front men's club, located a block from P.S. 50 and named after someone in the neighborhood who was killed in World War II. It had a large front room with chairs facing a TV, a couple of couches, and a small card table where people played hearts and pinochle. The back room was a kitchen with a stove and refrigerator, but the room was dominated by a large round card table, which was the center of action on weekends. There was always a game on Friday night and Sunday afternoon. The game was five-card stud, twenty-five-cent ante, one-dollar maximum bet, with check and raise. This was serious poker requiring a twenty-dollar buy-in stack, where people could win or lose the equivalent of a week's pay.

AVA membership was about thirty to forty men, about half in their forties and the other half World War II vets in their late twenties and early thirties. I joined the club in 1949 after I quit high school. I was the youngest member and was sponsored for membership by my uncle Charlie (my mother's brother). He didn't come to the club very often, but he was respected as a serious gambler. New members were voted in or out by members placing a black or a white marble in the hole of a wooden box; one black ball and you were out; for you to be accepted, every voting member had to want you in the club.

---

1. For a discussion of the functions of ignorance and the rationalistic bias in sociological writings, see Wilbert Moore and Melvin Tumin, "Some Social Functions of Ignorance," *American Sociological Review* 14, no. 6 (1949): 787–795; and Louis Schneider, "The Role of the Category of Ignorance in Sociological Theory," *American Sociological Review* 27, no. 4 (1962): 492–508.

Everybody in the club had a nickname (as in Italian mob movies): Fat Jimmy (to his face, just Jim or Big Jim), Charlie Longbeach, Legs, Squeaky, Eddie B, Jo-Jo, Nails, and others that I cannot now recall. I was Rab, short for rabbit, because I was the youngest. During my time at AVA, I learned a lot about playing cards and betting horses. But I had to work to eat, gamble, and hang out. My first job after quitting high school was in the new car department at F & M Habrich Oldsmobile ($1.10 per hour was the wage; I took home about $40 a week). I put accessories on the new Olds 88s and 98s. Sometimes I applied undercoat to cars (rust protection), but normally undercoating was done by two black guys, Alonzo Herod "Buster" Holmes and Ulysses S. "Niles" Niles. I ate lunch with Buster and Niles every day. We talked a lot about horses and placed our one- and two-dollar bets as often as we could at a nearby candy store. Garland "Burt" Burton, who also was black, worked with us. Often on Friday nights after work, Buster, Niles, Burt, and I would "go into a cool." (It was a TGIF thing). That meant we bought a bottle of whiskey and sat in one of our cars in the neighborhood and passed the bottle around until it was empty.

I quit my job at Habrich's (probably because of money) and joined several of my friends to become an asbestos sidewall shingler. We worked at Levittown in Nassau County, and I had to join the International Brotherhood of Carpenters and Joiners. I believe that my early experience with unionized work contributed to my later scholarly interest in unions.

Since shingling was seasonal work, I also worked as a writer for Joe F., a bookmaker and AVA club member. Joe F. was the closest thing I had to a role model. He dressed well and was very cool, a good dancer, and a good card player. I aspired to become a bookmaker like Joe.

What I did not realize until many years later was the profound effect the AVA had on me: I was learning about life from men who were much older and more experienced than I. They knew a great deal about gambling, mainly betting on horses and card games. I was "the kid" in the AVA and could watch card games if I didn't talk. The players were all smart. They counted cards and calculated the probabilities of outcomes for themselves and for other players as well. My current reflections on the serious horse players in AVA indicate that they were engaged in doing regression analysis before it was discovered by sociologists. Daily horse bettors would buy the *Daily Racing Form* (also known as the "Bible") each night and analyze races for the next day. For each race, the *Form* would report how each horse finished in its last five races along with data on the following variables: (1) the quality of the horses in past races, (2) how much weight each horse carried, (3) the conditions of the track (muddy or dry), (4) the pole position of the horse, and (5) the distance of the race. Taking these and other variables into account would enable the bettor to decide which horse had the best chance of winning.

What I was learning extended beyond poker and horse betting. It also had to do with deciding on whether or not to get involved in a particular hustle or jackpot that promised a return but also had risk (because it was usually outside the law). I didn't know how good a poker player I was until I was on the train heading to Parris Island with other marine recruits. To pass the time, we played nonstop poker games, and I couldn't believe how little the other guys knew about playing cards. I had been playing with really smart poker players for so long in the AVA that I never assessed my own skills, which were apparent on the train to Parris Island—I won over five hundred dollars, about four thousand dollars in today's dollars. When I got to Parris Island, I had the money put in the safe of my unit's commanding officer, who was very suspicious about my request. He questioned me about where I got the money, and I told him about the gambling, which seemed to satisfy him. But I am getting ahead of my story.

Second Trip out of the Neighborhood:
U.S. Marine Corps, 1951–1954

My AVA life ended with the Korean War and my being drafted into the marines. The Marine Corps taught me about self-discipline. I learned to deal with physical and mental stress far beyond anything I had ever experienced before, which led to self-discipline. I became much more confident in myself and what I was capable of doing. During boot camp and advanced infantry training I also learned to work closely with a small group of men—my five-person fire team—and to rely on them to do things that required reciprocal actions on my part. I was very different from them in background and can't say that I liked them, at least not like my buddies in the AVA, but I knew that I could trust them.

After training was over, I was assigned to a rifle company attached to the Sixth Fleet. I started out on a troop ship during its shakedown cruise in the Caribbean to work out all the problems the fleet might encounter before the actual tour in the Mediterranean. The Sixth Fleet was a big operation, with a carrier, battleship, and the usual complement of cruisers, destroyers, submarines, troopships for the gyrenes (or jarheads, as the swabbies called us), and supply ships. While in the Caribbean I also pulled duty in Guantanamo Bay. A small detachment of marines from the Sixth Fleet was assigned to guard a cluster of planes around the clock. I remember night-guard duty walking around small fighter jets and not knowing what it was about. It was very dark and very remote—probably CIA black ops. This was pre-Castro, when the United States was supporting Fulgencio Batista and undermining everybody else. Many years later as a sociologist I would write about the use of black ops as a part of U.S. foreign policy in *The Triple Revolution Emerging.*

After the shakedown we toured the entire rim of the Mediterranean for about a year, stopping at a great many ports in North Africa, southern Europe, and the eastern Mediterranean. My big break came with a reassignment to the *Coral Sea*, the Sixth Fleet's aircraft carrier (CV 43). That was great duty. No more stacked sleeping and better chow. It was also easier to hide on the carrier to avoid lousy assignments, like head duty (cleaning latrines). Compared to the troop ship, the *Coral Sea* was high-quality living.

The most important consequence of my time spent in the marines was the Korean GI Bill. Without it, I would have left the marines and gone back to the AVA for a continuation of fun and games that would have taken me nowhere. The GI Bill paid me to finish my high school degree in night school. I needed a course in English and a course in history to have the credits necessary for a high school diploma. Then I went back to the Veterans Administration and asked what's next. They said go to college. Where? They said pick a place that will accept you and recommended the New York state teachers college system. The GI Bill paid me ninety dollars a month to go to college (no books or tuition—but tuition was eighteen dollars a semester) for my B.S. degree in education from Cortland State Teachers College (now upgraded to the State University of New York at Cortland).

Second Life: 1954–1962

I came very close to leaving Cortland before the first classes started. All freshmen were required to be at Cortland the week before classes as part of a general orientation. I checked into a local motel to survey the situation and find a place to live. The first day of orientation we were handed green beanies that we were supposed to wear until some ritual date (first football game?). There was no way I was going to participate in such nonsense, and I was having second thoughts about whether or not to stay at Cortland or just go back to the neighborhood. Things only got worse. On my second night I left the motel with some of my favorite records (45s of Sax Stylists, Nellie Lutcher, and Eddie Condon), bought a bottle of wine, and went to a lounge in the student union where I had seen a record player. I put on the records, opened my wine, and settled into my own "cool." Before too long, I was informed that drinking was not allowed in the union and I was asked to leave. I couldn't believe it and was really ready to go back to the AVA. As fate would have it, however, on the third day I ran into Tony Lembo, who played softball against me in the old neighborhood. Tony's father had an umbrella hot-dog stand that he would wheel out every morning and set up in front of the railroad station near Jamaica Avenue. Tony had been in the army in Korea and was at Cortland playing football. He was at school a week early because of football practice. Tony said there was a vacancy in the place where he had a room. So I rented a room from Bud and Goldie Baker. If I hadn't run into Tony and rented a room from the Bakers, there is a very good chance that I would have checked out of the motel and driven my new car back to the city. Just another chance event that changed my life; not everything can be accounted for by structure and agency.

My first year at Cortland was difficult. I was doing more reading than I had ever done, and I was doing it with a dictionary at my side, which I consulted constantly. The courses of greatest interest to me were English (Lester Hurt), political science (Gilbert Cahill), sociology (Ephraim "Hal" Mizruchi and Leonard Goodman), and anthropology (Rozanne Brooks, who also taught me about wine). In my senior year I wrote a weekly column ("A Different Drum"; I stole the title from Henry David Thoreau) for the school newspaper. That's when I started to become more politically aware; the film *Operation Abolition* about the House Un-American Activities Committee's pursuit of radicals and communists had an impact on me. Some years later as a faculty member, I became the faculty adviser for Students for a Democratic Society (SDS) and Friends of Student Nonviolent Coordinating Committee (SNCC). Under my direction, students from these two organizations conducted a research project documenting racial discrimination in local housing. The research results were reported to the university president and the board of trustees, resulting in a change in university housing policies.

After my first year, things went well. I was preparing for life as an elementary school teacher in the suburbs. But several of my professors were pushing me to go to graduate school. Hurt suggested I apply to University of Minnesota in English; Cahill, to Colgate in political science; and Mizruchi, to Yale and Purdue in sociology. The rejection letter from Yale stated that it did not accept applications from graduates of vocational colleges. I published the Yale rejection letter in my "Different Drum" column as part of my ongoing critique of the quality of the education provided at Cortland.

I was accepted at three schools: no money from Minnesota; a preceptor position at Colgate (live in a dorm with students); and a fellowship from Purdue. The decision was a no-brainer, so I went to Purdue in 1958. I loved graduate school and sociology. All I thought about was reading sociology, doing research, and publishing. This was a heady time for me; I published three articles in the *American Sociological Review* (*ASR*) while still a graduate student. I was full of myself and received my Ph.D. in 1962. Purdue asked to me stay on, so I accepted a position as assistant professor.

Third Life: 1962 to Present

In 1965, I married Carolyn Cummings, a sociologist who at the time had a research appointment in the School of Engineering doing alumni surveys, and she switched to a tenure-track position in sociology. Over the years, our efforts to move to another university brought us face-to-face with academe's nepotism rule, which we had never heard of before. Our job interviews at the University of Wisconsin, Vanderbilt, Maryland, and Stony Brook produced offers of a faculty appointment for Robert, and research appointments for Carolyn, because of nepotism rules. Sometimes the shoe was on the other foot when Carolyn was interviewed at Michigan State to be department head and I was considered for a research position. In contrast, Purdue had no rule against faculty spouses being in the same department as long as one didn't have a supervisory position over the other. Today, most universities make extensive efforts to accommodate dual-career couples.

I remained on the faculty at Purdue for forty-five years, until 2007. During my career I developed a strong record of research grants and publication. I also served the profession as associate editor of the *ASR* and editor of the *American Sociologist, Social Problems,* and *Contemporary Sociology.* As a retiree, I go to the office every day and still work with students and faculty colleagues on research projects and papers for publication. My continued professional activities have not been facilitated by the university but by a colleague with a large office who provided me with space for a desk, computer, and bookshelves. I still enjoy my work as a sociologist, and although I do not have a regular teaching schedule, I give occasional lectures when colleagues invite me to their classes and have remained active with new research projects and papers for publication. Since my retirement, I have published two books and sixteen journal articles and have several additional papers in preparation for publication. The biggest problem with being retired is that you become a nonperson in the university community, reflected in small ways, such as being excluded from department/college e-mail lists, and in large ways, such as never being asked to serve or advise on an ad hoc committee that might benefit from your knowledge or experience. Most universities don't have codified procedures for dealing with their retired members and making use of their skills and experience. For example, when I retired, I met with the dean of the graduate school and offered to create a new position of ombudsperson for international students and to fill that position without pay to get things started. The dean declined, stating that my proposed new position would conflict with others already in place.

So largely, as a retiree, you do it on your own, which for me means to continue to be active as a sociologist, doing research, presenting papers at national and regional meetings, and publishing in appropriate venues. I cannot think of anything more interesting or more satisfying. The current effort by ASA to reach out to retirees is a great example of how to draw on their knowledge and experiences.

4

The Life Course of My Career

Glen H. Elder Jr.

In this memoir I tell the story of how my career in sociological studies emerged from a background of social change. My birth in the early 1930s in Cleveland, Ohio, exposed me to social forces that were transforming lives, from the Great Depression to World War II. My parents were college graduates, and they had the same aspirations for me. After they decided to move the family from "the big city" to a Pennsylvania farm in the late 1940s, Penn State became a natural choice in view of my newly discovered fascination with agriculture.

In telling this story I begin with my parents and relate how their lives generated my interest in the social psychology of change in people's lives and indirectly in the graduate-level study of sociology at the University of North Carolina (UNC) at Chapel Hill. From there, the professional connections of mentors placed me on the path to an appointment at the University of California, Berkeley, and to the development of a book that has literally shaped my career across half a century.

Impressions from Early Life

Whenever I am asked about the fascination I have with changing times in lives, I think about my parents and their influence. They were born around 1900 but came of age in very different worlds that reflected America's rapid transition from a life based heavily on agriculture to a more urban-industrial society in the Midwest. Mother grew up in the Buffalo (New York) family of a prominent Baptist minister, whereas my father came of age on a small stock farm in northeastern Ohio, near the city of Youngstown. Both attended liberal arts colleges in Ohio and entered the field of high school teaching, Mother in English literature and Father in mathematics along with coaching. They married in 1932 during the Great Depression.

The 1930s decade of hard times had reached bottom when I was born (1934), and my brother arrived three years later. The generally harsh impact of Depression life was not apparent to me or my brother, perhaps because of our later births and suburban residence. However, I had no such insulation from World War II. Flash-bulb memories of Sunday, December 7, 1941, picture members of my family sitting in stunned silence around a Philco radio listening to reports of the Japanese attack on Pearl Harbor. Newsreels on the local movie screen brought the Pacific and European war theaters into my experience time and time again, often against the wishes of teachers and parents who were trying to move their young charges away from "inappropriate material." But war news on radio and film surrounded us in the city much like the oxygen we breathed.

I grew up at a time when information typically was obtained from people at a point in time instead of at varying times across their lives. The social survey or questionnaire reigned supreme and conveyed a sense of timelessness about people's lives and community life. However, my mother introduced me to thinking about life histories, about people over time. And she did so through the many books she read and discussed. Eventually, biographies became a favorite way for me to gain insight regarding events and processes in lives and changing times. Historical biographies, in particular, gave me a sense of the intimate connection between change in people's lives and in their social world.

Personal experiences in Cleveland provided vivid examples, especially the many changes in people's lives through World War II. My parents invited young men who were in the navy to occasional dinners at home, and their stories filled my mind with accounts of how a changing world changes lives. Nevertheless, I became most aware of this impact when I experienced it. My father bought a dairy farm in northwestern Pennsylvania in May 1949, about 130 miles from Cleveland. This action was not unexpected, as he had talked about moving back to the land, but it happened suddenly and quickly transformed our lives.

I was asked to stay on the farm for the first week after we moved so that work could proceed on the farmhouse while my parents dealt with issues in Cleveland. Though I was only fifteen, I don't remember this solitary time as threatening. Instead it seemed like more an adventure in exploring an unknown world, but I was totally unprepared for the extent of change between my Cleveland suburb and the Pennsylvania farm. In some ways, the transition resembled an immigrant's experience, except that we were not moving as links in a chain to a place occupied by family and friends. We were on our own in a very different culture. The social discontinuities of this life transition increased my awareness of the personal effects of change.

Exposure to this new world of farming led me to agricultural studies at Penn State in 1952, but as so often happens when decisions are made on recent life changes, it proved to be premature. By the end of the third year, my interests had crystallized on how social change transforms lives, a social-psychological issue.

Education as a Career Bridge

By my senior year at Penn State, the mixture of courses had become such a smorgasbord that my adviser, the dean of the School of Agriculture, didn't know what to call it. I remember walking into his office one day, and he said, "Glen, what should we call your specialization? What about agricultural science?" I soon realized that a serviceable name for my curriculum did not provide any guidance on what my next step should be. However, a campus speaker for a service fraternity provided an interim step that helped me think through such matters—a one-year staff appointment with residence in a student dormitory as part of the Dean of Men's Staff at Kent State University.

A transition year made sense to me, and I signed up for it in the early summer of 1957. The dean required all staff members to enroll in a graduate program; I chose sociology over psychology because it focused on the changing world in which we live. My objective was to complete a master's in a year. Serving as a dormitory counselor for students peaked my interest in how community origins and attachments influenced their adaptation to college during the first year. Reference group theory became my conceptual perspective on the transition to the university. To investigate this change in the lives of students, I needed multiple waves of data that were not available. As an alternative, I turned to a survey in which I asked questions about the past, present, and future of students in the freshman class.

During my year at Kent State I had a decision to make about a preferred program of doctoral study in sociology. Theodore Newcomb's social psychology program at Michigan was one of my options, but the North Carolina program became most attractive through local Kent State faculty with ties to Carolina. I could study social psychology there with a major in sociology and a minor in psychology. Moreover, Charles Bowerman, the chair of UNC sociology, offered me a research assistantship on a three year National Institute of Mental Health (NIMH) study of adolescent orientations to parents and peers.

After moving to Chapel Hill in August 1958, I acquired a carrel for my library research on the project in the main library on campus. Unknown to me at the time, this carrel was in sight of a shelf of monographs on longitudinal studies. This turned out to be a profoundly important serendipitous event. During the next two years I immersed myself in these monographs and actually drew on them for the parent-peer project. After many years of exposure to cross-sectional surveys, I began to grasp what one could learn about human development and individual lives from longitudinal studies.

During my postdoctoral year at Chapel Hill, Bowerman told me about an entry-level position with sociologist John Clausen at the University of California. He had recently been appointed as director of Berkeley's famed Institute of Human Development and as a professor in the distinguished Department of Sociology. Clausen was in the market for a junior colleague who would collaborate with him on longitudinal studies at the institute—in particular, the Oakland Growth Study of Californians born in 1920–1921. I was enthusiastic about this chance to work with data records that depicted people over time and promptly accepted Clausen's offer. My library exposure to longitudinal studies provided valuable preparation for this appointment as a half-time research assistant at the institute and a half-time appointment in the Department of Sociology as an assistant professor.

The Berkeley Era: The Life Course and a Study of the Great Depression

My introduction to the institute and its immense longitudinal data archive began in the late summer of 1962. This pioneering institute included decades of intergenerational longitudinal studies that were launched with children during the late twenties and early thirties—the Oakland Growth Study, the Berkeley Guidance Study (1928–1929), and the Berkeley Growth Study (1928–1929). By the time I arrived, waves of data had been collected for nearly thirty years. The Oakland study members were entering their forties, and the Berkeley study members were approximately a decade younger.

My first assignment involved the development of a codebook on the Oakland data files. But first I needed a way of thinking about lives, their transitions and pathways. Strangely enough, this longitudinal study had not captured adequately the social process that the Oakland study members had experienced. I received some conceptual guidance on this project from the pioneering work of Bernice Neugarten at the University of Chicago and of demographer Norman Ryder—both had focused on age as a way of assessing life changes and the timing variations of events or transitions. Neugarten's thinking became a central component of my approach to the age-graded life course; and Ryder's thoughtful work on birth cohorts linked the birth year of people to their historical time and related social change.

With these age-based distinctions, I began to assemble a life-record codebook that included age-at-event information from each study member's data file in adolescence and another codebook on the adult years. Data on annual household income before the economic collapse and during the worst year, 1933, provided a revealing index of family income change. This led to the identification of relatively nondeprived and deprived families in the middle and working classes. Clausen expressed great interest in this work and gave me complete freedom to develop relevant ideas and research skills.

I viewed the family and its adaptations (change in household tasks, family relationships, and social-emotional strain) as a link between the economic deprivation of middle- and working-class families and the study members' early and later life course. The first part of the project focused on adolescents as they came of age in the Depression and assumed roles in the household division of labor, experienced change in family relationships, and were influenced emotionally. The next part followed the study members as they left high school and made the transition to adulthood, marked by entry into college, the military, employment, and marriage. I traced the Depression's income loss to educational and occupational attainment and marital and parental values. The final part of the study investigated the enduring effects of Depression hardship on emotional and physical health in later life.

Initial investigations on a complex project can be both encouraging and suggestive of the work that needs to be done. I discovered this to be the case when I had completed all chapter drafts of a proposed book, which I called "Children of the Great Depression." At the time I realized that I had not thought through the integration of the chapters in a life story that flowed smoothly. The challenge was to complete a life-course narrative for the Oakland cohort and to develop research papers informed by it on the educational, work-life, and family careers. I began this work on the men at the institute and continued with the women after returning to UNC in 1967 for an associate professorship.

Children of the Great Depression and Its Extensions

By the end of the 1960s the additional work on the book had produced a satisfying revision with a central theme of resilience in surmounting the disadvantages of hardship. The manuscript embodied distinctive themes of the early Chicago school of sociology, with an emphasis on the life histories of individuals in a particular time and place. One of the pioneering studies with this perspective was W. I. Thomas and Florian Znaniecki's classic study of immigration to the United States from eastern Europe, *The Polish Peasant in Europe and America*, published in five volumes during 1918–1920. Thomas was one of the leading figures in the development of the Chicago school of sociology, and he led the way in making a case for the study of people across their changing worlds. Considering this match, I mailed the manuscript, titled "Children of the Great Depression: Social Change in Life

Experience," to the University of Chicago Press in the hope that it would be accepted for publication.

At the same time, I wondered whether a younger birth cohort would experience greater developmental impairment than the Oakland cohort from stressful and dysfunctional families during the worst years of the Depression. One such cohort was that of the Berkeley study members, born in 1928–1929. They were two to five years old during the peak years of hardship and consequently were significantly more at risk of family stress and disruption. This longitudinal cohort also had the added value of coming from the same general region as the Oakland study members. With institute approval for access to the Berkeley data archive, I prepared a research proposal to the National Science Foundation (NSF) that provided support for a research team over the first year at the institute to develop measures on the Berkeley cohort (1972–1973) and over the next year at UNC–Chapel Hill for cohort comparisons. The early months of 1972 brought very good news from the University of Chicago Press and NSF on these initiatives.

In the course of developing measures at the Berkeley institute, we discovered an immense storehouse of qualitative and quantitative data on the parents that extended well beyond our needs for the cohort comparison. The Berkeley parents were interviewed periodically across the 1930s, as well as across the 1940s with a major intergenerational interview in 1946. They were also interviewed for the last time in 1969. This treasure trove of data opened my eyes to the extraordinary possibilities of an intergenerational study of the parents and their lives in an era of dramatic sociocultural change. Upon my return to Chapel Hill, I focused on ways the abundant parent data from the Berkeley archive could enhance our understanding of the impact of the resources and deprivations of the Berkeley families during the Depression on the experiences of their children.

In the summer of 1974, the University of Chicago Press published *Children of the Great Depression*, and it soon received positive reviews, which focused, in particular, on the life course as a promising theoretical perspective for studying individual lives. The first volume of the *Annual Review of Sociology* included a review essay I prepared on life-course studies, and national longitudinal data programs soon began to adopt designs that reflected temporal and contextual issues of the life course. Signifying this conceptual advance, Matilda White Riley organized a Social Science Research Council (SSRC) committee to explore applications of this perspective on human development. More than any other event, the establishment of this committee symbolized the potential significance of this paradigmatic perspective. I served on this multidisciplinary committee from the last half of the 1970s to the late 1980s.

In addition to doing theoretical work on the life course, the decade between 1975 and 1985 became a time when I focused on major extensions of *Children of the Great Depression*. Archival work at the Berkeley institute enabled us to compare the Oakland and Berkeley men, and we followed this work with a focus on their military service. A good many men who were born in the 1920s grew up in the Great Depression and were also recruited into the armed forces during World War II. Nine out of ten Oakland men served in the military during World War II, and three out of four Berkeley men served during the last half of the 1940s. Some of them were drawn back into active duty during the Korean War.

The cohort comparison revealed that Depression losses had different consequences for boys and girls who were born only seven or eight years apart in the 1920s. The younger Berkeley boys were more adversely affected by hard times than the Oakland boys, and their psychosocial disadvantage extended into the adult years. However, the older Oakland girls were more adversely affected by family hardship than the younger Berkeley girls, who were protected by their mothers and were too young to be exposed to the social pressures of early adolescence.

By the early 1980s, *Children of the Great Depression* was frequently used as an example of life-course study and as an approach to the study of economic cycles and their consequences for families and children. An Iowa study of the Great Recession in the rural Midwest from the early 1980s across the 1990s used the book as the longitudinal model, and I was asked to join the research team by the funding agency, NIMH. This invitation was appealing since it provided an opportunity to investigate a rural sample of families and children, broadening my perspective beyond urban families and children. The collaboration continued across the 1990s and produced several books and a number of articles.

The most significant theme in this rural study was the prominence of social connections or capital in the lives of rural farm youth and their families under socioeconomic hardship. The families were characterized by strong ties and networks that enhanced the resilience of young and old despite hard times. This resource was largely missing from the families and children being studied at the time in the disadvantaged inner city of Philadelphia.

Theorizing and Wrapping Up

By the early 1990s I had become aware of recurring conceptual themes of the life course extending back to *Children of the Great Depression* in 1974 and across subsequent empirical studies. My Cooley-Mead lecture in 1993 (at the American Sociological Association meeting in Miami) provided the occasion for assembling and discussing them. Four themes (linked lives, human agency, the timing of events, and historical time and place) depict key elements of the lived experiences of the Oakland study members who grew up in the 1930s. The fifth theme refers to the lifelong processes of development and aging.

The evolution of life-course thinking and research by the mid-1990s had occurred without the benefit of a major integrative chapter or book. But in 1996 the editors of the forthcoming fifth edition of the *Handbook of Child Psychology* decided to include such a chapter in the volume on theory and invited me to be its author. The empirical literature was now more substantial in North America and Europe, and major conceptual advances had been achieved. The development and clarification of core concepts, such as pathways, trajectories, and transitions, provided a rich conceptual toolbox. Most important were the paradigmatic principles that proved to be essential in defining the territory of the life course as a multilevel theoretical orientation. Preparation of this chapter and its publication in 1998 was seen as an important multilevel contribution to the emergence of an interdisciplinary field of developmental science.

The twentieth century ended with publication of the twenty-fifth-anniversary edition of *Children of the Great Depression*. This volume was now larger with a new chapter on developments, including the paradigmatic principles of the life course and a comparative account of the Great Depression and World War II on the lives of men and women in the Oakland and Berkeley cohorts. The new century opened with a symbolic recognition of the progress achieved in the field of life-course studies with publication of the very first handbook of the life course in 2003.

Up to this new century, my personal life had followed a steady course, with marriage to my college sweetheart, Karen Bixler, in 1958 and the birth of our three sons. But this life changed drastically when Karen was diagnosed in January 2001 with an advanced case of pancreatic cancer. She died four months later. With the support of my students and colleagues, I continued my schedule at UNC until 2003, when I selected a three-year phased decline in teaching that provided more flexible time for research and lecture invitations. My lecture at Rice University in February introduced me to a lovely woman on my return flight, Sandy Turbeville, a graduate of UNC in the 1960s. Our relationship developed rapidly over the year, leading to our decision to celebrate our marriage in a ceremony at the Carolina Inn on campus.

The last semester of my graduate seminar on the life course and teaching career occurred two years later when I was seventy-two. Moving off the teaching payroll proved to be seamless since I still directed a training program of pre- and postdoctoral students at the Carolina Population Center and managed research grants. My career focused now on research with flexible time for travel along with some mentoring and occasional university lectures. This mix of activities continues up to the present in my position as Odum Research Professor and fellow of the Carolina Population Center.

Shortly after moving off the teaching roll at UNC–Chapel Hill, I turned my primary attention to the completion of a book project that I first outlined in 1973 after a sabbatical at the Institute of Human Development. The project is based on the 1900 generation of Berkeley study parents who lived through vastly contrasting times. They experienced the relatively prosperous years of the 1920s followed by the economic collapse of the Great Depression. Next came World War II with its extraordinary industrial mobilization for war, leading to an unparalleled surge of postwar affluence into the 1970s.

This project was sidelined in the 1970s and 1980s while I carried out cohort studies based on the Oakland and Berkeley data archives. Nevertheless, I managed to draft a number of chapters by the 1990s. In combination, they followed the parents' lives from the early nineteenth century to the 1940s. All had married and were parents by the 1930s. My goal in the twenty-first century increasingly centered around the completion of this book, as well as finding an archival home for more than a half century of research records (from correspondence to grant proposals and life histories). Equally important, I realized that I needed to find a colleague or two who would collaborate with me in completing the book, caring for the archival data into the future, and continuing to use the Oakland and Berkeley data archives for life-course studies.

The senior archivist of the Davis Library of UNC and key members of the Carolina Population Center generously worked with me to create a collection of life-course materials. In addition, Richard Settersten, a life-course sociologist at Oregon State University with experience in the Berkeley archives, and Lisa Pearce, a family sociologist at UNC, agreed to work with me in turning the chapter drafts into a book and completing the unfinished chapters. They plan to use the archival data in the years to come. Effective management of data files is one of the great challenges in this line of work. As I have discovered, the preservation of longitudinal data archives cannot be taken for granted.

5

Six Sociologists from Wayne County, Ohio

Janet Zollinger Giele

After retiring in 2004 from teaching graduate students at Brandeis University, I had all sorts of projects to be completed—coediting a book on life-course research, writing a book on American family policy, and producing a guide for doctoral students on how to write a dissertation. When that was done, I planned to draw together all my work on the changing life patterns of American women and after that delve into my past in Wayne County, Ohio, and the coincidence that five other sociologists happened to come from there. The call for contributions to *Journeys in Sociology* suddenly changed my priorities. I put the last project first, located the other five sociologists, interviewed them by phone, and looked for what might be common threads in our past that led to our shared profession.

Over the years I had learned of the others. The discovery began in 1975 when I interviewed Phillips Cutwright at Indiana University while doing research on family-related social policies. In the mid-1980s, I learned that Joan Huber and I had the same high school English teachers and that John Meyer and Glenn Firebaugh were from the same area. In the early 1990s, David Snow introduced himself at an annual meeting and explained that he grew up next door to my family south of Wooster.

The city of Wooster in 1950 when I was in high school had a population of about twelve thousand. Located about fifty miles south of Cleveland, it sat at the intersection of the old Route 3 and U.S. Route 30, the Lincoln Highway. It was the county seat as well as the home of the College of Wooster, the Ohio Agricultural Experiment Station, and several well-known industries.

including Rubbermaid and Smucker, the jam company in nearby Orrville. On some weekdays the square in front of the courthouse contained the horses and buggies of Amish farmers who had come to town.

Given that six sociologists of roughly the same generation came from this small area, one might wonder whether there was something special in their background. In the following account I use my story as a lens for locating the significant influences and turning points in my life as a sociologist and then suggest what appear to be parallels in the lives of the others.[1]

There seem to be four common threads in all our life stories. We each came from a *distinctive family* that was a bit unconventional within the community. At the same time our families were embedded in a *small and friendly world* in which people knew and helped each other. As individuals, we were all *academic achievers*. Finally, each of us took on something of a *marginal position* with respect to community norms. Our knowledge of other worlds made us question conventional expectations in a way that fueled our interest in sociology and shaped our specialties within the field.

My Story: Janet Zollinger Giele (b. 1934)

My principal interests have been in the changing roles of women, modernization of the family, and various life patterns of contemporary women. After receiving a B.A. from Earlham College in 1956 and Ph.D. from Harvard in 1961, I became an instructor at Wellesley College but failed to receive tenure because of family obligations and a lack of publications. In the early 1970s at Radcliffe College, with sponsorship by the Ford Foundation, I conducted a massive review of emerging policies related to the changing status of women in the United States and abroad. In 1976 I was invited to the Heller School at Brandeis University, where I eventually received tenure, founded the Family and Children's Policy Center, and served briefly as acting dean.

Distinctive family heritage. My family was unusual in several ways. All four of my grandparents were immigrants. My mother's parents from Norway and Sweden settled in western Pennsylvania, where my grandfather and uncles were coal miners. My father's parents from Switzerland were taken into the Apostolic Christian church (an offshoot of the Mennonites) in the northeastern corner of Wayne County. Neither of my parents had a high school education, my father (1894–1985) having left his one-room school to help support his large family and my mother (1903–1989) at age sixteen having gone into domestic service to pay for business college and become a secretary-bookkeeper.

---

1. All quotations from the sociologists in the following sections come from my interviews with them unless otherwise noted.

Religious ideas and skepticism about dogma, as well as stories from the Bible and the evening news on the radio, were discussed at dinnertime. As a young adult my father had left threshing and hay baling to start his own excavation business. Around that time he was excluded from membership, even shunned, in the Apostolic community. So we children felt different from ordinary people and from our Zollinger relatives and went to the Methodist church that my mother had joined before marriage.

Community ties. My father had friends and acquaintances all over the county for whom he had threshed wheat or baled hay. He knew the county engineer, who gave him drainage work, and farmers who needed a farm pond. When he built our unconventional house using cement blocks and factory windows during the wartime housing shortage, he had help from friends and relatives who lent their time and tools. On Sunday afternoons we might visit people in the old people's home or drop by the farmhouses of friends or acquaintances. My parents could empathize with people who were different, like the Hungarian farmers who lived in the valley and spoke broken English, or the Jewish junkyard dealer, or one of my two best high school friends who was black. Their capacity for empathy was probably due to my father's being treated like a black sheep and to both my parents' knowledge of what it was to grow up with immigrant parents who spoke a foreign language.

Academic achievement. Both Wooster Township and Wooster High School had excellent teachers, and I did well in school. I first gained attention as the girl achieving the highest score in the Ohio Eighth Grade State Test and again four years later in the Ohio State Test. I became interested in sociology as a freshman in college when I stumbled across Émile Durkheim's *Division of Labor in Society* while writing a term paper for freshman biology. I suppose that Durkheim's comparison of simple societies to lower organisms, and complex societies to the more highly evolved, was fascinating to me because it was relevant to the borderline between town and country where I grew up. Sociology interested me also because it touched on familiar issues such as cultural differences, social class, and different religious beliefs that made sense out of my family's difference from other people. In another paper I described my family's position in our neighborhood as intermediary between the neighboring farmstead on the south and David Snow's more town-oriented family on the north. My other major in French literature took me to Paris for a year and immersed me in another culture. I graduated from Earlham in 1956 at the head of my class with honors in sociology and French. After receiving a National Woodrow Wilson Fellowship for college teaching in 1956, I moved to Massachusetts for graduate work in sociology at Harvard and was married the next year.

Marginality and a path to sociology. With a father who was an entrepreneur and the sole owner and operator of his own excavation business, it was very clear to me as the oldest of three daughters that I had to seek my fortune elsewhere. The principal struggle of my early adulthood was to reconcile my strong desire for independence and achievement with the desire to be a wife and mother. Critical to finishing my Ph.D. and continuing my career in sociology was my marriage in 1957 to David Giele, a war veteran and Harvard graduate ten years older than I. He decided to leave the family printing company in Dayton, Ohio, and move to Cambridge so that I could finish my doctorate and he could change from a career in printing to book publishing.

The 1950s were a heady time to be in the Department of Social Relations at Harvard, where all graduate students were required to study sociology taught by Talcott Parsons, social psychology by Gordon W. Allport, and clinical psychology by David McClelland and where Clyde Kluckhohn was the reigning figure in social anthropology. My dissertation topic on the early women's rights movement brought together three interests: the sociology of religion, deviance and social control (inspired by the shunning of my father), and the way social change occurs (which in that decade was a sociological challenge). It was 1959, I was ahead of the times, and Professor Allport tried to dissuade me with a caution that a topic about women would not advance my career. But Parsons encouraged me and became my dissertation adviser and a strong advocate of my work until his death in 1979. Another important influence was Alex Inkeles, who introduced me to personality-and-culture theories that informed my research on the lives of the early temperance and suffrage leaders. I learned to understand diversity in women's lives through a life-course perspective. Against the backdrop of the family in which I grew up, which combined production and reproduction in ways that are no longer possible in urban society, I now understand the modern safety net to be the main way that modern society supports its families.

Since retirement in 2004 I have published two more books and become active in Wellesley town affairs, feeling that up to then I had been a classic free rider. In 2007 I led the effort to establish the first Neighborhood Conservation District to delay or prevent teardowns and provide guidelines for compatibility of new construction in style and scale. I also helped found Wellesley Neighbors, a virtual retirement organization for mutual help and support among midlife and older adults that is part of the nationwide village movement. I continue to be involved in church affairs and the local community, which I see as the direct result of experiencing the friendship and neighborly support that I grew up with in Wayne County.

Joan Huber (b. 1925)

Known for her teaching and scholarly work on sex stratification and the family, as well as her administrative ability, Joan Huber was a cofounder (with Alice Rossi) of Sociologists for Women in Society and the seventy-ninth president of the American Sociological Association in 1988–1989. Following a delay in her graduate education, when she received her M.A. from Western Michigan in 1963 and Ph.D. from Michigan State in 1967, she rose quickly in the profession, through faculty and administrative positions at the University of Illinois and Ohio State University from which she retired in the mid-1990s as senior vice president and university provost.

A distinctive family. Joan's forebears came from Switzerland and Alsace and were Mennonites and members of the Church of the Brethren, although her parents joined the Presbyterian church in Wooster. The intellectual atmosphere in the home was one of independent and scientifically oriented thinking, even toward religion. Joan's father had a Ph.D. in entomology and worked at the experiment station. Her mother took college courses and earlier taught fifth grade. While others voted for Alf Landon or Franklin D. Roosevelt, Joan's parents voted for the socialist Norman Thomas.

The small community. In addition to the businesses that made Wooster prosperous, the Presbyterian-affiliated College of Wooster, along with the Ohio Agricultural Experiment Station, shaped its religious and cultural life. The Huber family were part of both, and friendships followed the same lines. They were close friends with Phillips Cutwright's family—her father and his both worked at the experiment station; Phill's mother was their pediatrician; and his sister, one of Joan's playmates. Acquaintances included the Presbyterian and Mennonite missionaries returned from the field as well as Joan's teachers and others connected to the station or the college.

Academic achievements. Joan was a bright child and placed first in the Ohio State History Test, was editor of the high school newspaper and president of the debating society, and graduated from Penn State at the age of nineteen. Yet an early marriage, birth of two children, and following her husband's moves delayed her graduate education until the 1960s, when she was finally able to commute hundreds of miles to earn her graduate degrees.

Marginality and sociology. In her autobiographical essay, "From Sugar and Spice to Professor," Joan recounts the double-talk that exhorted her to get an education to be a good mother but never mentioned the "domestic service" entailed in cooking, child care, and cleaning up.[2] It is not difficult to see the connection between this discrepancy and her sociological analysis of women's second-class status.

Since retirement, Joan regularly goes to her office. In her 2007 book *On the Origins of Gender Inequality* she delves into human reproductive biology to show how, prior to the invention of a safe substitute for human milk, women's child bearing and frequent breast-feeding kept them out of public

---

2. Joan Huber, "From Sugar and Spice to Professor," in *Academic Women on the Move*, ed. Alice S. Rossi and Ann Calderwood (New York: Russell Sage Foundation, 1973), 125–135.

life and consigned them to a secondary status. No man can bear a child, a fact that Joan reports is not recognized by many feminist sociologists. It appears that retirement has given her the time and space to challenge the reigning paradigm.

Phillips A. Cutwright (b. 1930)

Phillips Cutwright, a social demographer, is known for his pioneering studies of the connections between poverty, family size, fertility, illegitimacy, and family planning. With a B.A. from the College of Wooster in 1954 and a Ph.D. from the University of Chicago in 1960, he advanced through a series of appointments at Dartmouth, Vanderbilt, and Washington University to become a full professor at Indiana University in 1970, where he remained until his retirement in 1994.

A distinctive family. Both of Phill's parents had advanced degrees from Ohio State, his father a Ph.D. in entomology and his mother an M.D. His father was active in the Presbyterian church "but never seemed to be a believer," while Phill, at age nine, like his mother, refused to attend church. His father, an entomologist at the experiment station, was the author of over 175 scientific papers on insect pests and worked to discourage pesticide use by U.S. and Latin American farmers. Phill's mother was for a long time the only woman physician in Wooster and founded the local chapter of Planned Parenthood.

Community ties. Both of Phill's parents were leaders in the community. His father was president of the American Legion, a deacon in the Presbyterian church, and even a caller for square dances. His mother helped women avoid abortion by teaching them to use contraception. Both parents were members of the Board of Education, and as Phill remembers it, Wooster was a relatively classless town, in part because Wooster High School drew from all parts of the city as well as the countryside.

Academic achievements. Although his school grades were not outstanding, Phill played the trumpet in band and orchestra and participated in debate and extemporaneous speaking contests. At fifteen he became the youngest-ever Eagle Scout in the state of Ohio. In 1947, just before his senior year, he had a life-changing experience in a work camp during the summer in Chambon-sur-Lignon, France, a town made famous by the work of Protestants who saved many Jews during World War II. At the College of Wooster his interest in quantitative methods and social stratification was awakened by two memorable teachers, Ernest Q. Campbell and Cecil C. North. His independent study on the sociology of Arnold Toynbee would prefigure his interest in macrosociology during retirement.

Marginality and sociology. Of the six Wayne County sociologists, Phill Cutwright's is the least clear case of boundary crossing and role conflict that so often appear to fuel the sociological imagination. Nevertheless, the family's secular attitude toward religion, an unusual mother who was a practicing physician and proponent of contraception, and the experience of doing humanitarian work in France as a young adult sensitized him to complexity in the social world. His early work on political sociology with Peter Rossi; his voluminous research on fertility, family size, and poverty; and his current work on educational attainment all point to an effort to understand social issues that he first encountered in his youth.

Since retirement Phillips Cutwright has published seventeen papers in refereed journals. He reports that once he no longer had to teach enormous introductory sociology classes, he felt a surge in energy directed toward research. In the course of thinking back over his life, he has somewhat redefined his self-image as a "macrolevel quantitative sociologist."

John W. Meyer (b. 1935)

John Meyer, a recipient of many honors, is known for his insights about cultural scripts that shape individual behavior worldwide, especially in schools, organizations, and the global order. A graduate of Goshen College in 1955 with an M.A. from the University of Colorado, he received his Ph.D. from Columbia in 1965, moved to Stanford in 1966, and became a full professor in 1978, with joint appointments in education and international studies. His former students have collected portions of his signature works in *The Writings of John W. Meyer* (2009).

A distinctive family. John comes from Smithville, a few miles from Wooster, where his family were active in the Oak Grove Mennonite Church. His father had a Ph.D. in history from Harvard and taught at Case Western Reserve. His mother had taught school before marriage. Both John's parents, as well as his sister and brother, were graduates of Goshen, a Mennonite college.

Community ties. John's experience of the close-knit Mennonite community was largely negative—a world of "dull rural living" and "enforced community" from which bright young people tended to escape. Following a rule infraction during his junior year at Goshen, he was suspended and had to do alternative service before he could graduate. As a medical test subject in an army hospital, he "experienced some achievement of human freedom" from the "oppressive" rural midwestern Mennonite world. Yet Mennonite beliefs had their appeal: a suspicion of the state and large-scale organizations, opposition to war, and international work for peace.[3]

---

3. John W. Meyer, "Reflections on a Half-Century of Mennonite Change," *Mennonite Quarterly Review* 76, no. 2 (2003): 1–20.

Academic achievements. John clearly was a precocious child: He read the encyclopedia when he was six or seven years old. He skipped first grade and senior year and entered college at the age of fifteen. Especially interested in science, he read widely and majored in psychology. But Goshen was restrictive in many ways, and he did not find liberation until he became a graduate student in sociology at the University of Colorado and Columbia University. He noted that his "poor fit in the Mennonite world of the period, personal qualities that were seen as defects . . . became on entering graduate school virtues. . . . Unusual ideas indicated that I was 'imaginative,' [rather than] 'impractical.' My . . . arguments and their logical structure indicated scientific talent rather than 'immaturity' and 'irresponsibility.'"[4]

Marginality and a path to sociology. Meyer sees institutions and organizations as shaping actors from the top down rather than from the bottom up, perhaps because of his experience in the Mennonite world. Cultural ideas, myths, and ceremonies require conformity to increase legitimacy of organizations and states. Society then attributes certain characteristics to familiar categories such as "the college graduate" despite massive individual variation. These concepts help explain growing acceptance of universal human rights, equality of women, and a global civil society, even in the face of huge national and cultural differences.

Despite his formal retirement in 2001, John goes to his office every day, teaches about a third of his time, and continues with collaborative projects, largely because there is continued interest in studies of globalization for which many colleagues solicit his participation.

David A. Snow (b. 1943)

David Snow is known internationally for his work on social movements using a framing perspective and for his ethnographic research on homelessness. With a B.A. in 1966 from Ohio University, an M.A. from the University of Akron in 1971, and a Ph.D. in sociology from UCLA in 1976, he launched his major work at the University of Texas at Austin and continued at the University of Arizona and finally the University of California at Irvine, where he moved in 2001. The recipient of a variety of honors here and abroad, he served as president of the Pacific Sociological Association and Society for Symbolic Interaction as well as vice president of the American Sociological Association.

A distinctive family. David's parents came from Michigan, where his father was a farmer and his mother became a registered nurse. Following a move to Ohio, his father's work evolved from farm manager to salesman for a feed company to manager for the Wooster Lumber Company, in charge of

---

4. Ibid., 11.

building pole barns. David's paternal grandparents both had a college education, but his own father did not because at age eighteen he took over the farm
when his father died. David's mother was a public-health nurse in Wooster
and eventually the director of nursing for several nursing homes. The family
with their five children regularly attended the Wooster Methodist Church.

Community ties. Occasionally the family took in needy children from
Cleveland during the summer. His parents were active and highly regarded
in the wider community and among the Amish carpenters who worked for
David's father, as was evident when their foreman came to both his father's
funeral in 1999 and his mother's in 2013.

Academic achievements. David started school in a tiny town in northeastern Ohio where he remembers sitting in a dunce chair in the corner. At
Wooster Township he was a daydreamer and narrowly missed being put in
the vocational track at Wooster High.

The combination of winning a partial football scholarship to college,
a semester with a friend's family in Rome, and his antiwar thinking while
serving in the military gradually increased his academic self-confidence and
belief in his own intellectual ability. (David in fact contributed an article to
the antiwar publication *The Bond*.) After working as a juvenile parole officer in Cleveland, he decided to study urban sociology at the University of
Akron.

Marginality and a path to sociology. His younger sister's participation
in a range of movements while at Ohio State during the late 1960s and early
1970s coupled with his own antiwar sentiments led to his study of collective behavior. David's dissertation on a Buddhist-oriented chanting group
became his initial touchstone for insights on social movement processes,
including his much-cited 1986 article "Frame Alignment Processes" in
American Sociological Review. A crisis over where to relocate the Salvation
Army in Austin lent itself to an extension of framing theory and David's
continuing work on the problem of homelessness and poverty while also
serving on various related commissions and boards in Arizona and California.

Even though David is now at the age of retirement, he continues full
steam ahead with his teaching, writing, community service, and leadership
of a band of social movement researchers and advocates for the homeless.

Glenn Firebaugh (b. 1948)

Glenn Firebaugh is a demographer and methodologist who focuses on social inequality related to income, race, gender, ethnicity, and neighborhood
segregation. He graduated from Grace College in Indiana in 1970 and received an M.A. in 1974 and Ph.D. in 1976 from Indiana University. Beginning at Vanderbilt, he moved to Penn State in 1988 and served as editor of

the *American Sociological Review* from 1997 to 2000. He has been a regular instructor for courses on methodology here and abroad. He became president of the Sociological Research Association in 2016.

A distinctive family. Glenn was born in Charleston, West Virginia, where his father was a chemist with DuPont and his mother, a homemaker. His parents, both college graduates, moved the family to Wayne County in the 1950s when his father bought a farm, partnered with his brother, and set out to be his own boss. Not until later did Glenn realize that the family had gone from middle class to below the poverty line.

Community ties. Glenn started Wooster Township School in sixth grade, where his classmates ranged from children of a lawyer to farm kids. The family attended the Grace Brethren Church, where many members were politically conservative farmers and laborers who didn't appreciate the denomination's peace doctrine during the Vietnam War. The community helped each other and shared farm equipment such as a corn picker or his uncle's welder.

Academic achievements. Glenn attended the new Triway High School, which opened in 1963 and drew students from three semirural townships, resulting in a more sports-oriented and less academic ethos than Wooster High. Glenn was a successful debater and extemporaneous speaker, which had the effect of making him comfortable with public speaking later on. Although known as a "brain," he suffered a health setback during his junior year that made him choose a smaller school than Ohio State. At Grace College he became president of student government. As a result of good courses, a budding social conscience, and the social ferment of the late 1960s, he attended graduate school with a fellowship in sociology to study at Indiana University.

Marginality and a path to sociology. Glenn soon gravitated to quantitative methods and demography. His dissertation director was Phillips Cutwright, but neither knew at the time that they both came from Wayne County. Glenn loved to experiment with various kinds of quantitative methods and was particularly interested in the study of inequality, perhaps because of his early experience in a community with a "flat class structure." In a eureka moment one summer at the Institute for Social Research at Michigan he realized that the various coefficients for measuring inequality (such as the familiar Gini index) could be reduced to a single form of equation. From that insight Glenn has amassed an imposing body of work related to methodology and social inequality.

Although he has not yet formally retired, Glenn sees his approach to sociological research as becoming increasingly selective over time and attentive to matters of social conscience. Earlier he chose to work only on what was publishable, then only on what could appear in the best journals. But now his priority is on research that can have a significant social impact.

Parallels in Becoming a Sociologist from Wayne County

All six of the Wayne County group came from families that were unconventional in some way but valued education. All six excelled in school, either from a very early age or at a later point. They reached prominence in sociology by delving into questions that were personally important to them. Probably the same could be said of many other sociologists who come from other places. But why there is any connection between specialization in sociology and starting out in Wayne County is not obvious. My hunch is that there is some aspect of each person's small face-to-face community and eventual departure from it that is the common thread. This thread is one variant of the marginality that can be found in the lives of many artists and innovators.

Each of these sociologists had two kinds of experience that in combination appear to be distinguishing features. They lived in a family and place where give and take with other members of the community was a necessary and important fact of life. But at the same time they had some experience in that community or in another place that set them apart enough to stimulate a critical and analytical approach to social expectations that others took for granted.

Salience of community ties. All six of these social scientists lived in a remarkably thick community of informal connections, friendships, and social ties; many shared connections only one degree removed from each other. The result was a pattern of mutual help and trust, resulting in a relatively low level of class consciousness and a generous accumulation of "social capital" that James Coleman has shown is necessary to the general well-being of a community. Yet the small community also invites nonconformity because of its very closeness.[5]

Stimulus to a sociological career. Against this backdrop of mutual trust and exchange, questioning of normal routines led each one to sociological analysis precisely along the lines where each had strayed from accepted rules and expectations. To me, the limitations of the rural community were evident despite its neighborliness and mutual help. So also were the cramped expectations that confined women to home production and caregiving. Not surprisingly I studied the rural-to-urban transition in family life and the equal rights movement for women. For Joan Huber a similar conflict between expectation that she would be a well-educated homemaker and her own aspirations drove her to analyze the economic and biological reasons behind women's second place. Phillips Cutwright rejected organized religion at age nine, saw his mother's pioneering work in Planned Parenthood, and forged his early career in the demography of fertility and family size. John Meyer

---

5. James S. Coleman, *Foundations of Social Theory* (Cambridge, MA: Belknap Press of Harvard University Press, 1990).

resisted the enforced community of the Mennonites and became known for his sociological insight into the power of social and cultural scripts. David Snow saw the contrast between the trusting community of his youth and work as a juvenile corrections officer, antiwar draftee, and observer of exotic social movements. Glenn Firebaugh, experiencing the contrast between his family's middle-class beginnings and poverty-level farm life, came to focus on all kinds of inequality, particularly disparities across income distribution.

It may be, however, that this group of six is a generational phenomenon. There may be no comparable group of younger sociologists from Wayne County because the small communities that were once enclosed are now more connected to the world beyond. Marginality in that context may be of a different order that does not inspire a sociological career.

Given the fact that this account covers the lives of six sociologists of retirement age, it is remarkable that none of them has fully retired. They continue to go to the office, do research, and produce numerous publications. The common theme is one of enjoying the freedom that allows them to avoid unrewarding duties and instead focus on what they most love to do.

6

The Sociological Consequences of Choosing Radical Parents

The Political, the Personal, and the Professional

Peter Mandel Hall

One day when I was almost three, my mother came home from work and was greeted by an upset housekeeper, who reported that I had misbehaved. She had told me to get down on my knees and pray to God to forgive me. She said I replied, "I will not, and besides, what is he doing in my playpen anyway?" My mother told this story with pride. It represents the first accounting of my oppositional identity.

I am a red diaper baby, an announced and attributed, hidden and revealed, identity. My parents were American communists for twenty-five years. During the period 1934–1959 we lived in diverse places and different times: Birmingham, Alabama; Washington, D.C.; New York City; Berkeley, California; a depression, world war, and cold war. My father organized midwestern farmers, led the party in Alabama, and was Washington correspondent for the *Daily Worker*. My mother, a party activist, worked for left-wing labor unions and law firms and led local party branches.

Like my red diaper peers, I believed the centrality of Left politics for everyday life, a belief in political efficaciousness, historical and international awareness, and an oppositional identity. That background also came with emotional consequences that one writer termed the "shackled self" as repression, intimidation, and fear constrained development and expression.[1] There were lost adolescences, family ties, freedoms, and a sense of belonging. I did

---

1. Margaret Morganroth Gullette, "No Longer Suppressing Grief: Political Trauma in Twentieth-Century America," *Life Writing* 5, no. 2 (2008): 254.

not go public until 1994 at age sixty, when receiving the Mead Award from the Society for the Study of Symbolic Interaction (SSSI). That was a long time to hide.

I am writing a memoir about my youth linking the personal and political. I am also writing about how I became a sociologist, the consequences of that choice, and my evolution as a sociologist. The following narrative is part of a longer story. It is divided into three parts; truncated presentation of my pre-Ph.D. life, a summary of the evolution of my sociology from social psychology to social organization, and the still-evolving retirement phase and its relationship to sociology.

This American Life

I was born in Chicago in warm August 1934. My Jewish grandmother (Bubbe) came from New York to help my mother. Her "help" was to swaddle me with blankets. My mother feared Bubbe would, minimally, send me to the hospital, so she wanted her to leave. Fortunately, my grandfather (Zayde) staged a heart attack, and Bubbe had her first plane ride back home. Zayde was opposed to my parents' marriage because my father was not only a goy but a Red goy.

My father grew up in Mobile, Alabama, in a middle-class, Baptist family who had a history of several centuries in the South. My father's great-grandfather was sheriff of Dallas County in the early 1860s and led parades in Selma to send soldiers off to battle. Farther east in Monroe County, up the road from Monroeville, made famous by Harper Lee, a great-grandmother had a large plantation.

My father broke with his heritage and became a "race traitor," influenced by two socialist Jewish brothers who encouraged him to enroll at Columbia University. My mother, a Latvian immigrant at two, graduated from high school at sixteen and entered Hunter College, where she was politically active. In 1932 they both joined the Communist Party and were married. They were divorced in 1950, and both left the party in the mid-1950s. My mother returned to school, obtained a Ph.D. in anthropology, and became an expert on murals at Teotihuacan. My father became publisher of weekly newspapers in the Adirondacks and editor of the *Conservationist* magazine.

Having chosen my parents,[2] I followed them to Alabama (1935–1944), New York City twice (1944–1946, 1950–1953), and Washington, D.C. (1946–1950). There are many stories, but here I focus on some key events and formative experiences.

---

2. This is, of course, a joke; as sociologists who teach stratification tell their students, the best way to be successful is to choose your parents wisely.

My Alabama days were idyllic. I had great adventures, grandparents and cousins, and success in school. I was shielded from knowledge of my parents' activities. Their Alabama was dangerous and hostile. Close friends were beaten severely. My father was arrested and under surveillance by the FBI. My mother experienced a bullet coming through my bedroom window. She also was fired from a defense job during the war for being a communist. My father would be drafted late and harassed during basic training for political reasons. But they were also part of historically significant interracial organizations in the Deep South. My ideas about race were rooted in that experience. So it was of no consequence when we were readying to move north and a classmate said, "You're gonna go to school with 'niggers.'" What could be worse!

After several years in the Bronx where I had exposure to Jewish culture, the wonders of the big city, and the experience of being behind in school and uncomfortably out of place, we moved back south to Washington, D.C., just in time for the Red Scare, Cold War, and junior high school. I learned quickly that what my parents did was dangerous, radical, and un-American. The latter was a heavy stigma for a teenager. I learned quickly to keep secrets and not discuss household happenings. In school where there was sporadic "commie kid" harassing, I maintained a double consciousness of following my parents' perspectives but playing the class clown and not exposing myself.

In the spring of 1950 in the middle of adolescent angst, marginal social status, and hostile political context, I was called to the first and last family meeting to learn my parents were divorcing. Confused and upset, I wondered what this meant for me, how to express myself at the new uncommon status being added to uncommon circumstances. I responded by suppressing feelings and blaming my mother, which had long-term counterproductive consequences.

We moved back to New York City, where I found a place in a lively Left community. I became connected to a network of red diaper youth through being a counselor for three years at a small summer camp in Vermont run by two well-connected former party members. Many of the counselors and campers were children of prominent party members. Some campers had parents who were in jail or underground. The camp was a haven for kids who could be themselves, feel secure, and be with others who shared their values, secrets, and fears. Alumni recall the camp as a special time of their life during scary times. This was also a period, however, when I began to have questions about party orthodoxy and Stalinist Russia. I shared this with a few peers but got messages to either keep quiet or rethink my questions.

Those years were particularly difficult ones, being marked by the Korean War, trials of party leaders, and the specter of McCarthyism. I registered for the draft and took the Fifth Amendment when refusing to indicate any membership in subversive organizations. The most disturbing event during that period was the execution of the Rosenbergs. On the night of June 19, 1953, I stood with my mother and thousands of others near Union Square, hoping in vain that President Eisenhower would reprieve them. Many worried, if them, why not all of us? There was legislation that prepared internment for subversives. We knew that. And "They" knew where we were.

Moving west, I enrolled at the University of California (UC), Berkeley, in fall 1953. While wanting to study history where Reds were being fired not hired, I meandered through biochemistry, plant physiology, and beer and bridge to social welfare. I sought admission to the master's program, but at the interview I stonewalled when asked about my divorced parents. The dean was a strong anti-Red, and I believed if my background became known, I would be rejected. On advice from an alumna I returned, finished the interview, and was admitted. A blacklisted UC instructor, and then a longshoreman commenting on my social work plans, said, "Oh great, now you're pimping for the status quo!" I reflected on that while in the program and eventually decided I wanted something else but had no answer.

My field placements at a Quaker settlement house in a black community and a county juvenile hall were influential through revealing local reality and pointing me toward my interests in race and juvenile delinquency. I rebelled against the Freudian-dominated program perspective. I sought out Tamotsu Shibutani, a renowned teacher and esteemed interactionist, for entry into sociology to study the self-conception of delinquents. He advised to me go elsewhere, as the Berkeley department was not congenial to symbolic interaction.

Berkeley, of course, was more than academics. The university had a prominent legal conflict over a loyalty oath, and some prominent faculty left in protest in 1950. The campus also did not allow political speakers. The Sociology Department became the center of a student movement that challenged the university's policies, irrelevance, and exclusion of student interests. Toward an Active Student Community (TASC), formed in 1957, brought students together, mainly from social sciences and humanities. Many were grad students. Two factions emerged, one along lines of "Politics First" and a centralized organization to win elections and the other, "Education First," with a loose, evolving structure dependent on issues and discussions to alter consciousness, which I joined. The Politics First group won the debate, and the organization later became SLATE. In 1959 the campus elected a SLATE president and several council members. The following year the administration moved to disenfranchise graduate students and suspend SLATE, which reemerged several years later as part of the free speech movement in 1964.

While at Berkeley, I struggled with what to do with my life. I did not apply myself. I was not adopting Marxism as a perspective or going to work in a profession dominated by Freud. Sociology was a solution to a set of identity

problems I had as a prospective sociologist. I had a perspective that was neither Marxist nor Freudian. I had a problem to study, an area of interest, and
a place to do that. I had a future that would accommodate and enhance not
only study but praxis. While not wanting to follow my parents' old politics,
I was embedded in their values, but in a post-Stalin, New Left orientation.
Shibutani had recommended Minnesota, which admitted me. I set off for
Minnesota with a new sense of purpose, future, and identity.

The Making of a Sociologist

The transition from the Bay Area to Minneapolis was dramatic. Once you
got past the shock from others as to why one would do that, the weather hit
you with an early September snow and the 360-degree skid on the street. I
found some Lefties, heard Bob Dylan when he was Zimmerman, and joined
Fair Play for Cuba. I came unfunded and picked up a job on a research project doing coding. I came with no sociology so had to take three undergraduate courses. After that, funding came, courses were passed, relations with my
adviser were business-like, and adaptation to climate and culture happened.

I brought with me my bicoastal sense of being hip and politically attuned
to the Left ways of the world. Several faculty members chastised me for being
presumptive and even arrogant. I learned from two close friends who were
midwesterners to back off a bit, be silent for a change, listen respectfully,
and be more accepting of others. They accepted authority more readily than
I did. But I received awards from the department and high marks on com-
prehensives and was focused on finishing the program. Our one organized
rebellion was to get a reading list for the extensive comprehensive exams.

The program had some oddities and odd faculty. Sociological theory was
not learned through primary sources but the professor's textbook. Statistics
was not learning how to use tests but an abstract oration on philosophy.
Methods was a disjointed conversation between two faculty who did not
agree on much. My adviser read my dissertation in one sitting and found a
typo. My defense was not a defense but turned into a conversation among
colleagues. There were some excellent classes and teachers: a kindly gentleman teaching conflict, a Chicago school course on work, and a Mormon
one on the family. There was also an infamous alcoholic who inspired and
encouraged many interactionists. But much of learning sociology was self-
taught, learned from peers or done on the job later.

The biggest problem of my graduate career arose when I left the chair of
the department off my committee. He used a psychological test to study delinquency. I questioned its assumptions and was determined not to use it. At
a Midwest sociological meeting reception, he cornered me among a number
of graduate students and assailed my impudence, competence, ethics, and
future. Aside from that I was fine.

My fellow students thought I was smart to keep silent and were amazed at the flailing. I did learn to not respond, and I was humbled. It would take me a long time to adopt some of the midwestern style. I left Minnesota to become a real sociologist.

I came out of graduate school as a social psychologist who studied the self but also taught theory, race and ethnic relations, and collective behavior and social movements. My interest in politics, history, and inequality would continue to poke at me. There were some parallel developments at my first three jobs that set the stage for an evolving sociology. At Iowa I created the course on political sociology and chafed at the absence of critical or inter-actionist sources. In addition I was a member of an interdisciplinary faculty group encouraging campus discussion and action on southern segregation. A number of our students joined Freedom Summer in Mississippi.

At Santa Barbara I began to develop an interactionist political sociology using Murray Edelman's symbolic politics and my colleague Walter Buckley on power. I was also active politically on campus and in the community in antiwar protests and peace marches; mediating between black students who had seized a building and the administration; riding buses to Sacramento protesting Governor Ronald Reagan's university policies; and finally cochairing Gene McCarthy's county primary campaign. I taught political sociology in spring quarter 1968, and my last lecture wove concepts together with current events. I confess to being dramatic and urging engagement. I finished and silently walked out of the auditorium to the only standing ovation of my teaching career.

At York University in Toronto I cotaught a black studies course blending all of North America into the class material. After the kidnapping and murder of the labor minister of the Quebec provincial government, I witnessed the ease with which martial law was established without protest. Yet I was intrigued by the politics of the provinces and the existence of a social democratic party. Most significantly Kent State–Cambodia happened. Being distant but attentive, Jack Hewitt and I wrote an article published in *Social Problems* on how Presidents Johnson and Nixon used communication strategies and tactics to redefine or reframe political conflicts as problems of misunderstanding or ignorance. I began to draw out my ideas on politics and conception of power that culminated in "A Symbolic Interactionist Analysis of Politics," published in *Sociological Inquiry* in 1972.

That same year I was hired as the chairman of sociology and rural sociology at the University of Missouri. The university was under censure from the American Association of University Professors (AAUP) for punitive actions against sociology faculty for canceling classes in response to Kent State–Cambodia. My job was to get them off censure. That happened, but more as the result of the doings of others. I served only three years as chair, partly because I felt constrained by the administrative role on a very conservative campus and wanted to be freer and critical in a faculty role. My main contribution as chair was to foster a greater intellectual conversation about ideas. One example was a course on inequality that brought ten speakers to campus, including William Domhoff and Arlene Daniels.

In 1973 a number of us created the SSSI. I became the first regular editor of its journal and later president. In 1994 I received the Mead Award for career contributions, which were responses to the criticism of the symbolic interactionist perspective as being ahistorical, astructural, apolitical, and only micro. I disagreed with those contentions. My agenda became the development of a framework that would challenge those arguments and also expand the perspective.

Over the next thirty years I published a series of articles addressing power, social organization, and inequality. The work was done in the context of institutions, organizations, and policy, particularly in education. In 1986 my Midwest Sociological Society presidential address reviewed works by interactionists on social orders and social worlds in the 1970s and 1980s and constructed a framework that linked history, structure, and action contexts processually across space and time. Rereading George Herbert Mead, I found discussion of the role of the hand in sensing and manipulating the environment and objects. I used it to signify activity, a primary pragmatist tenet and a shift from conventional focus on symbol and meaning.

Today there is an important conversation taking place about the actual works of Mead and Herbert Blumer's formulation of symbolic interaction. Thirty-five years ago Anselm Strauss began a critique of Blumer and a derivation from Everett Hughes. I have been following that direction on social organization separate from social psychology. That work includes inequality in education, policy contexts and processes, metapower as conditioning expression of power, and, more recently, spatial inequality and natural resource extraction. This is in sharp contrast to the self, situation, and interactional social psychology where I began.

I Thought You Were Retired

At the end of my time at Missouri, I was chairing the campus promotion and tenure committee, serving on the campus strategic planning committee, and serving as a member of the campus institutional review board. There did not seem more to do there. I officially received my emeritus merit badge in 2000. There was still some writing left to do to finish developing ideas. I was also reading in science studies, biology, cosmology, and evolution. The university meanwhile was prioritizing and investing in the life sciences. A large, tall new building, named after a Republican senator, was erected to be filled by many new hires. However, sociology and other liberal arts faculties were absent from this largesse. I took my reading and went to the chancellor with a proposal for a life sciences and society symposium, which was greeted with encouragement and financial support. I organized the first two symposia, one on genetics and the other on stem cells in 2004 and 2005. The symposium continues to this day.

Meanwhile, my wife and I did a great deal of traveling in the go-go retirement phase. There were two long tent camping trips in the Southwest, a Route 66 road trip, two sunny beach vacations on Dauphin Island, several weeks in Hawaii, a road trip in Ireland, and two yoga retreats in Tuscany and Corfu with extended train and bus rides around Italy and Greece. Traveling, however, took a vacation as the economy tanked and our retirement account lost value. Simultaneously the tie to the university became attenuated as space disappeared and emeriti became has-beens. I had begun the work on the memoir so was reading and writing at home.

In 2009 we decided to move to Colorado to help with a granddaughter because our son-in-law was working on a Ph.D. That meant, sadly, leaving other grandchildren. We expected the move to be temporary, so we rented, but there were many unanticipated consequences. Not only were the state's natural beauty and the environment attractive, but there were explorations both to observe and to experience on a regular basis all year. Hiking, biking, snowshoeing, and just renting cabins were regular occurrences. There were also a number of unexpected opportunities. Volunteering with the local Democratic Party led to becoming a member of a community and the unofficial photographer of events and campaigns. The openness of the city community led to my becoming chair of the human relations commission after a short time as a resident. The Sociology Department at Colorado State University (CSU) gave me a courtesy appointment, office space, invitations to teach, and access to students and faculty across campus. But most significantly, I have colleagues who are collegial, interesting, smart, productive, and supportive. So we have stayed, bought a house, and settled down.

The watershed moment of my retirement came in 2011 when I was diagnosed with duodenal cancer. I lost many pounds, had fevers, digestive issues, and days in bed. Blithely, I even did a rafting trip one day with my daughter's family. Two days later, my primary-care physician knew it was cancer and sent me into the stream of treatment. I had major surgery, two rounds of chemo, and one of radiation over the next year. I had a feeding tube for six months. My digestive system was reconfigured and my gall bladder removed. Left behind is an eight-inch scar across the belly, which the surgeon admired. I had amazing medical treatment and counseling support from a dedicated, caring, and outstanding staff. My family had incredible support from extended family, friends, and my CSU colleagues. And I thank God for Medicare!

For reasons that still astonish me, given my usual pessimism, I was upbeat and positive about the outcome. I never wavered in my belief I would survive. Others with knowledge of my cancer were not so sure. The treatment was successful and quicker than my oncologist expected. It is an understatement to say my life and my caregiver's (my remarkable wife's) life changed during that year. I could have died. We can never forget that cancer, even in remission, is always with us, and relationships change with that recognition. Tests continue to show no signs of return now almost three years later. I am fortunate, but my best friend of fifty years has died and other friends have died. A reality of retirement sadly is that you will lose family and friends and they will leave behind grieving families, but lives still to be lived. Each holiday and birthday bring memories of those gone. I regularly burn a yahrzeit candle for my mother and grandmother in remembrance.

Recently, sitting on the patio at a local brewery, having a beer with friends, I was approached by a gentleman who wondered if he was older than I. He said he was sixty-seven. I replied I was eighty. He said, "Oh, I thought I was the oldest one here. You don't look eighty. I thought you were in your sixties." I continue to be told I look sixtyish, and I manifest being younger. So I am happy with that persona. It is a good life. L'chaim! To life! Tsim gezunt! To your health! The good life is facilitated by good health. But old age, whatever that is, inevitably means decreasing well-being and, with that, constraints on living. I was a runner for twenty-five years but am now hobbled by injuries and unable to run. I once smoked heavily but quit in 1967. However, I now recognize my labored breathing is respiratory disease, and hikes and stairs need inhalers to assist. Stomach discomfort is now a chronic condition to go along with long-standing sleep disorders. Even walking and balance are off-kilter due to recently discovered skeletal problems. So life is good but in a different way. It requires accepting and adapting to limits. Some things I cannot do. Some things require less perfection. Some things require new ways. And in the end, like our parents and grandparents, we will die. So I work to make the best of it while here but also prepare for when I am not. I want loved ones to know I love them and let friends and colleagues know they are appreciated.

In 2014 I celebrated my eightieth birthday with lots of family and friends, including a cousin not seen since 1958. Retirement has meant the easier ability to see and communicate with children, grandchildren, and siblings who give meaning and feeling to my life. One of the consequences of my parents' politics was that family ties were severed. For over fifty years, there was no contact with cousins on both sides. Their parents wanted no contact, and one even hid my existence. Joyfully, retirement has seen the rebuilding and reconnection on both sides. A big surprise was finding that my grandmother had six siblings, and I had cousins I contacted in Israel, South Africa, Canada, and the United States. I also discovered family members who died in the Shoah and who were killed by Stalin's police. I have ventured into genealogy and found documents on my grandparents' and mother's entry through Ellis

Island, and I shared that with family. On my father's side I have information on ten generations, as they moved from Virginia down the coast and across the South, clustering in Alabama and Mississippi. I have a stronger commitment to family, present, past, and future than I did before retirement and before cancer.

The truly amazing development is that I am a still an active sociologist. I have a new research agenda on space, time, natural resources, and environment. I am affiliated with an environmental governance group, a center on disaster, and a school of global environmental sustainability. I will teach introductory sociology for the first time in a generation but will do it my way, through a focus on time, space, and environment. With several CSU colleagues, I will become a coeditor of the *Sociological Quarterly*. It is unfortunate that emeriti across the country often lose their offices and their places. Of course, I had to move for all this to happen. So I laugh when a senior colleague walks by the office and says, "Peter, you are giving a bad name to retirement." The meaning of sociology in and of my life is still evolving.

Coda

The consequences of growing up as a child of the old Left and its demise contributed to skepticism about assertions of truth and authority. This background contributes also to a sense of marginality and an imperative to express and act in opposition. My responses to Stalinism, Freud; study of delinquency; involvement with protest movements, educational reform, and now environmental issues; and the Missouri symposium all reflect that oppositional identity. The choice of sociology and study of inequality and power were confirmational. For me, sociology comes with a critical spirit, and that power and metapower are the mainstays of inequality. It is a conversation of critics, skeptics, and alternatives. Getting here was not a straight line but the right place to land. Not comfortable but accommodating, it fits, in part, who I am and what I do. It helps keep me in sufficient trouble. An oppositional identity could not ask for more. But it would be a false characterization to proclaim that is all I am. I find myself in places of peace and silence, friendship and community, collectivity and cooperation, ancestors and family. I feel a greater sense of being whole and grounded now than in the past. L'chaim!

7

My Professional Life

A Brief Memoir

THOMAS SCHEFF

My father wanted to be an engineer, but he had to go to work after only one year of college. So when it was my turn, he advised me to be what he had wanted. However, I flunked my first course, drafting, so I had to change my major. I picked physics out of the hat. I got a bachelor's degree in physics at the University of Arizona and went on to three years in graduate school at the University of California, Berkeley. To be on my own there, I also got a full-time job tending a cyclotron in a radiation lab.

It wasn't long, however, before I got bored with my courses and the lab. At first the lab seemed to me the height of glamour and income; I was dumbfounded with my good luck. But the repetitiveness of the work was beginning to tell. Also I noticed that my fellow workers were not into much conversation. Most of them wanted to talk about gadgets of various kinds. If I brought up anything else—politics, literature, film, and so on—little response. I began to look around for a new road.

During my last year in grad school, I sat in on courses in history, anthropology, sociology, and psychology. The psychology and sociology classes seemed the most interesting. Through a mutual friend, I met Arlene Kaplan (later Arlene Daniels), who solved my problem of picking between psychology and sociology. She was an English major, but she was also visiting sociology classes because she was enraptured with a professor. It was through Arlene that I met Tom Shibutani.

Arlene and I followed Tom and his grad students around as hangers-on. Their talk was of great interest because it seemed to be about important matters. Since Tom was a sociological social psychologist, he attracted students with broad interests in social science. When I talked to him about switching from physics to sociology, he was encouraging.

I thought, What the hell, you're young only once. The graduate adviser in sociology was also encouraging. Although I had only one sociology course, he said I would be admitted to the grad program if I took six courses in sociology and got As in all of them. By this time I was no longer a physics student, but I continued to work in the lab for income.

I took five courses in one semester and the statistics course by exam. I was then admitted as a graduate student in sociology. I also did something else completely on my own: I tried to interest the radiation lab in a union. Not the one where I worked, Crocker, which was a small unit on campus. I gave up on them; they had no interest at all in any kind of politics. Instead, I handed out leaflets at the gate of the big lab on the hill, which employed thousands. Some of them seemed interested, but never enough to get involved.

However, the FBI was very interested. My life was suddenly filled with young men in suits and ties. Since no one else in Berkeley dressed that way, it was a dead giveaway. They interviewed me several times, as well as my colodgers, my coworkers, and probably my teachers. There were always photographers at Sather Gate political forays, taking pictures of the crowd. But after I stood outside the gates of the radiation lab, one of them usually seemed to display interest in taking pictures of me.

I couldn't understand why there was so much interest in me, strictly small potatoes. I was a solitary figure making no headway, Cuchulain fighting the invulnerable tide. Years later, I found out, when reading a book about the head of the lab at the time, Robert Oppenheimer. Shortly before I began my organizing attempt, he had been denounced by Edward Teller as disloyal. The FBI was taking no chances, not even with small fry. I could have gotten busted, but I didn't.

There was one detail related to my switch to sociology at the age of twenty-three that I should mention. I knew that as soon as I switched, I would lose my deferment from the draft. This was no small issue, since the Korean War was waging hot and heavy at the time. I knew it, but I switched anyway. I was bored with physics; sociology was exciting. As I said to myself on many occasions in those days, "What the hell!"

The English poet William Hazlitt wrote that no man under forty thinks he will ever die. That was certainly true of me. Impulsively I made a decision that would inevitably land me in the army during a dangerous war. Politically, I didn't approve of the war, and I didn't want to kill anyone, let alone get killed.

I am completely uncertain what was going on the mind of that twenty-three-year-old idiot that was me in those days. Perhaps I thought that it would be an adventure. Or only slightly less likely, I didn't see why I should be deferred when others were going. In some hidden abyss of my consciousness, I might have thought that I owed it to my country. Shortly after my switch, I received an induction notice from my draft board.

I lived through sixteen weeks of arduous basic training at Fort Ord, California, in a company that was going to Korea. But at the last minute, the army somehow found out about my background in physics, so they sent me to a technical center in Maryland instead. Dumb luck! In the minimum possible time, twenty-one months, I was released from the army to go back to graduate school. Because of my political background, I got no promotion to private first class, perhaps the only instance in the history of the army, but I didn't care. Compared to the army, or even my past life, Berkeley beckoned with its aura of glamour and glory. I was infatuated.

Berkeley

I had had time to take only one semester of classes before being drafted into the army. The most exciting class was from Philip Selznick, who used the discussion method. It was much more stimulating to me than Tom's polished lectures. It allowed students to participate, a roller-coaster ride of anxiety and exhilaration. It took me awhile, but I finally got around to using the same method in my own teaching.

Our social psychology gang got together once or twice a month at Chinese restaurants in San Francisco. I helped Arlene make it through statistics. In return, she taught me how to write an essay. I had failed my first attempt at the written examination for the master's degree, since I gave what I considered to be the answer without any introduction or framing, without showing my work. The graders couldn't recognize what I said to be answers since they were so brief.

When I spoke to the graduate adviser about failing the exam, he told me that I might be better off in another field. But Tom Shibutani encouraged me to try again. He was on the top floor of a huge old building, sequestered like a monk in a tiny office. I was rattled when I came in. In his slow, ceremonious way, he calmed me down by asking questions about my life and my family. Then finally he allowed me to voice my doubts about continuing. He said I was an independent thinker, a rare thing, and that I would one day contribute to the field.

As it turned out, I was more influenced by Tom than by any of my other teachers. I was unimpressed by his lectures, unlike my friend Arlene. She was captivated. But in informal discussions with him, both alone and in his little coterie, I must have learned to think like he did and about the kinds of problems that he was interested in. It took me a long time to realize and appreciate the extent of his influence.

Teaching

My first job in sociology was five long years at the University of Wisconsin. I was nominally an assistant professor but no more than a research assistant to two senior professors. I was also writing my dissertation and teaching very large, mostly introductory classes made up of around three hundred students. I felt worked to death and missed seeing my two children. I stayed alive by ignoring messages from one of the senior professors but couldn't do that with the other one. He sought me out if I hid and sent me all over the state on his research work. I searched desperately for a job elsewhere.

Over the years, I developed a style of teaching that was radically different from lecturing. I began rearranging the seating so that students would form a circle or, in a large class, concentric circles. If possible, I would have at least the inner circle sitting on the floor. So that I would not to be the center of attention and students would see and talk to each other, I joined them in the inner circle. As I saw that the changes increased student participation and the depth of student learning, I lectured less and less.

By the last two years at Wisconsin, I had cut down on lecturing, but not entirely. Several years later in Santa Barbara, my role became more and more a coach and resource, with students taking over parts of the traditional teaching role. I sat on the floor with the students in the inner circle. Volunteers chaired the meeting, planned the agenda, and kept time on the various agenda topics. After a few years in Santa Barbara, I had found what I was looking for, the discovery method of teaching. A Yale professor of art made the point quite clearly: "If you tell someone something, you keep the person from learning it."

But as I changed the format of teaching, I also included more of the things that I knew myself, at first hand, for sure. In addition to reporting the state of the field, I began to include my own explorations in my classes. With this change, they became more and more hands-on and therefore more richly satisfying to me and to a majority of the students, but not for all. There were usually some students who were confused by or resentful of the new format and content. Only a small minority, they occasionally introduced some static into the proceedings.

The changes had many benefits. My classes became lively, even at times exhilarating. The improvised style created high drama in the classroom. As the students became participants in a dialogue, there were moments of humor, discovery, and solidarity. In this vein, I was free to go very deeply into issues. But there were also costs. Some students complained that although they were learning very useful things, they might not be learning enough about the field. Even though these students were only a tiny minority, their complaints stung because I could see their point. I tried to strike a balance.

Intellectually, I felt justified in not focusing entirely on teaching the field because I believed, and still believe, that most of what is accepted in the field verges on being useless—either untrue or unimportant. This attitude has been liberating for me in one way. Rather than just repeat what the authorities are saying about mental illness, attunement, catharsis, or emotions, I have been free to explore them for myself. But my attitude has also isolated me from most of my colleagues. I am no longer part of the City, as Aristotle put it.

Research Areas: Labeling, Attunement, Catharsis, and the Social-Emotional World

I more or less stumbled on my first direction, the labeling of mental illness. After I had passed the Ph.D. exam, Tom Shibutani found me a six-month internship at Stockton State Hospital, near Sacramento. I accepted because it would exactly tide me over financially until my job started in Madison. In the hospital, I was just an observer. At first I visited all the wards but, after a month or so, began to concentrate on back wards and soon just one. I picked it because, like the other back wards, there was virtually no treatment going on. On the ward that I focused on, I was sure there was no treatment at all. So I decided to find out what it was that was happening there.

This experience led to the next one. While I was working in Madison, the legislature offered to pay a research assistant for a study of the statewide mental health system. Since no one else applied for the grant, I got it. The social work grad student I hired turned out to be a hard worker. Between the two of us, we traversed the state gathering data. My first book, *Being Mentally Ill*, was the result and continued my interest in labeling. This book was mostly responsible for the writing and passage of new California law that effectively closed all state mental hospitals. Other states and countries followed suit: a big help in ending the oppression of the mentally ill.

I can't remember how I got started on my second topic, what I call degree of attunement. Since I had been Erving Goffman's teaching assistant at Berkeley and he later served as mentor, it could have rubbed off from him. If so, it would have been quite indirect, since I hadn't read any of his work until many years later. The idea is that there are different degrees of solidarity between individuals, ranging from complete connectedness, on the one hand, to complete isolation, on the other. At the heart of the concept were different levels of connection: (1) I know something, (2) I know that you know the same, (3) I know that you know that I know, and so on. Isolation is not even reaching the second level; attunement is reaching the fourth level. My first publication in this vein was about the concept of consensus, at both the interpersonal and societal levels.

My interest in this idea continued through the publication of several articles and most recently, a book. It is based on my systematic study of top pop-song lyrics between 1930 and 2000. One of its tasks was to try to define genuine love, which turns out to be problematic both for the public and for researchers. My book defines family love in terms of attachment and attunement; romantic love adds attraction, usually sexual. Unlike my first book, this one has been like the others, attracting little attention.

Emotions!

My final path has been the social-emotional world. Once again, I stumbled on it. In 1969, after I had divorced my first wife, she took the children with her to Hawaii for a year. To my surprise, I got so depressed that I could hardly work. In fact, I stopped research and writing entirely. I did the absolute minimum of work possible. Since I was chair of the Sociology Department at the time, I filled those obligations. But when I was alone in my office, I put my feet on the desk and stared at the wall. Without my children, I had lost interest.

I made arrangements for a trip to Hawaii to see the children. In the meanwhile, I tried various forms of therapy, but to no avail. Finally, I found one that worked for me. I went to a six-hour self-help group psychotherapy class called reevaluation counseling. I understood almost nothing of what was said but was envious of the students who were crying during the class. I really wanted to cry also, but something was missing. I found out what it was that evening when I was telling my lover about the class.

When I got to the part about the crying in class, I started to cry myself. At first it was painful. But after only a few moments, I fell into a crying spree that was like nothing that had ever happened to me before. I didn't feel in control of my body: it was crying me, and it was wonderful. After some fifteen minutes, the crying stopped, but my tears had soaked the pillow. I thought it was over, but it had been just a first step.

A few minutes after the crying stopped, I was catching my breath when a new episode began. With no volition on my part, I began to growl, writhe, and bite at the air. The writhing became so pronounced that I fell out of bed. Apparently I was violently angry but without a clue what I was angry about. Finding myself lying on a shag rug provided an actual target; I began to bite the rug. But then a thought, "What will Rachel think of me acting in this ridiculous way?" I stopped and looked up at her, saying, "Are you okay?" She smiled and said, "Go ahead. Do your thing." Reassured, I resumed writhing, growling, and biting. In retrospect, the fact that I could stop and start seemed important; how could I possibly have so much control when my body was in the grip of an intense emotion? Years later I understood it in terms of a safe zone for resolving emotions at what drama theorists call "aesthetic distance."

The anger stopped after fifteen or twenty minutes. It wasn't long before I began shaking and sweating. The shaking was quite extreme, and the amount of sweat was surprising, drenching my pajamas. In a previous class the discussion was about shaking and sweating as the resolution of fear. Otherwise I wouldn't have known what was happening, since I had no consciousness of fear or any thoughts for that matter. Like the other two episodes, it was quite pleasurable, this time riding a completely safe roller coaster. Again, after some fifteen minutes, I grew still.

Very quickly, however, a thought entered my head, unbidden: "I believe, Lord; oh, let me believe." (The reader should realize that this biblical language was being used in its poetical, not religious, sense.) Having this going on in my mind, unbidden, made this episode somewhat different from the other three, but it was mostly quite similar. Once again my body took over, this time with laughter. But it was a different kind than I had ever experienced: I wasn't laughing in the usual way; instead, my body was laughing me. It was joyful, even more than the other episodes. Because of this bout I began to have some understanding of the spell that Beethoven's "Ode to Joy" had always cast over me. After some twenty minutes of nonstop, whole-body-grabbing laughter, I stopped. Exhausted, I fell immediately asleep.

The next day on the plane to Hawaii, I felt transformed, as if I had become a different and better person. It took only a few weeks, however, for me to realize that I wasn't a different person. Instead, it now seemed that I was mostly the same person, but somewhat improved. I laughed and cried much more frequently, and I could feel fear, which might have kept me from being arrested or injured in subsequent antiwar protests. But my poor management of anger persisted with only slight improvement. I came close to realizing that I would spend most of the rest of my life tracking down my hidden emotions and writing about emotions.

Why didn't all this happen in the first and subsequent therapy classes that I took? After some years of puzzlement, an answer occurred to me: Rachel made the difference. She had watched and listened to my outbursts with complete sympathy; she made no attempt to interfere in any way. Perhaps she was completely attuned to me, much more than I to her. She was an angel. In modern societies, angels are hard to find, even in psychotherapy.

Most of my work since has concerned the social-emotional world. My first publication on this topic dealt with the catharsis of emotions. To the extent that it was noticed at all, it was ridiculed in reviews by psychologists. They still think, mistakenly, that their studies of venting anger have disproved the idea of catharsis, but it hasn't. They make this mistake because they are still unaware of the huge literature in the humanities on the *distancing* of emotion. Since then, I have published many books and articles on both interpersonal and societal aspects of the mismanagement of emotions. I have been particularly interested in the origins and treatment of depression and of violence. It has been a hard sell, but I enjoyed doing it anyway.

Joys and Costs of Retirement

I took early retirement in 1992, almost ruinous with respect to income. But somehow it was worth it. Retirement liberated me from my official duties and from the daily tensions of life in a department. I think that enabled me to get closer to fundamentals, both in my professional and personal lives. When the administration offered an early retirement option at 60 percent of salary, I repeatedly asked if there would be a later offer at a higher percentage. The answers I got were always no. So I took the plunge into retirement. But the answers to my question turned out to be not the case: in the following year, another offer was made at 80 percent. And finally in the next year, a 100 percent offer was made. At first I was somewhat bitter, but after only a few years I realized that for me, at least, the financial loss was worth every penny. Ah, freedom!

A big plus for retirement is that one has much more time, freed from the various departmental and campus duties. More important still, retirement helped me ease out of departmental, campus, and even disciplinary politics. Saying farewell to the tensions in my department was particularly important. It wasn't long, perhaps only a few weeks after retirement, that I realized how much tension I had been under in the department. I felt like a different, liberated, more energetic person. No more department meetings, ever! No shouting fests as chair or with the chair. A new world appeared before me, with most of the tension removed or at least eased. I was a born-again sociologist/psychologist, with the promised land now at least visible, if still not reachable.

I had expected that retirement would mean losing my office and other privileges on campus, such as a campus mailing address, perhaps even use of the campus library and parking places. But to my surprise, the university was quite generous. I was able to keep my office and other privileges but now do most of my work at home. Even though I soon shortened my visits to the campus from four a week to one, it was (and still is) handy to have the privileges. I have the use of campus facilities but without the responsibilities.

The reason the privileges come in so handy is that since retirement, I have been working just as hard as I did but now with complete freedom. I continued to teach, but only small classes. I became particularly fond of freshmen seminars, which have only twenty students, meeting for two hours once a week. Over the years I have found that teaching freshmen is ideal for me, because they have not yet had time to learn to keep their mouths shut in class. Since I use the discussion method rather than lecture, they form an ideal group for me. I find teaching these classes quite stimulating.

I am also experimenting with different forms for teaching independent studies. The latest format is the tutorial: two or three students write papers on a project and discuss it once a week when we all meet. I call the outline for their scholarly project P-h-d, which stands for problem, hypothesis, and data. The students catch on very quickly to writing, thinking, and discussing within this framework. And they laugh in my face when I tell them it has nothing to do with a real Ph.D., because they know I am just kidding.

After many years, I have begun to think that I understand the high level of tension that I experienced when I was a full-time professor at my university. Part of it was certainly my own fault, my habit of talking too much, or even worse yet, treading on the other person's toes. I think this tendency played a large part in producing tension between me and others at the university, particularly with my departmental colleagues. I have been working on this fault ever since, but it's not easy to remedy.

But there is another component, I now think, that is easily just as important. Since my student days, I have had a strong push toward interdisciplinarity, particularly between sociology and psychology. I have also written about political science, history, and literary matters, such as the extraordinary novels of Virginia Woolf. Recently I have begun to publish articles about the effects of rigid adherence to dogma of the discipline.

Sociologists, for example, are insistent on avoiding the psychology of individuals. This separation seems to me an enormous disaster for both disciplines. Émile Durkheim found that suicide rates are correlated with religion. However, the correlations are so small that what he has really shown is that religion is not a major cause of suicide. But all the other disciplines, especially the social and behavioral ones and the humanities, are held back also. It seems to me that very little new knowledge will be discovered until integration at least begins. Much of the impetus for discovery in the physical sciences comes from integration of disciplines (such as physical chemistry). I would like to see a large percentage of the members of each discipline integrating into at least one other discipline. Let the marriages begin!

8

My Life in Sociology, Sociology in My Life

ELINORE E. LURIE

This chapter presents my life in sociology from college through retirement. My career was influenced by prevailing belief systems in general and in sociology and by the organizations in which I worked or from which I received funding. Themes of nontenured academic appointments and doing applied work run throughout my career; they had implications for me and are relevant today for sociologists working in nontenured positions and applied sociology.

Work Life

Becoming a Sociologist

The 1950s and early 1960s had traditional role expectations for women. My college professor father and elementary schoolteacher mother wanted me to do well in high school and attend a good college, teach high school English for a few years, then leave for a financially secure "good" marriage. At

Acknowledgment: I thank those who helped me think through and edit this chapter, including three anonymous reviewers for the book; the editors, Rosalyn Darling and Peter Stein; my colleagues on the American Sociological Association retirement Listserv; Rachel Kahn-Hut, Marilyn Little, and Joyce Bird of my retired sociologists' book club; Renee Berger; Helene Lecar; Susan Zacharias; and my husband, Lawrence Lurie.

Oberlin College, where I was an undergraduate Ford Scholar, the model was different; women were intellectual equals and many held leadership roles. I majored in sociology at Oberlin, which excited me as a way to understand the world and, with social psychology, prepared me for later work in the sociology of mental health. I received my M.A. in sociology from Yale and my Ph.D. in sociology from Columbia University in 1970. Columbia had a tradition, exemplified in its Bureau of Applied Social Research, of applied sociological work leading to developments in concepts and theory.

I married in 1959, after a year of graduate coursework at Columbia. My husband persuaded me to spend a "honeymoon" period in California while he interned at Stanford Hospital. We moved to the Palo Alto/Menlo Park, California, area and afterward to San Francisco, where my husband took a psychiatric residency. In my first three major California jobs, I learned skills that I used later and was exposed to specializations in which I eventually worked.

In Menlo Park, I worked for the Stanford Research Institute, summarizing social science and psychological research for businesspeople. Project leaders sometimes preselected their conclusions and wanted research used selectively in their support. My research training made this approach very uncomfortable. However, I learned to write clear, short summaries for decision makers of the main points of research, without technical terms and footnotes.

In San Francisco I worked on two major projects that influenced my career development. The first was a study of alcohol-drinking practices conducted by the California Department of Public Health. Under the direction of Ira Cisin and Raymond Fink, I learned contemporary survey research methods that I used through most of my career.

After two years there, I began work on the Studies in Normal and Abnormal Aging (SNAA), directed by Marjorie Fiske Lowenthal at the University of California, San Francisco (UCSF), a health professional training, care, and research campus. The SNAA used qualitative interviews and quantified hospital records for those hospitalized for psychiatric reasons to construct life histories of people sixty and over living in selected census tracts in San Francisco. The SNAA's purpose was to tease out determinants of eventual state psychiatric hospitalization. Fiske Lowenthal, a powerful professional woman in an era where there were few, became an important role model and mentor.

My job at the SNAA was to write and conduct life-history interviews of the community-resident sample. I loved these interviews for what they revealed about individual perspectives on American society and history, from the Alaska Gold Rush through the early 1960s, and the often complex life stories of ordinary and frequently very poor people. I used the SNAA's combinations of qualitative and quantitative research techniques in later work, such as the program evaluation of On Lok Senior Health Services, a study of hospital discharge practices and family support in the 1970s–1980s, and the Homeless Prenatal Project of the 1990s.

In 1963 my husband was ordered back to New York for a two-year assignment as a U.S. Public Health Service physician. I used those years to finish sociology coursework at Columbia, take qualifying exams, and plan my doctoral dissertation, using data from the SNAA and analyzing family and friendship relations in later life. Then called informal support, now caregiving/receiving and social networks, this became an area of specialization for me. Mental health and the study of services to help older people age in the community rather than institutions also became career research interests.

Work–Family Life Balance and Feminist Issues

I had our first child, our son, just before we returned to San Francisco, which we now considered home. I felt I couldn't wait longer to have children; at age thirty, I was considered an "elderly primipara." Although I wasn't thinking of it then, in returning to the San Francisco Bay Area from the Northeast, I was returning from an area with many colleges and universities to one with fewer, potentially limiting my choices of academic employment. My husband began his clinical practice of psychiatry, further rooting us in the Bay Area. Eventually I was offered a job at the psychoanalytically oriented Human Development Research Program (HDRP) at UCSF, which under Fiske Lowenthal was studying life-course themes at four stages of life. Working gave me professional colleagues, although it restricted dissertation writing time. It was difficult to write in absentia from Columbia in the pre-Internet era without easy electronic access to faculty.

Having a second child, our daughter, in 1968, because I again felt time pressures to complete my family, made balancing child care, dissertation work, and further work at the HDRP very hard. I persisted in my efforts but felt isolated, lacking support from women friends who stayed home with small children.

Good child care was a particularly difficult issue. My housekeepers/ nannies often left after a year or two. I and other women campuswide at UCSF formed the Chancellor's Committee for Establishing a Child Care Center, but this effort eventually took ten years and did not help me personally.

Child-care issues continued to be difficult until my children were in high school. Roughly ages eight to twelve were worst, because the children resisted babysitters but could not fully manage alone at home: for example, my son, in bed with a feverish cold, got scared the very day I was coaxing a reluctant secretary to work on a grant submission with an immediate deadline.

Luckily my colleague said she would oversee the grant preparation, and I went home. My daughter, at home alone on a school holiday, got spooked by a friend's suggestion that a bad man was in the neighborhood. I coaxed her on the phone to feel safe; I also called the police, who were still patrolling the block when I got home (no such person was found).

During the 1960s–1970s, the culture at UCSF was unsupportive of work-family issues. Most women in positions of authority, including those at the HDRP, were no more supportive than men. Many successful women faculty never discussed their children. One colleague concealed the fact that she had a child until the child required hospitalization and she had to take time off. Not initially understanding this, I twice brought my small son to HDRP office parties to see where Mommy worked; I later heard this had been viewed negatively. I learned not to mention home or school at work. But other family work-life issues continued, such as trying to rush home during lunch hour to relieve a babysitter or see a child's school performance. I focused on the job and did not schmooze in the coffee room; a colleague told me later that not being visibly present schmoozing had worked to my disadvantage.

In the 1960s and early 1970s, overt sexism in the workplace was common. For example, in an article, a male professor said he would rather talk to women graduate students but would seriously recommend only men for jobs; in another, a male professor claimed that women sociologists chose "handmaiden" fields, such as mathematical sociology. I remember teasing about my appearance from male colleagues, which I pointedly ignored (requiring my emotional energy), and a job interview in which I was asked how my husband would feel about the commute I would have to make to take the job.

But times were changing, thanks to increasing and organized feminism. During the early 1970s, a Bay Area chapter of Sociologists for Women in Society (SWS) formed. The local SWS chapter held meetings at which research was presented by us and outside speakers. These meetings enabled us to come together as professionals, socialize, and share information. We also formed an SWS writing group in which we critiqued each other's papers for oral presentation and publication, which I found immensely helpful. Throughout my career, I received referrals to consulting jobs from SWS colleagues. Our mutual support and friendships continue through retirement. Four of us from the former local SWS chapter meet today as members of a social issues/sociology book club, organized by Rachel Kahn-Hut.

SWS national advocated for better positions for women and defended against sexual harassment—common in "benign" forms like the teasing I had experienced—as well as overt sex discrimination. SWS national became a major source for me and other women of professional socialization and career support. It provided peer groups, advocacy, and guidance (e.g., how-to sessions on building a sociological career, taught by Pam Roby).

Changing My Interests

In the late 1960s and 1970s, the San Francisco Bay Area was roiled with antiwar protests and the counterculture. There was a push for relevance in research, which influenced me. Although I was presenting and publishing on life-course issues, I began to want applied work directed toward social change. After my HDRP grant funding ended, I worked with Henry Lennard on alternative treatments for addiction. Eventually I was referred by my colleague David Chiriboga to two program evaluations consistent with my major interests. One was of a day-care program for the elderly at the San Francisco Jewish Home for the Aged. The second referral was to On Lok Senior Health Services (now called Lifeways), which was developing a new program model of integrated social and medical care for the elderly. Through working at the Jewish Home and On Lok, I developed relationships with San Francisco aging services agencies that have continued through retirement.

Midcareer Issues: Professional Achievement and Recognition

For the next nine years, during my forties to early fifties, I worked both at On Lok and as director of program evaluation for a novel Adult Nurse Practitioner Training Program in the School of Nursing at UCSF (UCSF-SN). At UCSF-SN, I was now teaching and serving on some committees without a formal teaching appointment. Previously at UCSF-SN, some faculty positions had been held by psychologists and sociologists. But during the 1970s and 1980s, as the profession of nursing developed new professional roles, it also developed a more independent identity. "Nurses will be taught by nurses" was a frequent theme in contemporary *Nursing Outlook* articles. At UCSF-SN, faculty positions supported by university money were now allocated to nurses; a psychologist colleague sued unsuccessfully to retain his position.

I became interested in getting an affiliation for myself and other social and behavioral scientists at UCSF-SN with the Department of Social and Behavioral Sciences. I thought this would provide us with a home and professional legitimation. Initially the department was unreceptive. Some symbolic interactionists, including the chair, were unhappy with our diversity of theoretical and methodological orientations. Other faculty were concerned with the potential consequences of having affiliations with sociologists and psychologists outside their department. Later, when Carroll Estes, an important mentor and support, became chair, the department offered nontenure-track adjunct appointments; I became adjunct associate professor of social and behavioral sciences. Although I was not required to teach, this seemed to me to be an important part of my career and professional university life.

I continued to teach seminars and offered independent study, primarily in aging and health-care delivery. I served on dissertation, thesis, and other committees from the late 1970s until shortly before I retired.

Even with an adjunct appointment, however, I felt that there were disparities in recognition of the work I and many others were doing and the reward system in sociology in general and academia in particular. It could be difficult to obtain grant support in untenured positions unless the awards committee understood the use of adjunct faculty. A stable academic position still was the respected norm in sociology in the 1970s–1990s, although the number of available academic positions was decreasing. I saw little understanding or support of sociologists having untenured positions and/or doing applied work, both inside and outside academia. Tenure and tenure-track positions in academia always have had structural advantages that untenured faculty do not, such as access to financial resources, priority access to support staff, the right to a permanent office, decision-making power on committees, and other prerogatives.

Within UCSF then, academic appointments and promotions depended in part on where your students were teaching and their academic careers. Many women students in the department were unable to leave the Bay Area for teaching appointments, essentially my situation, and many consequently took nonacademic jobs. To address this for myself, I worked with others in the ASA's Sociological Practice Section in support of applied and non-university-based work. But like my child-care center work, this became a long-term approach with no immediate personal benefits.

It has been suggested on the ASA e-mail list of retired sociologists that there was little legitimation of nonacademic work because sociology during the 1970s–1980s was organized around departments of sociology. The American Psychological Association, in contrast, was organized around psychology as a profession for those inside and outside academia.

While still working on the nurse practitioner evaluation in the late 1970s to early 1980s, I began work as coprincipal investigator in the Department of Family Medicine at UCSF. This study, funded by the National Institute of Mental Health (NIMH), was of hospital discharge planning and the social supports of elderly people leaving hospitals after episodes of hip surgery or heart disease. Our findings on discharge planning processes and caregiver stress have since been replicated and further developed in other studies.

In 1985, I received fellowship status in the Gerontological Society of America (GSA), largely for my work on informal social support. This, like an earlier GSA award, was important to me because otherwise there was no conventional recognition (e.g., promotion in academic rank) acknowledging my work.

NIMH changed its funding priorities during the Reagan era to focus on clinical and basic research with mental health outcomes. For a while,

I was between funded positions. I subsequently received a contract from NIMH aimed at presenting summarized research on aging to directors of state mental health departments. The directors who composed our governing board chose the research topics. I, my coprincipal investigator Jim Swan, and my research assistant team, mostly graduate students, used the writing techniques I learned at the Stanford Research Institute to do this (without predetermined conclusions).

We published our work in *Serving the Mentally Ill Elderly*. By the time of publication, there were cuts in the community mental health and health services created for the elderly (and others) after the SNAA. We made suggestions to create more integrated care and better coverage, but in that funding climate, with additional complications of different funding streams and bureaucracies, it was difficult to make changes.

Seeking Stability

In the mid-1980s I applied to be and was appointed executive officer (EO) of the Society for the Study of Social Problems (SSSP). The position was advertised as half-time. I was hoping for a stable part-time base for my professional life in an organization in which I had been active. I brought skills from years of grants management. Under Carroll Estes as chair, the department hosted SSSP. I involved the department's students as assistants, adding to their professional socialization as sociologists.

The previous EO at SSSP, whom I liked, had held office for many years, which I assumed was a sign of organizational stability. When I asked, he just told me that he was retiring, not why. Board members I spoke to encouraged my application. But unknown to me, there had been conflict over his resignation and opposition to it by some continuing board members, who were not happy to see a new EO. These factors resulted in a difficult transition. I then learned that SSSP's finances were precarious, partly because the journal was running late and therefore not generating subscription and advertising revenue and partly because membership had dropped.

Some SSSP board members were also unhappy that I worked toward rapprochement with ASA, especially over annual meeting hotel room credits, to avoid spending my time and energy in conflict rather than SSSP's financial stabilization. There was an internal schism between some older politically left-leaning board members, who stated that SSSP ought to lose money as a policy, and the more pragmatic outlooks of younger members and section chairs.

SSSP had been using its strained resources in support of the Association of Black Sociologists (ABS), I thought paternalistically, rather than in support of the independent development of ABS, which I thought would work better for both organizations. However, I had not obtained prior support for this approach, a major mistake that was taken badly by many in both organizations. I eventually made the annual meetings profitable and worked successfully with the Southern Sociological Association and SSSP members to raise membership, which brought in dues money. After some conflict, our journal finally published on time, regaining subscribers and advertisers. SSSP stabilized financially. The board then decided to lower future expenses by moving its executive office to a lower-wage area and hiring professional association management. I left for another position before SSSP's transition. SSSP work gave me valuable experience in organizational dynamics for my future nonprofit board service. But the greater than half-time work required as EO did not result in a stable base for my career.

Late Career

One of my last three jobs was at Sociometrics, a Silicon Valley for-profit firm that acquired large studies and databases in the social and psychological sciences, substantively coded variables, then marketed the coded databases to researchers. Funded by a National Institute on Aging (NIA) grant, I wrote workbooks to teach gerontology and beginning statistics using three major studies in aging. I thought Sociometrics' working atmosphere, including casual dress, flextime, acknowledgment of family life, and problem resolution by direct confrontation rather than academic-style politicking, was wonderful. However, I lacked the technical computer skills for further work there.

I worked with Beverly Ovrebo evaluating an innovative program for homeless pregnant women, the Homeless Prenatal Project (HPP). After I called the HPP executive director's attention to a Robert Wood Johnson Foundation request for proposals, she obtained a grant, the first step in HPP's becoming a major community resource. Both the Sociometrics and HPP grants led to papers on innovative teaching methods.

Finally, I returned to UCSF to work with Carroll Estes on several program evaluations in the areas of day programs for elderly and AIDS patients and nursing home ombudsmen. I happily began work as coprincipal investigator on an NIMH-funded study of mental health services for the elderly and was starting to write a large mental health grant when I experienced a major disruption: cancer. Treatment was rough; I had to take time off. When I returned to work and grant writing, I got sick after each grant submission. I was uncertain (there were no verified findings) about whether my stress would contribute to a cancer recurrence. I finally retired in 1998.

Professional Organization Work

From 1970 to 1998, I was active in many professional organizations, including the Pacific Sociological Association, ASA, SSSP, GSA, American Public

Health Association, and American Society on Aging. I presented papers, organized sessions, held office, and edited journals. While I worked on the Nurse Practitioner Study, I became active with the Medical Sociology Section of ASA, continuing for about ten years. I served as an editor for the Arnold Rose Monograph series, the *Journal of Health and Social Behavior*, the *Journal of Applied Sociology*, the *Sociological Quarterly*, and four gerontological journals.

My professional association and editing activities represented normal parts of a sociological career, gave me collegial friendships, and made me feel a part of the larger sociological community. Like the honors I received, they were especially meaningful because I did not have the amenities of a regular teaching position.

Professional Work with Community Organizations

Outside the university I did many program evaluations of innovative social service programs in addition to On Lok. Interesting applied work with San Francisco's Department of Mental Health Services included a survey of residential care homes for the elderly. In the early 1990s, I was hired to design a survey of the elderly and people with disabilities in a low-income area of San Francisco, similar to the respondents in the SNAA. I trained service providers to do the survey and use the data in planning service delivery for a new agency, Planning for Elders in the Central City (PECC). After the survey's completion, I was invited to serve on the PECC board, including one term as president. There I oversaw three student assistants who worked on further data collection and drafts of reports.

Volunteer Work with Community Organizations

I began serving on nonprofit boards in the 1980s, starting with San Francisco Suicide Prevention, which reflected my mental health interests. When the PECC executive director left to found another organization with a similar mission and clientele, the Community Living Campaign (CLC), she invited me onto CLC's board. I stayed for six years, two as president. At CLC, I enjoyed using my skills in developing surveys, editing grants, and developing low-cost evaluation designs. I relayed findings from scholarship on social connectivity, which supported CLC's mission and funding.

In retirement, I've connected to other community organizations. I've been active in San Francisco Village, a "virtual village" for older people providing mutual support among members (informal support) along with access to paid services (formal support). As a member of the Advisory Council to the San Francisco Commission on Aging (which oversees publicly funded services for the elderly and adults with disabilities), I've written papers using public data on the geographic district I represent. I served on the governing board of the pilot San Francisco Transitions Program, which offered services to elderly patients to facilitate safe hospital discharge and reduce rehospitalization.

Reflections on Discontinuities in My Career

Overall, I had about an equal number of academic jobs (based on grants) and nonacademic jobs. My work built on my professional interests and skills and was continuous in that way.

But increasingly during my work and career course, particularly as federal funding was cut or priorities changed, and particularly under Nixon, Reagan, and Clinton's Republican Congress, there were periods of unemployment or underemployment. During these periods, my work became applying for jobs, writing grants, making or cultivating contacts, and maintaining an even emotional keel. My adjunct faculty colleagues soon went through similar experiences.

Then as now, career advice for building a résumé was to appear continuously employed. I always had some consulting work or short-term teaching stints that counted as employment. However, although I did not feel good being without major work, I felt it was unwise to be too open about my situation or feelings. My career both inside and outside academia, with its discontinuities, would have been easier psychologically if there had been ongoing support groups, perhaps online and/or hosted by ASA. (This might also be helpful for contemporary untenured professionals.)

The changing priorities of funding sources also had implications for the further conceptual development of my research interests. Because my work consisted of discrete positions funded by separate grants, I had limited ability to build on my research interests and concepts over a long time period. I always had to write the next grant or find the next position. I suspect this issue is relevant today for sociologists working as adjunct faculty and in research or policy institutes.

However, although my employment was discontinuous, my career shows what can be done with sociological skills and concepts. I was able to work as a sociologist in a broad range of substantive areas, both in the university and outside.

Retirement

For most of the first decade after I retired, my husband and I found ourselves providing intensive informal support—caregiving and care management— to our very aged parents. I used my knowledge of the field and contacts as much as I could.

My husband and I share continued interests in health and mental health care. Because life in retirement, especially my volunteer work, has been continuous with my work life in many interests and skills, I think retirement was somewhat easier than if I had been a full-time academic. But I realized soon that successful retirement for me would require more than continuity of interests, good times, and absence of stress. As my connections to work colleagues grew distant, I needed new friends with new common interests. After I began to structure retirement life around my new interests, such as San Francisco Village, Spanish and other classes, and my hiking and writing groups, I made these new friends.

Implications for the Profession and My Life in Sociology

Working conditions in the profession for women have changed for the better since I began my career. There is less overt sexism and apparently more egalitarianism among working spouses. I now could more easily negotiate for equal consideration in areas such as where to live and child care and would feel safe postponing children a little longer while establishing my career.

But in other ways, I feel my professional life is representative of many sociological lives now, with implications for our profession in legitimation of and preparation for nonacademic careers and some career discontinuities. My experience suggests that applied work will further our profession, as working sociologists employ and disseminate sociological perspectives and skills in a range of institutions.

Although there were difficult periods, I'm very happy with my career overall, especially my contributions to innovative, socially relevant work inside and outside the university and my service to the profession of sociology through organizational work, teaching, and research. In retirement, I've retained my personal perspectives of sociological analysis, continuing interests, and skills. My life in sociology continues.

9

Have You Noticed . . . ?

CORINNE KIRCHNER

Have you noticed that not all accounts of sociologists' retirement feature their techniques for participating in activities in spite of age-related losses of physical function? Nevertheless, we know from national health statistics that such loss is common after usual retirement age. I have chosen to focus on this topic, which relates so closely to my work and my life.

I am eighty-one years old. It has been nearly a decade since I retired from my full-time job of thirty years as director of social and policy research at a nonprofit organization in the field of disabilities—blindness and low vision, to be precise.

Before that, from childhood onward, I showed signs of being perhaps overly committed to some kind of work and to the independence that generally goes with the status of "worker." As early as age twelve, I organized small groups of young children whom I took care of after school until a parent came home from work. During high school years, I took summer jobs, such as being the receptionist in my father's solo-practice medical office in New York City. Then, for two summers, in sharp contrast, I became a farmworker in Vermont as part of an "exchange program" for U.S. urban or suburban children, as I was, to encounter the very different culture of U.S. rural community life.

When I went off to start college, I had no clear intellectual or vocational interests but was driven more by wanting *not* to follow my father's choices. I chose the state teacher's college at which, aided by scholarships and some local housecleaning, I could finance myself. While there, I did encounter some classes about the various ethnic groups in U.S. national history, which piqued my interest because of my experience of being the U.S.-born child of immigrants from Hungary. I had even spoken Hungarian briefly before age five and then learned and spoke English exclusively. My father was part of the early 1900s immigrant generation that attempted to assimilate as fully as possible, so his children were directed away from the foreign language. (Our mother, as typical then, let him dominate such decisions, though she was multilingual and would have preferred that we be too.) I soon learned that Hungarian was not useful in U.S. society but that it was linguistically interesting because, unlike most European languages, it did not derive from the Latin base. I did think about studying linguistics to understand how and why that came about, but in fact, my path was slightly deflected into immigrant history and from that into sociology, which became my under-graduate major.

It would take far too much time and space in the current context to offer up details from my whole career in sociology, so I'll be highly selective. My career began, arguably, while I was still in college—my third year—when I transferred to Barnard College and later, graduate school at Columbia University, specifically because they, as affiliated institutions, had great strength in sociology (Mirra Komarovsky, Bernard Barber, Paul Lazarsfeld, Robert Merton, and more).

At the same time, my private life changed drastically. Unexpectedly, I discovered I was "expecting" and married the father, another student. In rapid order (1950s, before common use of daily birth control), we had two daughters, while I was also completing my junior and senior years. He was completing undergraduate and law school. Both of us fitted in part-time jobs when we could.

Looking back, I know that seems impossible. My mother-in-law came to live with us when our girls began kindergarten and was a big help. Of course, for me, it meant doing part-time research work for some years and delaying the start and eventual completion of my Ph.D.

After earning my B.A., I started working full time as research assistant, eventually co–project director on social research grants at Columbia's Bureau of Applied Social Research (BASR), and subsequently at its School of Public Health. That was an extraordinary opportunity to begin doing sociology, getting published in two books, and getting to know a dynamic network of sociologists.

But I was always limiting my time in work and with any network in favor of my children. I'm sure that having had that fortunate BASR early position helped me stay in the survey field for a very long time. I chose not to enter a traditional academic career. Raising my children and working (having divorced after about fifteen years) meant that it took me a very long time to finish my doctorate.

From BASR, I moved to the Ford Foundation for a period, then back to Columbia's School of Public Health, and then took the opportunity of the job I became intrigued by, and entangled in, during the turbulent period (1970s and 1980s) of several social movements—the civil rights movement, feminism, and, closest to my work interests at the time, the disability rights (DR) movement.

I became quite involved, in ways consistent with my paid job, with organizational aspects of the DR movement, mainly helping develop the professional association of the emerging discipline of disability studies. In that last respect, I was following renowned sociologist Irving Zola.

We and the other founders named the new association Society for Disability Studies (SDS), well aware that those initials also referred to the name of a radical student group (Students for a Democratic Society) that had made news in the politically charged then-recent period of the late 1960s. We also aimed to influence policy on disability issues. I served on the board, became president of the professional group, and later was coeditor for three years of its professional journal, *Disability Studies Quarterly.*

At age seventy-one, healthy and very active, I still loved my job but was eager to shift my setting and substantive focus. Having from so early been interested in the sociological aspects of languages (generally referred to as sociolinguistics), I looked forward to having some time to pursue this interest more deeply. Lest anyone get the common impression that retirement means slowing down, I insisted to all that I was rewiring, not retiring! I began to take courses very selectively in linguistics, though not for credit, at Columbia University and helped organize and run an interdisciplinary seminar on sociology and languages. I became interested in dictionaries and the profession of lexicography. I became active with the research group on language and society in the International Sociological Association (ISA). I published a paper in the research group's new journal and presented papers at its conferences in Spain, Sweden, and, just last year, Japan—having never traveled to any of those places before. I also continued teaching a master's-level course on disability studies and public health as an adjunct lecturer in the Socio-Medical Sciences Department at Columbia University's Mailman School of Public Health.

Early in my involvement, colleagues would sometimes ask whether I was so committed to disability rights because I might have had some invisible impairment or because my younger brother, as an adult, had become a wheelchair user. My answer was simply no, but with an explanation that I agreed with disability activists' cause and complaints, feeling identification with them by analogy with my understanding of the civil rights and social constructionist perspectives of the feminist movement.

In fact, my personal experience with even temporary impairment was very limited, probably about what is typical in our U.S. society—a couple of incidents many years earlier, involving broken arms that each had put one of my arms at low functioning for some months.

My Socialization to Real-Life Disability and Disability Culture

My first "casualty" had been my right arm; the break was at the elbow, and the method of treatment at that time fifty years ago—arm immobilized in a solid cast for six months—had to be followed by six months of physical therapy to recover full function. I was a teenager then. About twenty years later, as a young employed sociologist and mother of two, I broke the other arm, also at the elbow. But treatment had changed greatly; this time a light-weight but sturdy cast was used. It had a kind of flexibility that allowed me to move the elbow increasingly as it healed, so by the time the cast could come off (about three months), I had full function of my arm.

Also, I now realize but didn't then that I had no contact or even aware-ness of the "disability culture" mainly because it barely existed then but also because my disability was of a mild, fairly common, and merely temporary nature. Today disability culture is still largely invisible but beginning to have public venues and occasionally become perceptible. Its visible products— paintings, poems, dances, and so on—are rooted in attitudes of pride and possibility, expressed by people with often severe impairments. This year marks twenty-five years since the signing of the Americans with Disabilities Act (ADA), and disability culture has been more on view, such as in parades, books, and movies.

Similarly to almost all people of my generation and of those following close after, I grew up in the years before the DR movement had even begun to stir. There was no special education, no curb cuts, no signs of efforts to make everyday life more accessible to people who had trouble, or could not, climb stairs, read books, or read print on public signs, type letters, or had any other impairment that limits one's participation in our culture. For de-signers of buildings and of consumer products, their implicit model of a user is a young, nonimpaired person.

It's possible that you have begun noticing in your environments, at work or shopping, many new design features that promote accessibility. That has occurred mainly because the requirements of the ADA, passed in 1990, are gradually being adopted. Certainly college campuses have adopted many accessibility features, such as ramps and elevators as alternatives to stairs inside and outside some buildings, wider doors on bathrooms, and more use of microphones in auditoriums and sometimes in classrooms.

But it is also possible that you haven't noticed those things. There is much less public awareness of the ADA, and of disability issues in general, than you might expect. It is also very possible that some such physical alteration has been an annoyance to you. Any feature designed as an accommodation for one type of impairment might pose a barrier or slight obstacle to someone else.

Why is there an increase—albeit slight and slow—in accessible environments and products? It is not only as a result of the ADA requirements. As more environments have become accessible—wheelchair-adapted buses, for example—more people with visible disabilities are seen out and about. Whether that greater visibility increases the general public's acceptance of, or irritation with, people with disabilities is a delicate question. I am not aware of any longitudinal research trying to determine that. In any case, that would be a difficult study to do convincingly because people are generally aware that the socially desirable (i.e., politically correct) response is to welcome all people with disabilities and may give that response even if they don't really feel it.

But the important point is that older people and their families are most likely to hold the conventional negative views about what one can do, or should do, if they have one or more impairments. The prevalent view is *restraint*: the older person restrains herself for many reasons, and her relatives urge restraint for some of the same reasons and some (possibly irritatingly) different ones.

My own views, when I first found I was somewhat impaired in walking and talking as the result of a stroke, were complex. That stroke occurred almost three years ago. To explain my complex reactions, I return to describing my background with respect both to my career, which affected my knowledge about disabilities, and to my attitude and behavior toward physical health and fitness through most of my life. By describing my experience, I hope to close a gap I have noticed in the retirement literature and to help others learn about managing their situations to accomplish their retirement goals in the face of unexpected disability.

Physical Fitness: A Highly Independent Variable

In early childhood and through my teens, I was overweight and a desultory sports person, but at age twenty, pregnant with my first child, I knew (emphasized by my physician) that I had to lose weight. And, surprisingly, I did. Subsequently, then with two little children, and finishing college and working part-time jobs such as tutoring, I kept it off.

As nearly everyone who has been overweight or obese knows, you see yourself that way for decades after you have slimmed down and strive to keep your weight down and fitness up. That applied to me. At age thirty-five, I began a daily home-based exercise routine that I have modified over the years but have followed in all circumstances—even on camping trips and

European vacations with my kids—up to age seventy-seven, until that first stroke (what I now call "S1 Day"). I had also been working with a fitness trainer at a gym twice a week.

Without warning, S1 Day broke into my longtime workout routine and my whole life more dramatically than I realized at the time. Here are a few of my thoughts on that event: Not surprisingly, I had a major twinge of bitterness that my regular exertions and healthy eating habits, which were supposed to keep me healthy as well as fit, apparently failed so greatly. But I quickly realized there is no such magic protection from *everything*.

After all, I had made it to seventy-seven with no chronic illnesses, no aches or pains, or any slowing down. Indeed, I now speculate that my intended "preventive" measures may have helped keep the stroke less serious. And with greater certainty, I can now appreciate that my previous good habits have helped me regain function and keep active, although much less than before (mainly because of reduced energy).

I needed a cane at first and was very self-conscious about my slightly distorted speech (because of a slightly distorted mouth). At home, I had vigilant help from my grown daughter who lives quite nearby, from the other grown daughter who flew in from the Midwest, and from my college-student granddaughter. For a week or so, one of them stayed each night in case I fell or needed some help. After that week, we started discussing other possible living options for me. But since I had had no mishaps, we realized I was able to manage safely. So I "threw out" my family members (lovingly and gratefully, of course). I did still have some difficulties because my left side had been affected by the stroke, but I could walk and had some household help and therapies from the visiting nurse service. My long-term biweekly cleaning lady did my laundry and heavier-duty housework, as she always had. Basically, I could manage on my own.

I even resumed teaching my course at Columbia's Mailman School of Public Health. The class was a small seminar (seven students) in disability studies; they were graduate students for an M.P.H. degree, and I knew most of them from a previous course I had taught on aging and social factors. They and I realized there could be educational benefits from their sharing my real-life socialization to living with disabilities. That course ended in late May. In mid-June, "S2 Day" occurred.

This second stroke was more serious—my doctors assured me I had not brought it on by my activities. When I returned home from the ten days in the hospital, I had a feeding tube through which I could ingest only liquid nutrition. I did that for several weeks, then joined a clinical trial testing a new method to recover swallowing ability, and recovered it in about two months. I then had some weeks of physical, occupational, and speech therapy. Here I highlight the more generalizable features of the lasting impairments I have and how they have influenced my experiences with, and *feelings* about, retirement.

Retirement with Disability

What are the important functions that almost everyone, regardless of his or her chosen retirement activities, wants to perform? I venture they include getting around within his or her city or town; talking with friends, relatives, or students; reading books or journals; and writing (which in effect means using a computer).

For me, compared to my prestroke years, all of those functions have become harder and slower to accomplish, some perhaps due just to old age but more significantly to the strokes. Still, I do acknowledge that an important factor in my continuing activities is that my impairments are not severe and can be worked around, in part because of several positive circumstances in my life, which are not rare and can be approximated. Even the circumstance of nonsevere impairments will probably be temporary, and as I get older, I will likely acquire new or worsened impairments. But I have learned from my disabled acquaintances that severity, considered in terms of consequences apart from the biomedical conditions, can be modified by strategic ingenuity, such as locating or developing environmental adaptations or alternative techniques.

I place my career in sociology high in my roster of positive circumstances. Mostly that is a very general asset—a way of looking at the world that prevents one from seeing one's problems as unique and keeping alive the recognition that, most likely, there are socially constructed solutions or groups devoted to helping develop solutions.

But my career has been helpful also in more specific ways—notably because of the courses I taught: social dynamics of aging and disability studies. Through them I had systematic exposure to current and evolving standards for successful aging. I don't agree with all of it (mainly its exclusion of people with disabilities from the picture of elderly success), but I do agree with its emphasis on physical and social activities as helping foster and actually constitute the notion of "successful old age."

Most fortunate, without question, have been my friendships and working relationships with leaders and other members in the DR movement. There even is a small part of me that reacted positively when I first recognized that I had finally achieved the status of being a person with a disability. However, that spontaneous thought was a superficial reaction; but at a deeper level, I did know that for many people whom I admire, their disability was truly part of their proud self-identity. And I genuinely believe that when I become more competent using the abilities I have and accomplish some retirement/career goals, I can also feel that way.

From my work in disability studies, I learned and adopted the "social model" of disability, which contrasts with the "medical model." Stated most concisely, the social model recognizes that it is the *interaction* of one's bodily impairments with their environment, including attitudes, policies, and physical design, that may create functional barriers, and not the bodily condition alone, as the medical model presumes.

As part of a pattern of negative feelings that I had to combat in myself was a sense of *shame* when first being seen by friends after my strokes or meeting new people. I realized that was inappropriate and have gotten over it (mostly). Or to put it in better terms, I have identified a scenario that makes me most comfortable in such situations. When I happen to be with people I don't know, I wait for a suitable moment (and there always is one) for me to quickly bring up my limitations and assure them that no one should worry about it; I will ask if I need help doing something and will not do anything that may seem dangerous to me. I am comfortable with that, and it seems others are too.

I also learned that some of my initial feelings as a person with impairments worked counter to my efforts at participation but were common among newly disabled people and typically are overcome. People who were born with impairments or acquired them at an early age tend not to retain those negative feelings about themselves, but we older adults have imbibed over *many* years our culture's negative expectations for people with disabilities. We need to learn to appreciate how modifiable the conditions are that contribute to our disabilities and to learn who is working on changing them and how.

As you probably have anticipated, very important for me was the chance to return to working with my trainer weekly and to resume a daily round of exercises. I did so a few months after the second stroke. I accord my trainer much gratitude for his willingness and ability to modify our routines to suit my now-limited strengths. He is certainly one of my fortunate circumstances. Also fortunate is the fact of a well-stocked gym in my building, so I can do my daily workout there.

I consider living in New York City one of my fortunate circumstances because of its public transportation system. I had learned from readings for my course on aging, and earlier from work in the blindness field, that a visually impaired or old person having to plan for giving up driving is a major issue that many families face, so I was glad to take control of that decision early. I gave my car to my grandson several years ago, happy to be carless, as are many people in the city.

However, when I was beginning to return to my retirement activities, I worried greatly about getting around. I applied and was tested for the "handicap" van system (every city must have some form of that, according to the ADA). I was granted coverage but only for nine months; as it turned out, I never used that service. I found that buses were usable, and I can use the subways, though I avoid them because of the stairs and pushy crowds.

There are other fortunate aspects of my situation. Most sociologist retirees probably have access to the university library and many university facilities and events. The online world allows extensive resources to pursue new learning, and I look forward to participating in the American Sociological Association's conference via computer. I had attended every year for about four decades and regret not seeing some colleagues now.

I have learned that the most significant consequences of my strokes have been my feelings, more than the physical limitations. I have not stated fully here the range of my negative feelings and of sociolinguistics-related activities forgone because of my reduced energy. Since there are little acts every day that I can no longer do swiftly or well (e.g., getting dressed, cooking), I experience an abundance of frustration. Frequent frustrations are a sure recipe for some degree of depression.

But that is well balanced by the pleasure of work and other activities that I can still do; also, I have figured out how to evade, or deal with, many of those little frustrations. And there is the real pleasure of learning how caring many friends are. Also, it has been more surprising to me than perhaps it should have been to realize the joy of my relationships with family, students and friends, and (some) therapists.

Finally and importantly, a virtue of *feelings* over bodily status is that feelings can be analyzed and evaluated by one's self as positive or negative and then, accordingly, nurtured or minimized. (That is not easy to do, but I can testify: it is *doable!*)

PART II

Coming of Age in
the Postwar Years

10

A Life in Sociology

CHARLES S. GREEN III

Early Life

I was born in New York City in 1937 but raised in Princeton, New Jersey. My father was an osteopath, as were his father, his younger sister, and her husband. My mother had some college education and was a dancer in several Broadway musicals before her marriage. She remained a housewife for all of her married life. Thus, in terms of occupational prestige and education, I was born into a middle- or upper-middle-class family. But the Depression and World War II made a significant impact on our income. My father conducted his medical practice in the dining and living rooms of our two-bedroom apartment until after the war, and he was not able to buy a home for us until 1950.

First Encounter with Inequality and Injustice

As a teenager I worked one summer in a nursery that was hybridizing fruit trees by grafting buds from one species onto another. The grafting was done by teams of three. The budder was the leader. He carried a box full of slim tree branches with buds on them. Into each tree to be grafted he would make

---

Editors' note: Sadly, Tuck Green passed away on April 20, 2016. We will miss this kind and gentle friend.

a T-shaped cut, cut and peel a bud from one of the branches, and insert it into the T cut. Next, the wrapper placed a rubber strip around the newly grafted bud to keep the bud firmly in place. Preceding the budder and wrapper along a row of saplings were the strippers, all of whom were black but me. We had to strip the leaves from the trunks of the trees, cut off small branches with a pruning knife, and then make sure the trunk was smooth by running our hands up and down it. Even the slightest error in cutting those small branches would leave a jagged edge that would cut your hands when you again ran them up and down the trunk. Of course, we wore gloves, but it was easy to ruin a pair in less than a day. So even the most skilled strippers typically had bleeding hands by the end of a workday. Infections were rife.

The incentive system the nursery devised consisted of piece rate for budders and wrappers and hourly pay for strippers. This meant the budders and wrappers were constantly hollering racist insults at us in an effort to get us to work faster. This pressure to work faster forced us to make more errors in cutting and more cuts to our hands.

Can you imagine what C. Wright Mills would say about that exploitative incentive system? Unfortunately, I had at that time no knowledge of such concepts as Mills's private troubles and public issues or of such ideas as "divide and conquer." But my experience at the nursery made me sympathetic to the plight of workers and minorities and aware of just how privileged I was.

Encounters with Sociology as an Undergraduate

I entered the University of Virginia (UVA) majoring in aeronautical engineering. After three years it became painfully obvious that I was not suited for engineering, and I transferred to the School of Commerce. There I blossomed. Besides the usual required courses in business and economics I was able to take electives in other social sciences. Though I did lots of reading in sociology, I never took a course. My senior thesis, "Student Employee Turnover in Summer Jobs: A Case Study," drew on the sociology of small groups, especially on William Foote Whyte's and others' work in industrial sociology. I left UVA in 1961 with the hope of studying with Whyte at Cornell's School of Industrial and Labor Relations (ILR). My intent was to obtain a master's degree in preparation for a career with the International Labour Organization.

Sociology at Cornell

At Cornell I took courses and seminars in the School of ILR as well as in sociology and several other disciplines. I did extremely well in my first year so was invited to switch to the Ph.D. program in organizational behavior. In my second year I received a research assistantship with Bill Whyte and Larry

Williams to work on their studies of industrial relations in Peru. My assistantship focused on the comparison of surveys of Peruvian workers with similar surveys of American workers. We discovered that Peruvian workers scored lower on a scale of trust or "faith in people" than American workers and preferred a very different relationship with their supervisors. Our article, "Do Cultural Differences Affect Worker Attitudes?," reported these results.

Like many students in the 1960s, I was frustrated at the time spent studying, guilty at not being more actively involved in applying sociology to solve the injustices we were studying. So in the summer of 1964 I got involved in a voter-registration effort. It was not part of the better-known Freedom Summer effort but a smaller program in rural Tennessee sponsored by Cornell United Religious Work. I didn't last long there. While I was driving a local black student back home on the third day, we were picked up by police and beaten. I left the next day. In retrospect, it's hard to believe how naive I was. Even a budding sociologist should have known that driving with a black man in a VW Beetle with New York license plates might attract unwanted attention in rural Tennessee.

By the late fall of 1964 I decided to take a break from academia and moved back to my hometown to help my father cope with my mother's long battle with cancer. While in New Jersey I sought a job where I might apply my sociological knowledge.

Applying Sociology in State Mental Institutions

I found a job at Marlboro State Hospital as the coordinator of placement activities in the Department of Psychiatric Social Work Services. The hospital was engaged in an effort to rehabilitate and place a very large number of mental patients into the community, an effort shared by many state hospitals across the nation. John F. Kennedy's vision was that these patients' care and supervision would be taken over by community mental health centers, but few were ever built. Consequently, many ex-patients wound up unemployed and homeless. Those were not the short-term results at Marlboro, however. We placed patients in small boarding homes or nursing homes and shipped any medications they needed to those homes. My job was to recruit and train boarding home owners, inspect the homes at least once a month, and train volunteers to work in the homes to engage ex-patients in a variety of activities and even employment. I was often called on to translate theory into practice, for example, by helping a pair of volunteers resolve a serious conflict between two groups of ex-patients in the boarding home where they volunteered. These efforts were quite successful; very few ex-patients needed to be returned to the hospital, and most became integrated into their communities.

In the spring of 1966 I moved to the Delaware State Hospital to become the social science research analyst. In that capacity I supervised the statistical data-processing section, which kept track of patients. I also oversaw the writing of a number of project proposals funded through War on Poverty grants. I designed and carried out the evaluation procedures built into these projects. Little had I realized in graduate school that I would become a Poverty Warrior!

In the fall of 1968 I returned to Cornell to complete the residence requirement for the Ph.D. and get a start on my dissertation. The years 1968 and 1969 were full of turmoil across the country. Cornell was no exception: Antiwar rallies and protests were frequent, and race relations deteriorated to the point that in the spring of 1969 black students took over the student union building and armed themselves. I tried to ignore what was going on there in hopes of completing at least a draft of the dissertation. But my topic, based on what I had been doing in mental institutions for four years, was going nowhere. In the early spring of 1969 I shifted my topic to a study of processes of economic and political development in new nations. Searching for employment that spring took up a lot of time because I was invited to interview for nine positions, which was a reflection of how the increasing enrollments in higher education were affecting academic labor markets. Therefore, the dissertation was incomplete when I accepted a job offer at UVA.

Doing Sociology at UVA

When I returned to UVA eight years after earning my undergraduate degree, the university was transforming itself. As was the case with many other universities at the time, enrollments were expanding and many new faculty were hired to accommodate the boomer generation. Research was burgeoning, in part in response to the federal government's Cold War–related quest for such things as better weapons and spacecraft and private industry's quest for increased productivity and new products. In short, UVA was becoming what Clark Kerr, head of the University of California, called a "multiversity."

Two years after I was hired, the new department chair specified the criteria for tenure. Nothing published before being hired and no articles or books based on the dissertation (since it was already published in University Microfilms) would count toward tenure. What was expected were at least two articles in the *American Sociological Review* or *American Journal of Sociology* (or one in each) or four articles in specialty journals or "lesser" general journals. A book would count toward tenure if it was well reviewed. Edited books would not count.

We assistant professors panicked. Each of us was teaching three courses per semester and supervising several graduate students. Several of us were still writing our dissertations. Where were we going to find time to do all that publishing? Were we competing for just one or two tenured associate professorships, or was it at least theoretically possible we could all be tenured?

Perhaps surprisingly, once past our initial panic, we never discussed our shared predicament and anxieties with one another. Teaching was a taboo topic at UVA anyway, and we did not discuss much about our research. However, we did discuss other issues of the day, such as the Vietnam War and how to incorporate the newly arrived women into what had been until 1970 an all-male university.

Since teaching was not seriously valued by the department at that time, I became a closeted teaching enthusiast. Yet I was dissatisfied with the sage-on-the-stage model of teaching so prevalent in academe and began experimenting with a variety of approaches to get students more actively involved and applying what they learned to their lives as family members, employees, and citizens. For example, I used William Gamson's simulated society (SIMSOC) game in my race and ethnic relations class. Students spent an entire weekend involved in the simulation, competing for positions and Simbucks. The objective was to get students to understand from an emotional and intellectual standpoint the origins of inequality and what it is like to be in the lower class and/or a minority group member. I got involved with the International Studies Association's Education Commission (ISAEC), which provided me with a National Science Foundation grant to develop two learning packages that were published by the International Relations Program at Syracuse University. Of course, they didn't count toward tenure! Indeed, I was advised that they were a waste of my time. But sharing ideas with others in the ISAEC made me realize for the first time that there were other people who cared deeply about the teaching enterprise.

Though I drafted two book manuscripts and published six papers based on new research, I didn't get enough published in time and in the right journals to beat the tenure clock. This was the fate of four others of the six of us hired at about the same time. The one exception was granted tenure based largely on success in securing several hundred thousand dollars in government-funded research grants. This foreshadowed what was to become a much more important criterion for promotion at UVA and other colleges and universities. Corporatization was in full swing.

Doing Sociology at the University of Wisconsin–Whitewater: Teaching as If Learning Matters

I joined the Sociology Department at University of Wisconsin–Whitewater (UW–W) in the fall of 1976 following a job search that yielded only two interviews, a reflection of just how much the academic marketplace had changed since my 1969 job search. Whitewater started in the late nineteenth century as a state normal school. It later became a state college with a full liberal arts curriculum and in 1965 became a university. Though there was increasing emphasis on research during my time there, teaching remained the most valued activity.

When I arrived, our department was grappling, as were departments throughout the country, with the increasing emphasis on vocationalism among students and their parents. Symptomatic of that emphasis was the shift in enrollments from the humanities and social sciences to business and other "practical" fields. We decided not to dilute our liberal arts curriculum with courses such as Handcuffs 101. Instead, we devised an innovative program that involved advising students about courses in the major and minor to prepare for twenty career paths; expanding internship opportunities; and offering a capstone course, sociology in practice, to prepare students for internships, job hunting, and applying sociology after graduation. The program received the teaching award from the Wisconsin Sociological Association. Importantly, the program led to steady increases in enrollments in the 1980s when sociology enrollments nationwide were in steep decline. Even more important, our surveys of graduates showed them to be more satisfied with the career guidance they received and with the jobs they secured than had been the case in the mid-1970s.

I continued the efforts started at UVA to kick the lecture habit. I found through surveys of my classes that by the end of a semester students retained little of what they had learned in preparation for exams. The literature on teaching suggested that to retain learning, students need to be taught the various ways in which that knowledge could be applied. I introduced debates into my lower-division classes and found that, in comparison with students in another professor's lecture-based classes, my students became more-critical thinkers and writers. Team research projects were introduced into my advanced courses with gratifying results: team projects not only were typically well done but served as models for how individuals' term papers should be crafted.

Like many other professors I found that trying to get students to participate in class was a real struggle. One source of low participation was that students either didn't bother to read assigned material or misunderstood it. I therefore developed "checkers," which involved students writing up answers to questions I provided for each day's reading assignment. As class began, students assembled into their teams and reviewed the assignment and their answers. If one or more teams had questions, I answered them and we then proceeded to a critical discussion of the readings or an exercise of some sort that involved applying that day's reading.

During my years at UW–W I became even more actively involved in the ASA Section on Undergraduate Education (now the Section on Teaching and

Learning) than I had been at UVA. I served as a member on several committees, as the organizer of many ASA sessions on teaching and learning, and as
chair of the section. In addition, I served on the editorial board of *Teaching
Sociology* and for several years as its deputy editor. I was also involved in
the Teaching Resource Group (TRG, now the Department Resource Group),
conducting consulting visits to over a dozen departments and coauthoring
the first version of the *Department Evaluation Visits Manual.* The members
of the section and the TRG were the source of many ideas about teaching
and learning that I adopted for my courses. I was honored with the section's
Hans O. Mauksch Award for Distinguished Contributions to Undergraduate
Sociology in 1989.

I joined the Wisconsin Sociological Association (WSA) and the Midwest
Sociological Society (MSS) as soon as I moved to Wisconsin. Both organizations were sources of inspiration for teaching and the sociological enterprise
in general. I organized many sessions for WSA meetings and served as editor of the *Wisconsin Sociologist* for five years. I organized many sessions on
teaching, applied sociology, and assessment for MSS meetings as well as
served a term on the board as Wisconsin state representative.

In short, the UW–W department was a wonderful place in which to
work. Though there certainly were disagreements and even a few serious
conflicts, we muddled through because there was a spirit of egalitarianism
and a great deal of cooperation and collegiality. For example, we successfully
resisted efforts by the state legislature and the UW System to implement
highly unequal allocations of merit pay, and we did a great deal of collaborative research and publication.

I began to think about retirement in the late 1990s. Much as I was enjoying teaching, the innovations I had made required a prodigious amount
of grading, at least several hours every day. I thought such intensive and
extensive feedback was important for student growth, but it was also tedious
work. Included in my retirement plans was a research program in the sociology of the arts. I had longed to do such research and introduce a course on
it but had never gotten around to either. I decided to look first at a neglected
area of the topic: the socialization of artists. One of my colleagues referred
a student, Jenni Brant, to me because she had expressed an interest in the
topic of creativity when she had taken his introductory sociology course. I
was hoping she might be able to help me with a literature search and, since
she was an art major, with some ideas of her own about socialization.

Jenni and I talked over our shared interests, and after a couple of weeks
it dawned on me that she might be able and willing to undertake a very
ambitious project. In fact, she agreed to undertake a comparative study of
four art programs that differ in prestige and public versus private sponsorship: the School of the Art Institute of Chicago; the Milwaukee Institute
of Art and Design; and the art departments at UW–W and UW–Madison.

Her observations and interviews at these programs were spread out over a three-year period. She discovered that the experiences of art students were remarkably similar despite some important differences among the four programs. She also managed to elucidate the subtle interplay between agency and structure in the socialization process. The resulting paper won a writing award from UW–W's College of Letters and Sciences and awards from the WSA's and MSS's student paper competitions. The paper was also published in a book. I couldn't have asked for a more fitting end to a career as a teacher of sociology. Jenni earned her MFA degree and is now a successful potter.

Sociology in Retirement

I had a retirement plan worked out well before I retired thirteen years ago at age sixty-five. First, I expected to realize a lifelong dream of becoming involved in the arts. Specifically, once we decided to leave the bitter winters of Wisconsin for the milder climate of North Carolina, I decided to become a volunteer docent at the North Carolina Museum of Art, an effort that I thought might involve about two days a week. I also expected to engage in research in the sociology of the arts and had worked out a fairly detailed plan for doing so. What happened when we got to North Carolina? One expectation was modified, the other abandoned, and a new interest emerged and was pursued.

First, I discovered that the commute between where we live and the Museum of Art would be at least forty-five minutes each way in heavy traffic. I had no interest in such a commute. But I ran across an ad for a new docent class at the Ackland Art Museum of the University of North Carolina (UNC) at Chapel Hill, just ten miles away. I was interviewed for that class and became quite enthusiastic over the active learning approach stressed by the museum's educators and the prospect of teaching youngsters as well as adults. When I announced my enthusiasm to my wife, she was incredulous because she had spent her career teaching and counseling K–12 children and young adults—and I had taught just at the college level. What did I know about managing a group of second-graders? She decided to interview to become a docent as well. We were both accepted in the year-long docent training program.

We now spend one morning a week in training and part of another day team teaching school groups and occasionally adults. On a typical one-hour tour we take the kids into three galleries. We spend about twenty minutes in each gallery, sometimes focusing on just one painting or sculpture. The activity we choose for each work of art is designed to achieve objectives specified in advance with the teacher or teachers sponsoring the tour. One activity might involve having students look very closely at the work of art and share with their peers what they see. Then they might be invited to interpret the whole work of art, at which point we chime in with some information about the artist, the work of art, and the social and historical context in which the work was created. Other activities can involve such things as students learning the difference between abstract and realistic art and between portraits, landscapes, and narratives; and learning how innovations in technology can affect the content of art as well as the processes by which it is created.

I have offered a number of insights from research in the sociology of the arts to our docent classes. For example, the insight that has proven most surprising to them is that artistic creativity is not based on some spark of genius (or a warped personality!) but rather by the influences of race, class, gender, and the institutions of the art world.

Early in our first fall in North Carolina we were invited to attend a lunch-and-learn session sponsored by the local chapter of the United Nations Association (UNA). I had long been interested in the UNA but had never lived close enough to a chapter to get involved. Therefore, I was enthusiastic about attending. The monthly lunch and learns turned out to be very intellectually stimulating because the speakers were typically UN officials, ambassadors, or faculty from UNC, Duke University, or North Carolina State. It also turned out that the chapter members, mostly retired, had had a variety of career experiences in international affairs. So my wife and I continued to attend these sessions. In early 2003 we were invited to join the chapter's board and to head up the Education Outreach Committee. That committee had been trying for years without much success to get curriculum materials about the UN into the hands of teachers and to establish Model UN Clubs in the schools. We decided to introduce the changes we sought by focusing on curriculum coordinators and social studies teachers rather than on superintendents and principals as previous committees had. We knew that the former were in a position to introduce (or resist) change, whereas the latter were not. Our strategy worked: We have gotten curricular materials into the hands of several thousand teachers in the four school districts served by our UNA chapter. There are now active Model UN Clubs in eight high schools.

Finally, we have organized a UN contest for local high school students. The projects these students produce involve creative problem solving: devising a better way for the UN system to deal with such issues as conflict within or between nations, poverty, human rights, environmental pollution, and climate change. A good example of such a project is "The U.N.'s Role in Reproductive Health Care and Female Empowerment," the first-place winner of the most recent contest. The author researched the history of the UN's efforts in dealing with reproductive health care and the literature critical of those efforts. She incorporated in her project recent sociological research that shows that providing reproductive health care not only reduces infant and maternal mortality but empowers women in a number of respects. She then proposed a number of reforms in existing UN practices and several new initiatives that our diverse nine-member judging committee found to be a real tour de force. Her oral report was based on PowerPoint slides. She also created a collage that dramatically illustrated key points in her project.

Thus, my original research plans in the sociology of the arts have been put on a back burner. But I have no regrets because I have been doing sociology, albeit of an applied sort, at both the Ackland Museum and the UNA.

I would be remiss if I didn't mention how disease can affect one's career and retirement. I was fortunate in that for most of my career I had few serious illnesses—mainly just an occasional bout with flu or bronchitis that did not require my missing classes or slowing writing projects. More serious illnesses, a pair of spinal fusions and prostate cancer late in my career, also had little impact on teaching and research because of the support provided by several institutions that we take all too much for granted: spouses, paid sick leave, and, in my case especially, collegial coverage of one's classes.

More recently, however, I have been receiving treatment for fourth-stage lung cancer. A six-week series of five-day-per-week radiation treatments in the fall of 2014 meant that I did not have time to do tours at the Ackland. This spring I underwent twelve weekly chemotherapy infusions. I was fortunate that I had few serious side effects from these, though they did leave me too tired to do any tours. Late this summer (2015) I completed three intense radiation treatments for a tumor on my adrenal gland. A recent CT scan has revealed those treatments to be successful, and we've just completed our first tour of the academic year for the museum. Again, support from my spouse, friends, and UNC's Lineberger Cancer Center were crucial in minimizing the disruption I experienced.

11

Permission Slip for Life as
an Applied Sociologist

ARTHUR SHOSTAK

In the spring of 1958 I asked for life-changing advice from a genial gentleman I had just met, Professor Mel Tumin (1919–1994), then Princeton University's adviser to sociology graduate students. I wanted to know what I
might study if I enrolled in the university's Ph.D. sociology program. I knew
very little about the subject, as I had had only one sociology course back
in 1955 during my sophomore undergraduate year—one among forty-eight
courses taken over four college years. To be sure, I vaguely recalled appre-
ciating its wide scope and the instructor's heartfelt belief that it could help
repair the world, but other academic fields, such as political science, or even
the study of the law, also appealed to me.

What made me decide in favor of sociology and led to a forty-two-year
career as an applied sociologist was the professor's many-splendid answer,
which, as best I can recall, went something like this: "You can study whatever
you are drawn to explore, as sociology is a permission slip to look at any
aspect of life—past, present, and future—on behalf of uncovering unknown
possibilities: the good, the bad, and especially the hard even to imagine."

Born in 1937 in Brooklyn, New York, I grew up in the 1940s as a member of one of only two Jewish families in a dense Italian American urban
village. My folks ran a small neighborhood grocery dependent on the good-
will of our working-class gentile customers. As an after-school and weekend
grocery boy I intuitively learned much of sociological value about ethnic
folkways and cultural norms. I was especially impressed by the tight grip

working-class culture had on Italian American generations and the pride many took in their insularity, nationality, patriotism, and religiosity.

My parents walked an existential tightrope of sorts, as anti-Semitism (fanned by Father Coughlin on the radio and the local German American Bund) posed an ever-present, if veiled threat to our well-being. It helped that my mother was a registered nurse and my father was a columnist for the neighborhood free paper (even though he had not earned a high school diploma). My mother provided free medical advice, and my father carefully flattered influential neighbors (some of whom had alleged ties with the local Mafia).

Anxiety and marginality were at the core of my childhood. Preoccupation with the status and role of an outsider—the need for adroitness, creativity, and resiliency—accompanied me into adulthood.

I attended gritty public schools alongside poor urban youngsters headed everywhere but into higher education, and I resolved at an early age not to follow their unambitious example. A handful of especially good high school teachers covertly encouraged my academic aptitude, and I became the first-ever graduate of my old Queens, New York, high school to go off to Cornell University, my ticket out of what otherwise could have proven a prosaic passing-time way of life.

At Cornell I attended a brand-new State University of New York (SUNY) college, the School of Industrial and Labor Relations (ILR), where I honed pro-labor and pro-activist values that forever guided my academic and personal life. Since my folks had no funds to help support me, I worked eighteen hours a week as a pot boy in the kitchen of a girls' dormitory, many hours as a librarian at the ILR School, many evening hours as librarian at the student union, and weekend hours as keeper of a campus coin-operated laundry.

Fascinated in my freshman year by my five required courses (and a sixth elective course I eagerly took every term), I earned the highest GPA of my seventy-five-member ILR class. Three years later at graduation I was awarded a prize for having had the best GPA throughout all eight semesters. That award helped me win a very generous, multiyear Woodrow Wilson Fellowship for a Ph.D. program in any subject, provided, that is, that I became a college teacher.

During my first two years at Princeton (1958–1960) I was required to pass written exams in the history of sociology, industrial sociology, social problems and social issues, sociological theory, and statistics. I also had to pass reading exams in French and German, neither of which language I had previously studied. As I was by then the father of a baby boy and lived with my wife among other graduate student families off campus, I found life at Princeton quite a challenge. While not then aware of its existence, I was guided in large part by a NASA slogan: "Failure is not an option."

In my third and final year (1961) I did field research and wrote and defended my dissertation. It was published by the ILR section of Princeton University as the first-ever sociological study of single-firm independent unions (sometimes unfairly deemed company unions). The book broke ground with its attention to the Jeffersonian democratic culture of the best of the unions and took issue with overreaching condemnations of these unions as employer dominated. Its challenge to unexamined prejudicial views became characteristic of my thirty-four books (to date) and well over 160 articles.

On graduating from Princeton in 1961 I became an assistant professor at the Wharton School of Finance and Commerce at the University of Pennsylvania. (The College of Arts and Sciences had long before declined to accept a sociology department, which had then been housed in the Business College.) Being naive in the matter, I welcomed a joint appointment in two departments—sociology and industry—a choice I have ever since urged others not to make. It became very difficult to handle two sets of department expectations and assignments and to coexist with two very different sets of faculty personalities. I found myself an outsider in both departments, an unenviable position for a twenty-four-year-old academic newbie.

At Wharton I taught both M.B.A. courses (often being the youngest person in the classroom) and sociology courses (as a father now of two young sons, I was possibly the poorest person in the room, a spur to my attention in lectures to issues of income inequality and possible remedies). I also participated in a Ford Foundation–sponsored research experiment to prepare prisoners for parole, a program that took me inside Graterford Prison once a week for ten weeks. I learned much there about what Gresham Sykes called "the society of captives,"[1] and I draw now on this in my current research on the lives of Jewish prisoners in Nazi camps during the Holocaust.

Although on the faculty of a business administration school, I earned acceptance by the Philadelphia AFL-CIO Labor Council and was able to help unionists strategize about ways to secure new members. I also got involved with (ill-fated) predecessors to charter schools that sought to aid low-income African American youngsters. These ventures sorely lacked people with managerial skills, and while their educational goals were sound, their execution of business fundamentals left much to be desired, a lesson I noted repeatedly when teaching would-be change agents how they might improve their chances of accomplishing lasting reforms.

I was denied tenure at Penn in 1966, in part because I shunned the writing of arcane articles for jargon-heavy sociology journals in favor of such outlets as the *Harvard Business Review, Social Forces,* and the plainspoken like. A few days later I accepted an invitation to join the faculty at nearby

---

1. Gresham M. Sykes, *The Society of Captives: A Study of a Maximum Security Prison* (Princeton, NJ: Princeton University Press, 1958).

Drexel University. Founded in 1891 to help upper-working-class and lower-middle-class youngsters qualify for high-skill posts in cutting-edge trades, it offered them an escape from the unambitious lifestyle I had myself rejected as a Brooklyn teenager. With a very different student body (first-generation college-goers) from that of the predominantly affluent one I had known for six years at Penn, I soon felt comfortably at home.

At Drexel over thirty-six years I had the latitude to introduce courses in futuristics, race and ethnic relations, and the sociology of science and technology, along with eighteen other courses. I revamped an existing course in industrial sociology to focus more on labor-management cooperation than on conflict, and I changed the course in social problems to concentrate on alternative solutions rather than "sluts and nuts," the student shorthand for the previous blame-pasting and sensationalizing orientation.

In the early 1980s I volunteered as a faculty adviser so that an LGBT group could start a pioneering campus-based chapter, and I joined two other faculty in promoting development of a Judaic Studies Center. Throughout most of my stay at Drexel I served as an elected member of the Faculty Senate and as head of its Student Affairs Committee. I helped organize a Drexel chapter of the American Association of University Professors. I also enjoyed the confidence of several of five successive university presidents (1967–2003) with whom I discussed campus sociological issues. On my retirement in 2003 the College of Arts and Sciences gave me its first Lifetime Award as a distinguished faculty member.

Across my career I developed my own notion of "Sociology Citizenship," what a sociologist owes to his or her profession. Accordingly, I kept up membership in the statewide organization, the Pennsylvania Sociological Society, gave papers at its annual meeting, and even served as president one year. I was a member of the Sociological Practice Section of the American Sociological Association (ASA), and chaired it for a year. I attended nearly every annual meeting of the Clinical Sociological Society, the Eastern Sociology Society, the Society for Applied Sociology, the Society for the Study of Social Problems (SSSP), and the ASA, and I served on committees of them all.

In 1987 I was chosen for the Distinguished Scholarship Award of the Pennsylvania Sociological Society. Also in 1987 I was chosen for the Outstanding Practitioner Award of the Clinical Sociological Society. In 1990 I was given the Lester F. Ward Award for Distinction in Applied Sociology by the Society for Applied Sociology. In 2006 I received the ASA Distinguished Career for the Practice of Sociology Award.

On the Philadelphia scene I was a member of the Citizens Committee for Public Education, the Citizens Committee for Public Policy (which I co-directed one year), the Philadelphia chapter of the Industrial Relations Research Association (which I chaired for a year), and various neighborhood organizations focused on improving public service and redefining grassroots citizenship. As ours was a racially troubled city, I helped promote dialogue among race and ethnic groups, worked on redistricting projects, and aided a major (ill-fated) Urban League effort to convert the school system into one reliant on educational parks. I partnered with Ross Koppel, a local sociologist, on a wide range of applied reform projects for the public good.

At the same time I was attracted to professional consulting openings and always had moonlighting posts with various major polling and/or problem-solving organizations. This took me behind the scenes where corporations, labor unions, and school systems were concerned—a rich source of timely and little-known material for my teaching and writing. I worked for every level of local, county, state, regional, and federal government and conducted paid research on such sociological topics as energy usage forecasts for the fifty states, forecast metrics for the state of Ohio, assessment of innovation in Department of Housing and Urban Development (HUD)–backed planned communities, and strengths and weaknesses of alternative modes of computer-based schooling. As such matters were of wide public interest, I gave on average twenty or more commissioned off-campus talks a year either here or overseas (Brazil, Canada, China, Denmark, England, Israel, Japan, Netherlands, South Korea, and Taiwan).

Between 1975 and 2000 I enjoyed spending a winter and a summer week as an adjunct sociologist at the AFL-CIO George Meany Center for Labor Studies in Silver Spring, Maryland. I became the first sociologist there to teach several sociology courses to up-and-coming labor unionists (e.g., futuristics, race and ethnic relations, social change, and social planning). My students sent me several required papers during the six-month recess. Many are now highly placed union leaders, hopefully better for their exposure to sociology.

Easily the most ambitious of my extra-campus activities involved membership on the board of a unique multi-million-dollar organization that tried—unsuccessfully—to persuade labor unions to pool millions of dollars in union pension funds in our one giant fund. It would have provided good financial gains and also steered union investment dollars away from antiunion companies. We had many high-level talks with AFL-CIO leaders and made some progress but not enough to withstand the 2008 recession. None of our investors lost any money in our venture, and I continue to hope it is resurrected someday soon, as its financial clout could make a desirable difference for organized labor in particular and America in general.

Across my academic career I kept in mind Professor Tumin's highlighting of "unknown possibilities—the good, the bad, and especially the hard even to imagine." With help from others I studied and wrote about fresh ways to alleviate poverty and reduce stress in blue-collar lives. I also did a monograph about ongoing innovations in organized labor that might help it soon reverse its downward slide. I coauthored the first-ever study of

American men who accompanied women to abortion clinics and urged clinics to upgrade services to these significant others. I wrote a book advocating a wide range of modern social reforms, and I also contributed to *The Readers' Guide to the Social Sciences* and the *Encyclopedia of the Future*.

I especially liked editing other people's writing. I edited the first-ever book about the part very personal taboo topics have played in the lives of introspective sociologists. I also edited a book that featured accounts of contemporary sociologists helping to make change. There was, as well, a series of four books of original futuristics essays for use by high school students, along with a series of five high school–level books of original essays about the Iraq War. I edited a book about how college life was seen through a sociological perspective and books about how two major institutions—K–12 schools and the nation's labor unions—might better employ computer power.

Two of my recent books explain why and how futuristics can be brought into K–12 schooling. I was a founding member in 1969 of the World Future Society, the cofounder and longtime director of its Philadelphia chapter, and a regular presenter at its annual meeting. I spoke often as a long-range forecaster at national and regional meetings of school superintendents nationwide and at meetings of the major labor unions of teachers (American Federation of Teachers, National Education Association).

Nowadays I have reinvented myself as a Holocaust scholar. I have been studying the 1933–1945 provision by European Jews of Nazi-prohibited support for other Jews. I share my research findings on both a website and in my 2017 book, *Stealth Altruism: Forbidden Care as Jewish Resistance in the Holocaust*. My wife, Lynn Seng, and I have made self-financed visits worldwide to forty-eight Holocaust museums and education centers, where we have found little or no attention paid to this subject. In contrast, much is made of the matter in 195 survivor memoirs I have studied and in many related interviews with survivors. So my latest crusade is to help rectify this provocative oversight, as I am convinced Jews and gentiles alike will gain from knowing that at least some victims of Nazi tyranny rose to the occasion, fanatical Nazi opposition notwithstanding.

I have always worked simultaneously on several book projects, and at this time I have three under way. One focuses on movie scenes viewers believe led them to change a major aspect of their lives (the working title is "Scenes of Consequence: Memorable Movie Moments"). A second discusses ongoing changes worldwide that might foreshadow a better or a worse future (the working title is "Touring Tomorrow Today: 100 Places That May Preview the Future"). And a third is a memoir I tentatively call "Swashbuckling Sociology: Adventures of a Recovering Change Agent," a colorful nonacademic book with which I intend to go far beyond this essay.

In 2014 I developed an informal advisory group known as the Sociologists Advisory Group on Elder Societies (SAGERS). Our group offers free advice to retirees anywhere wrestling with sociological matters. We have thus far advised parties wrestling with tough questions regarding governance, landscaping, and related matters. Members also participate in the ASA's Opportunities in Retirement Network (ORN), and SAGERS eagerly welcomes new members (please contact me at arthurshostak@gmail.com).

SAGERS calls to mind remarkable mentors of mine, such as E. Digby Baltzel (1915–1996), who, in my first year at Penn, discretely advised me to graciously accept all invitations to department committee meetings and never attend. Jessie Bernard (1903–1996), a personal friend, modeled going where few had dared go before, both in subject matter and in the world. Amitai Etzioni proved sociological counsel could be valued at even the level of the White House. Ross Koppel, a close associate, demonstrated the value of advanced statistical methodologies. Joan McCord (1930–2004) pointed out the unlimited advantages of writing on computers. Wilbert Moore (1914–1987) demonstrated the value of wry comments in otherwise straightforward material. And Mel Tumin (1919–1994) lived a life of social action that has endlessly inspired me. I was very fortunate to have known this cohort of larger-than-life social scientists.

Where retirement per se is concerned, Lynn and I, once tried-and-true East Coasters, recently experimented with living in Oakmont, a gateless, self-governing, fifty-three-year-old retirement community of 4,634 residents located seven miles from Santa Rosa in Northern California. We chose to relocate across thirty-five hundred miles for four reasons: First, three of our four adult sons with three of our four grandchildren live nearby on the West Coast. (We miss the family of one son back in Brooklyn, New York, and thrill to cross-country visits.) Second, our physical and mental health were being threatened by extremes in Philadelphia winter (climate change) weather. Northern California's year-round climate is all that its boosters claim. Third, the progressive nature of California was a magnet. We want to grow old in a dynamic state, one that has outstanding green achievements and major social welfare gains. And finally, Oakmont offers much of distinctive worth, such as a weekly Current Affairs Club, where I for a while offered novel sociological comments, and a dance studio where Lynn taught Zumba Gold three times a week.

In Oakmont I served as a sociological consultant on the community's first self-managed Futures Survey, one that drew survey responses from 47 percent of the owner-residents. I was instrumental in getting attention paid in survey analysis to social forces that have affected my own life course, including growing income inequality, seeming contraction of middle-class well-being, the persistence of racism (however disguised), the fragility of the American dream on predictable intergenerational gains, and the troublesome like. The community now has valuable baseline data and plans to repeat the survey (improved and expanded) in three to five years' time.

Sociologists will be interested to learn Oakmonters (a majority of whom are women in their early seventies) want to preserve what exists in the community and are almost as one in resisting colorful calls for change from retired boomers who favor flashy, large-scale, and expensive improvements (such as development of pickleball courts, modernization of the assembly hall, and possibly even development of a dog park). Nearly everyone wants to keep community dues as low as possible. How amenable the staid attitudes of the majority are to change remains unclear, and this polite rift between younger and older retirees will probably be a major factor in shaping the near future of many such retirement communities. From our new home in Alameda, California, a more diverse, multigenerational community that is closer to our family in San Francisco, Lynn and I will keep up with these developments.

Finally, three open-ended retirement matters especially warrant our attention as sociologists, attesting as they do to fault lines of consequence. First, *virtual* retirement communities are now appearing coast to coast, and they are likely to raise the bar where quality of life for seniors is concerned. Second, an ever-greater income gap between well-heeled boomers and fixed-income elderly residents is likely to impact significantly in retirement communities. And third, research attention is owed to the implications of voluntary senior citizen segregation (lily-white and solely nonwhite retirement communities). Visiting grandchildren, for example, may mistakenly think such racial insularity is the only way to live in retirement, a serious and costly constriction of possibilities.

These three aspects of the retirement scene should not go unattended by those of us who have always aided social integration. Having been privileged to have an adult life as an applied sociologist, I know we can help turn all of this to society's advantage.

12

What's It All About?

Reflections on Meaning in a Career

GARY T. MARX

> What's it all about?
> —**Michael Caine in** *Alfie*

> All these tidal gatherings, growth and decay,
> Shining and darkening, are forever
> Renewed; and the whole cycle impenitently
> Revolves, and all the past is future
> —**Robinson Jeffers, "Practical People"**[1]

In 1851 Herman Melville wrote to Nathaniel Hawthorne, "I am so pulled hither and thither by circumstances. The calm, the coolness, the silent grass-growing mood in which a [person] *ought* always to compose,—that, I fear, can seldom be mine."[2] At the height of an active career as a college professor, I knew the feeling. But that is the case no longer. In 1996 I became an emeritus professor, retiring but not shy. With retirement I have given increased attention to the "aboutness" of the personal meanings of a career, beyond the substantive issues I study. I next offer a short biography and then consider teaching (as broadly defined) as a central factor that gave meaning to my career.

I was born on a farm in central California, raised in Hollywood, and grew up in Berkeley. I moved to Los Angeles when I was two. I attended the University of California, Los Angeles (UCLA). As a junior meeting college breadth requirements, I happened into a class on deviance and social control

---

1. Robinson Jeffers, "Practical People," in *The Collected Poetry of Robinson Jeffers*, vol. 1, *1920–1928*, ed. Tim Hunt (Stanford, CA: Stanford University Press, 1988), 112. Copyright © "Practical People" Jeffers Literary Properties. All rights reserved. Used by permission of the publisher, Stanford University Press, http://sup.org.
2. "Letter to Nathaniel Hawthorne, June [1?] 1851," in *The Life and Works of Herman Melville* (2000), available at http://www.melville.org/letter3.htm.

and loved it (and not only because I had never before gotten an A in college). I became a sociology major.

After graduation in June 1960, I left the pastel womb of Los Angeles for Europe. I left as a clean-shaven, saddle-shoed fraternity boy, conspicuously consuming America's material abundance. I returned bearded and sandaled on the cusp of adulthood, inconspicuously consuming European history, culture, and geography. With hardly a look back in either anger or nostalgia, I simply flew away from the insular, smug, homogeneous, material status world of an adolescence, so bounded and defined by growing up in Hollywood in the 1950s.

At Berkeley, as a righteous 1960s student from Los Angeles (a place at that time that seemed to be the capital of materialism and media-induced superficiality), I was lucid about what I didn't want rather than what I did. With mentors such as Erving Goffman, Charles Glock, Marty Lipset, and Neil Smelser the latter quickly changed. After the Ph.D. orals exam, I spent a year traveling around the world, including going by land from Iran to Calcutta.

To varying degrees the question asked in the epigraph that opens this chapter underlies the life of scholarship. My academic work consisted of trying to understand the aboutness of topics involving race and ethnic relations, collective behavior and social movements, social control and science, technology and society. I pursued these topics through articles in academic and popular media and in books such as *Protest and Prejudice, Racial Conflict, Muckraking Sociology, Collective Behavior: Structure and Process, Undercover: Police Surveillance in America, Undercover: Police Surveillance in Comparative Perspective,* and *Windows into the Soul: Surveillance and Society in an Age of High Technology* (see www.garymarx.net).

My first job was in the Sociology Department at the University of California, Berkeley (UC Berkeley), but in 1967 I left for a job at Harvard in the Social Relations Department and the Joint Center for Urban Studies, working with Daniel P. Moynihan, and later at the Harvard Law School Criminal Justice Center. I have written about moving as a farm boy from a state school to the very heart of American academic life in "On Academic Success and Failure: Making It, Faking It, Forsaking It and Reshaping It." In 1972 under threat of deserting Cambridge for a tenured position at Columbia, I extended my appointment at Harvard. But after mentors Marty Lipset and Alex Inkeles left for Stanford, it seemed prudent to move down the street (literally) to Massachusetts Institute of Technology (MIT).

At MIT I was in an urban studies department, and that was wonderfully broadening, as I came to understand, with A. N. Whitehead, that all ways of seeing are also ways of not seeing. I became a *social studies* scholar combining scientific and humanistic ways of knowing. I have had visiting appointments, beyond sociology, in political science, law, psychology, science, technology, and society departments; have taught in Belgium, France, Spain, Italy, Austria, and China; and have lectured in Chile, Japan, and Australia.

The energy of the 1960s and the ideas of C. Wright Mills, along with the experience of being at MIT with its focus on the practical uses of knowledge, led to a concern with public policy issues. I have tried, to paraphrase the poet Wallace Stevens, to patch the world as best I can. I have worked with government agencies and commissions, congressional committees, and nonprofit groups on issues of intergroup relations, civil liberties, social control, and technology and society and written op-ed articles that helped bring national and international awareness to the social and ethical issues raised by new information technologies.

I moved, in a trajectory I could not have predicted, from initial work in race relations and stratification to social movements and collective behavior, to social control, to technology and society and from quantitative to qualitative methods.

In 1988, at the age of fifty, I became the person I wanted to be with the publication of *Undercover*, a new course on surveillance and society, a large National Science Foundation (NSF) grant for comparative study of covert police, involvement in public policy groups, publication of op-eds in the major papers, editorial positions, and reprinted articles and translations. Restlessness set in over the next few years. When the dog died and the kids left home for schools in the west, and with aging parents in California, it was time to move on. We had never planned to stay in Boston and had initially viewed it as a short-term cultural experience. Having been so focused on my research, I was ready to give something back. in 1992 I took a job as a reconstruction engineer, charged as chair with improving the Sociology Department at the University of Colorado Boulder.

Great departments are easier to envision than to build. In an article on thirty-seven moral mandates for sociologists, I indicated what I would like to see in an ideal department. The article was a response to what I saw too little of in Boulder. After four years it was time to move on. Phyllis Anne Rakita Marx, my wife of fifty years, who passed away in 2013, first developed cancer in 1986. Although she had her own career as a social worker and later teacher and practitioner of landscape design, she always followed me wherever career opportunities led. Now it was her turn, and she wanted to be near our grandchildren for the time remaining. So in 1996 we moved to a farm on Bainbridge Island near Seattle. There were some great fellowships in Palo Alto and Washington, D.C., fancy visiting professorships, and shorter-term teaching jobs, but for the majority of the time retirement offered a fellowship for life with nothing but discretionary time to think, recreate, garden, and be with family and friends.

Cultural Influences on Identity and a Career

A mélange of values, preferences, orientations, and beliefs formed the psy-chic backdrop that ordered a career and defined a sense of self and personal style. These include appreciation of the intellect, rationality, empiricism, irony, paradox, thresholds and curvilinear truths, the concrete as against the grand abstraction (but appreciation of midrange ideal types); authenticity/ honesty; surprise; humor; nature reverence and transcendence; resilience, individualism and a naive belief in an almost presocial self, able to endure the slings and spears of destiny and the pressures of the crowd; fascination with the outsider; courage; challenges, perseverance, and struggle against the odds; performance; awe, enthusiasm, cool and hot, precision and pas-sion; testing but respecting legitimate limits; asking, "Says who, and why, and based on what empirical, moral, legal, and measurement standards, and serving what interests?," "Are things what they appear to be?," and "Who or what is behind the mask and screen?"; initial skepticism and tentativeness, but with awareness of the need to believe and act.

The cultural backdrop for these includes (particularly in my formative years) Ayn Rand and her sophomoric characters in *The Fountainhead* and *Atlas Shrugged*; Sinatra's swingingly having it his way; Hemingway, Chan-dler, Hammett, Bogart, Brando, Newman, Dean, Traven, Kipling, Sartre, Camus, and Kerouac; the lyrics of Cole Porter and the Gershwins; the sing-ing of Chet Baker, June Christie, Chris Connor, Anita O'Day, Johnny Cash, Buddy Holly, the Beach Boys, and Mose Allison; Southern California in the 1930s, 1940s, and 1950s; the hazy, lazy days of summer; the beach and des-ert; palm trees and stucco homes with red tile roofs; on a clear day you can see Catalina; convertibles and girls, girls, girls. In the background were Sandburg, Mencken, Twain, Whitman, Thoreau, Emerson, Conrad, Kafka, Orwell, Huxley, and Europe. And closer to home were Groucho Marx, Jack Webb, James Dean, Natalie Wood, Lenny Bruce, Mort Sahl, Shelley Berman, Martin Luther King Jr., Malcolm X, Bobby Kennedy, and Erving Goffman.

My gratitude to sociology is unbounded. The discipline has provided many things to me over the decades: role and antirole models, road maps, an occupational identity and community, remuneration, status, and tools to make sense of questions about justice, inequality, social control, and change and authenticity. The university setting offered the lovely illusion of being forever young, with endless summer vacations and the cost-free asking of questions without having to provide answers. One didn't have to take risks in the world beyond the cloister (and with tenure, anonymous reviews, secret ballots, and professorial authority, few within it). The calling in the form of the job offered legitimacy and a megaphone to report research findings in-volving social issues and public policy questions I felt strongly about. In the beginning it also offered optimism.

A Little More History

Early in my career I was fortunate to encounter national leaders of the civil rights movement and to directly experience historical events. As a student at Berkeley I was active in the Congress of Racial Equality (CORE). Under the sway of positivism and the idealism of youth, it seemed like a career in sociology would be meaningful because it offered a way to bring about social change.

I knew some of the early Black Panthers. Richard Aoki, one of my best students, was a neighborhood friend of Huey Newton and Bobby Seale and was among the first members of the Black Panther party in Oakland. He legally provided them with their first weapons and weapons training and became a Panther field marshal.

One of my friends in CORE was Jack Weinberg, a graduate student in math responsible for popularizing the statement "never trust anyone over thirty" (which with the wisdom and tentativeness of aging I would suggest reversing to "never trust anyone *under* thirty" or maybe even forty). Weinberg's arrest for sitting at the CORE table at the entrance to the campus on Telegraph Avenue and Bancroft Way was the event that triggered the free speech movement. I sat at that table a few months earlier, giving out information and seeking donations (the table can be seen in the film *Berkeley in the Sixties*).

Malcolm X came to Berkeley in 1961. He was an amazing speaker and a marvelous illustration of C. W. Mills's call for showing how personal troubles could reflect broader social problems. His personal tales of victimization, imprisonment, and redemption; his energy, eloquence, delivery, humor, and cries against racial injustice were stirring and affecting. Yet when with the same forcefulness and passion he began talking about Yakub, a black scientist who created the evil white race thousands of years ago, I was in disbelief. Earlier in the semester I heard Eric Hoffer speak and was troubled to see so many remnants of the true believer in Malcolm X. I was incredulous and wondered if this might not just be a mobilizing device and was pleased but not surprised when he later rejected the more debatable aspects of that theology.

Shortly thereafter I was inspired by hearing Norman Thomas speak. He ran for president many times on the Socialist Party ticket—important aspects of his program were taken over by Franklin D. Roosevelt in the 1932 election. Thomas said, "I am not the champion of lost causes, but of causes not yet won."[3] A few months later we picketed a more successful presidential

---

3. Harold Meyerson, "A Democratic Socialist Campaign? It's about Time," *Washington Post*, May 14, 2015, available at https://www.washingtonpost.com/opinions/a-democratic-socialist-campaign -its-about-time/2015/05/14/05634e18-f9a1-11e4-9030-b4732caefe81_story.html.

candidate, John F. Kennedy, over issues of disarmament and discrimination in federal housing projects and then went to the Berkeley Greek Theatre to be inspired (perhaps against our initial will) by his eloquence and his substance as the first U.S. president born in the twentieth century. A bit later I was on the outer circle of policy advisers for Robert F. Kennedy's presidential bid.

Bayard Rustin, a founder of CORE, strategist for the civil rights movement, and leader of the March on Washington, wrote the introduction to *Protest and Prejudice*. The book helped in fund-raising and in fighting the backlash against the civil rights movement as a result of the rise of black power and the urban disorders of the late 1960s. In CORE we had some notable successes in combating discrimination in employment. I worked for the Kerner Commission (National Advisory Commission on Civil Disorders), which investigated the 1960s disorders and focused on police responses and contributed to the report of the Senate Select Committee on Undercover Activities.

Lowered Expectations

It was incredibly exciting to be at Berkeley and Cambridge during the 1960s. But under the somber weight of historical events and knowledge from my studies about revolutions and too many reforms gone bad, the heady optimism of youth was replaced by disillusionment and being happy with small favors. The limits of politics, let alone social science, to bring about rapid, deep-lying social change without an avalanche of unwanted consequences became clear. That awareness suggested endless topics for research to find out why the best-laid plans so often went awry and reflections on what sociological scholarship could contribute. My 1972 edited book on "muckraking sociology" was an effort to come to terms with the pulls between passion and scholarship.

In spite of lowered expectations, I am glad to have been able to apply social science knowledge to public policy through writing and speaking about racial issues and civil liberties. It is satisfying to have helped secure a seat at the table (even if not at its head)—most recently for privacy and surveillance questions—and to have contributed to the national conversation on these issues.

Certainly there is satisfaction in contributing to the empirical and theoretical development of knowledge and in understanding puzzles, inventing concepts and well-turned phrases, being cited and invited, and garnering awards. The subsidized opportunities to pursue topics of one's own choosing and to think and write freely are a precious gift.

But research would not offer any Rosetta stone for building the heavenly city on the hill, and the limits and downsides of utopian projections and of the ego become ever more apparent with age. No matter the satisfaction you take in social research or how worthwhile you think a given publication is, it is likely to be little noted nor long remembered. The star quickly burns out, even if some memory of the flame remains. In contrast, our training of students, and in particular those who will become teachers and researchers, has a longer shelf life because it is self-renewing.

So when the dust settles and the lights dim, what's it all about? What endures? Certainly not the accolades that nourish needy egos and the plaques that tarnish in boxes in a barn. The research grants are expended; articles in journals and the popular press are replaced by the latest issue; books go out of print (and with digitalization our remnants find new homes only in landfills); new social issues and research themes continually appear and displace the old; and the mentors, colleagues, editors, publishers and officials in schools, foundations, and government one worked with move on, or out, whether to warm pastures or cold ground.

Perhaps more important and certainly more enduring than the fleeting and quickly forgotten publications, awards, and direct encounters with the policy and political worlds are the interactions with students. In reviewing some of my earlier career reflections in preparation for writing this chapter, I was surprised to see how ego focused many of them were.[4] It was a way to enliven the silent grass-growing mood as one moves from "Who's Who" to "Who's he?" The writing served to relive (relieve?) the past and as an advertisement for myself for those who missed the 1960s and 1970s. The writing was mostly about how *I* responded to the opportunities, vicissitudes, and successes of a wonderful career and tried to make sense of failures.

Students

But with this deconstructive warning and call for humility and perspective, I said little about what brought abiding satisfaction and what today brings the fondest memories—teaching and working with students. Given the informal culture of sociology at leading universities, it is easy to slight the importance of, and the personal rewards from, teaching.

In looking back, the most satisfying aspect of my career has involved the education of teachers and researchers to whom I communicated the values of the university, the excitement of learning, and the flame of Erasmus. I tried to socialize students to the traditions and values of the Renaissance, the Enlightenment, and civility and to the high ideals of scholarship, freedom of inquiry, and critical reflection. I encouraged their curiosity and ability to ask questions about and seek answers to matters that matter.

---

4. These personal reflections are available at http://garymarx.net. They deal with topics such as Berkeley in the 1960s and the civil rights movement; encounters with and studying surveillance; sociology and travel; mentors S. M. Lipset, Erving Goffman, and Neil Smelser; muckraking sociology and dirty data; success and failure; and moral mandates for aspiring social scientists.

Under the best of circumstances their energy and fresh experiences and thoughts provide a reason to bound into the classroom each morning, particularly if one teaches in a Socratic fashion and makes question raising and learning from students the core of instruction. In the beginning there are the questions, and our goal is to provoke wonderment, to cultivate asking why, and to provide the tools to help with answers. The satisfaction in training teachers is equaled by having worked with students who chose the world of public affairs.

With the occasional contacts over the years, memories of many students stay fresh. Then there are others I lost contact with but observed at a distance.

Richard Aoki, the Black Panther mentioned earlier, was a very smart student, and I had many discussions with him—we had no disagreements about racial and economic injustice but many about the best way to bring about social change. In our discussions I encouraged him to continually question his assumptions just as I do mine and also to look at the empirical base for the beliefs held and to think about the logical structure of an argument. I like to think that our interaction helped guide him toward a successful career in Asian studies and administration, though luck as well may have prevented him from being killed or jailed.

Then there are students such as Vicki, who wrote:

Professor Marx how can I thank you for giving us so much? More than any other professor, you challenged me to think more analytically, to be more objective, and to work harder. You have always been personally warm and receptive, willing to talk, anxious to listen.

As I sat in your last lecture, I tried to comprehend not having someone like you to be here encouraging and helping us to think, to question, to learn. I felt very scared and realized the ultimate goal of the best professor is to teach his or her students to do all of those things for themselves. And, I felt better, confident that once I'm "out in the world" all by myself, your lessons will be with me, confident that now I am prepared to think for myself, to question, to wonder. And for that, I thank you. —Vicki

Wow. I'd like to have a teacher like that! But who is Vicki? I have no recollection of her. I have stayed in occasional contact with many of my students. Receiving messages such as "I hold you in the highest regard as a mentor, scholar, and human being. You provided encouragement, scholarly guidance and words of wisdom on living the good life" makes it worthwhile. To be asked to write introductions to colleagues' books or to have students dedicate books or articles to you based on what you have offered is a price far above rubies.

In an overflowing cauldron of teaching experiences, among the more memorable was having a student from India introduce himself and say, "Just call me Sid." His full name was Siddhartha, a name hallowed by 1960s seekers of the way. The occasional unsigned love notes were interesting, as was the careless student who wrote a fine paper on riots that seemed familiar. It should have, as it was taken verbatim from my article in the *Encyclopaedia Britannica*.

One can even wring some wry satisfaction from displeasing a student. Consider the student who gave me a poor grade in the course evaluation because "he uses far too many big words that get you lost in what he is actually trying to say." There can even be some satisfaction from students who fail the class. Note the curious case of the student who failed the midterm and the final yet wrote a note saying, "Professor Marx, I just wanted to let you know that I really enjoyed your class even though I may not have shown it through my work. Through the class I have become so much more interested in law and I now know that this is the direction I want to head in. . . . I wanted to thank you for a great class and for helping me find what I really am interested in." God save the law. What might have been written if the student had received an A grade?

Over the years students I did not work with directly have kindly thanked me for the impact my writing had on their thinking and careers. A leading scholar of the civil rights movement told me reading *Protest and Prejudice* while working in a factory led him to want to become a scholar.

An Italian student wrote, "Sometimes I think the world is terrible. I see corruption. I see cynicism and people without solidarity. Then I met people like you and I come back to smile because you give us hope. I feel myself stronger than before because I see that another world is possible. What can I do it is Italy? But I will try not to change my mind about my moral integrity."

A letter from Rebel, an articulate outlaw biker:

Dear Professor Marx: I usually detest sociologists. About a year and a half ago, I was very tempted to stomp [author of a book about Vietnam veterans]. . . . But I want to tell you, even though you are a sociologist, how much I appreciate your work. I promise you, I pose no threat to you at all. I am just appreciative and excited. Thank you very much. You now have a new fan. Rebel.

Maybe he could help me with the critics!

In spite of the hierarchical nature of the relationships, students can also be colleagues. Fundamental to the sociological sensibility with its attention to roles, subjectivity, and personhood is taking the role of the other and being a good listener. Engaging students' ideas and writing can aid one's own

work. As Anna in *The King and I* sang, "If you become a teacher, by your
students you will be taught."

The individual must go to bat alone, as C. W. Mills observed. Yet the bat-
ter is also a member of a team, and that team nestles within a broader series
of overlapping communities. As ET said, "We are not alone." Students often
overflow with the raw materials for an article but need to be encouraged to
believe in themselves and to learn the craft of asking questions and converting ideas into publishable form.

Like baby birds, they require nurturing and protection but shouldn't stay
in the nest too long. It is important to support and complement (as both
supplementing and praising) one's students—but this must be toward the
end of setting them free to follow their own path, not replicating yourself. I
am very proud of having written papers with so many of my students over
the years (in most cases this was the student's first published paper, and we
did only one together).

Students can be the vital vacuum pulling us from the powerful isolating
forces of solipsism, and they are the conduit through which we learn to speak
to broader public audiences. In addition, we need allies and torchbearers.
Cream might rise to the top if it's not in the freezer, but academic reputa-
tions and opportunities require supporters and networks. Given the reciprocal nature of much interaction, there can be more direct payback. Those in
subordinate positions we encounter today may later be in positions to help
(or harm) us tomorrow. Graduate students seem so young and jejune when
first encountered (and that intensifies as one ages) that it is hard to remember
that pretty soon they will be on editorial, hiring, grant-giving, and award
committees to which, in a role reversal, you may come to (or be offered) as
a humble supplicant.

In Gratitude

Students both in class and when they become colleagues sometimes thank
their teachers; the reverse is less common. Yet basic role analysis will
show the dependence of teachers on their students and the gratitude we owe
them. They offer not only a captive audience but, in a curious economic reversal, don't require payment for what we receive from them.

Wordsworth tells us that we should not grieve for the splendor in the
grass or for the glory of the flower but should seek strength in what remains
behind. Yet we can also gain strength in what lies *ahead*.

When Ruben Rumbaut of the University of California, Irvine (whom I
had contact with when he was a student in Boston), asked his mentor, the
late Egon Bittner, "How can I ever repay you?," Egon gave a wry look and said
in his understated way, "In the great chain of being, one day it will be your

turn." And so it is and will be. As Henry James observed, "We work in the dark—we do what we can—we give what we have."[5]

Egon was correct. If we are fortunate, it will be our turn. I saw that with respect to my article "Of Methods and Manners for Aspiring Sociologists: 37 Moral Imperatives," written for graduate students. Ruben wrote that he found the article

> such a refreshing antidote to so much of academic sociology and of the "training" of graduate students that ever since I've made a practice of sending it with a personal note to all the students of every seminar I've taught. I've also sent it to colleagues and former students who went on to become sociologists and noticed subsequently that some of them even included it in their syllabi to *their* students. (Nobody ever keeps a citation count for that but it matters more.) . . . In front of my computer I have a handcrafted sign on a 3 × 5 white card with this personal motto: ASPIRE TO INSPIRE BEFORE YOU EXPIRE. I'm looking at it now. Every time I send out your 37 moral imperatives, I think I'm living up to the spirit of those six words.

In validation, one of Ruben's students decades ago, Professor Pierrette Hondagneu-Sotelo of the University of Southern California (USC), graciously wrote, "Thank you for your moral imperatives. I teach a 2 semester grad seminar on participant observation and interviewing at USC, and I always use that article from *The American Sociologist*. It helps students, and it inspires me every time." I like to think that some of her students now teaching are passing on the ideas to their students.

As teachers we are rewarded in knowing that through our students and their students ad infinitum some of what we give seeps into the culture and geometrically trickles across generations. I am grateful to my teachers (and their teachers) and to those I have taught and worked with over the last fifty years for their complicity in the great chain of being that involves the delivery, receipt, and transmission of knowledge. Knowledge, unlike other forms of wealth, is enriched as it is shared and exchanged.

As it does for the Dude in the film *The Big Lebowski*, the giving of ideas abides—that is our satisfaction and our solace, our sustenance and perhaps even our salvation, so thanks to all of my students and to theirs and theirs.

Finally, in retirement sociology has continued to impact my life in the effort to understand what it's all about. I am very appreciative of the values, questions, and worldviews it has offered. There is greater time now to reflect

---

5. Henry James, "The Middle Years," in *Henry James: Complete Stories, 1892–1898* (New York: Library of America, 1996), 354.

and for family, recreation, consumption, and citizenship activities. I am thankful for the indulgence of imagination and the faded memory-maps of biography and place with the quest for a life lived with truth, integrity, love, civility, beauty, humor, fun, and the continuing challenges of discovery. As Michelangelo is reputed to have said late in his life, "Ancoro imparo" (I continue to learn).

For colleagues approaching retirement my advice (perhaps trite but certainly right) is to be in the moment. Don't put off things you have wanted to do. "Let it be," as the Beatles sang—both your expectations for and your anger at others. Be appreciative of all that has been, and continues to be, good in your life and in life; stay active within your physical limits; stay engaged à la Sartre with whatever moves you and doesn't hurt others; keep the faith and the passion; come to terms with the transitory nature of recognition and success and see their accidental and environmental correlates; try to merge means and ends; appreciate dualities, polarities, and ironies and the fascinating elements of the individual and the social in which individuals die but the culture that nourished them and that they contributed to lives on; share the knowledge; and finally, stay curious and be filled with wonderment and laughter. And if it is true that that's all there is, then by all means, as the enigmatic song "Is That All There Is?" suggests, let's keep dancing.

13

My Journey with Sociology

Joyce E. Williams

Beginnings

My journey with sociology is framed by a Millsian intersection of biography, history, and social structure, as my life and my sociological journey are inseparable from the intersection of class, race, and gender in a sociohistorical context that spanned reference points from the Great Depression to 9/11. In many respects the telling of my journey with sociology is about mentors, my own and the one I attempted to become for my students. My life began toward the end of the Depression, which actually made little difference to an already-poor family. My early years were spent in rural Texas without indoor plumbing or electricity. My father died when I was nine, after which my mother and I moved to a nearby small town where we lived on the "wrong side of the tracks" and where she worked at whatever jobs were available. I was the last of four children, separated from my siblings by considerable age difference and by the fact that they left home in their midteens. I was not only a first-generation college student but the only one of the siblings to complete high school. From age twelve, I worked at various part-time jobs: waitress, carhop, and once as a dishwasher. I am sure that it did not occur to any of my teachers that I was college material. If we had school counselors to assist with career goals, I never knew of one, and no teacher ever mentioned college to me even though I was always a good student. In fact, after earning a Ph.D., I chanced to meet my high school English teacher, who made the comment, "Joyce, if I had been shooting students that I expected to get a doctorate, you would have been very safe."

I never perceived my life as difficult or unfortunate, although after joining the ranks of academics, I realized my background was different from that of most of my colleagues. The only handicap I ever felt I needed to overcome was in college, where I was disadvantaged by not having taken college preparatory courses. Because I was a female and no doubt perceived as not college material, I had been advised into typing and shorthand classes—skills that would prepare me for an office job and provide some degree of upward mobility. A Sunday school teacher and a pastor were my earliest sources of support and saw in me the potential that others overlooked. Their personal interest, intervention, and influence resulted in my being awarded an all-inclusive college scholarship at a small Baptist girls' school (all white at the time) where everything was provided except spending money, and I worked on campus for that. Even though my own journey with religion later diverged from this early beginning, I will always be indebted to the good, religiously motivated people who believed in me and set me on my journey to becoming a sociologist.

My Discovery and Pursuit of Sociology

Having taken none of the preparatory classes needed in science, math, and foreign languages, I struggled with these subjects in my first year of college. It was not until my sophomore year that I enrolled in a sociology class with a new faculty member who was just beginning her teaching career. Sarah Frances Anders was the first woman to complete the doctoral program in sociology at Florida State University, where she had studied with William Ogburn and Meyer Nimkof. Thus, my first introduction to the discipline was mostly traditional positivism but with a humanistic overlay. It took only the introductory class in sociology for me to know that this was to be my major and my field of study. A methods class made me realize that I could pursue and find answers to some questions. If I ever entertained any doubts about sociology as a career choice, it was as I struggled through a statistics class. Dr. Anders, a product of her training, assumed that sociologists should be quantitative. Not until I was doing doctoral work at Washington University did I discover the world of qualitative research. My initial attraction to sociology was that it was a means of understanding the social world and *my* social world constructed by gender, by class, and, not incidentally, by whiteness, with windows of opportunity opened by my church and subsequently by education. I excelled in sociology classes, and after my freshman year my performance improved in all subjects. Dr. Anders became my academic adviser, my role model, my mentor, and my friend. Shortly before graduation, she approached me with the suggestion that I pursue graduate work and think about a career in college teaching. I followed her suggestions but with several detours because of a short-lived marriage and financial constraints that necessitated full-time employment.

My first job out of college was as a social worker in Dallas, where I also began taking graduate courses in sociology, one or two per semester, first at a state school within commuting distance and then at nearby Southern Methodist University (SMU). One of the first classes I took at SMU was race relations with Morton King, who became my second mentor. As Dallas and the country as a whole grappled with desegregation, the topic of race relations captured my attention and was to become for me a primary area of interest. King helped me formulate a plan for a master's degree, including a thesis project that I could carry out while doing my job in a residential children's home. Later, after I began teaching, I wrote an article from this research and submitted it to the *Journal of Marriage and Family*. I was so insecure about what I was doing that I told no one about the submission and was unaware that it was customary to publish thesis work with your adviser. When this first article was accepted for publication, I knew nothing of the process and, upon receipt of galley proofs, almost missed the deadline for returning them because I was not sure what they were and was intimidated by looking at them. My classes at SMU were interesting although most combined graduate and undergraduate students or were independent studies. I received faculty support and guided reading from King and Lewis Rhodes and in 1962 earned my master's degree. While the SMU program had served me well by allowing me to study part time, it did not provide exposure to a graduate subculture both because I worked full time and because there was little of it at SMU where sociology had fewer than half a dozen graduate students at the time.

On the recommendation of Sarah Frances Anders, I returned to my undergraduate alma mater and, one semester before my M.A. degree was completed, became an instructor in a growing department of sociology. I taught four courses my first semester in addition to completing my thesis. Teaching made me aware that I would learn more as an instructor than as a student because my need to understand a topic before attempting to explain it kept me busy each day preparing classes for the following day. For that first year, I stayed just one lecture ahead of my students but was constantly inspired by them and by what I soon knew to be a love of teaching with its circular and linear patterns. Every semester offers a new beginning, a chance to do better, with fresh faces and new converts to sociology, but there is also the linearity of mentoring and in the continuous flow of students as they are absorbed into various careers, audiences, and unknown generations ahead.

After three years, in need of expanded opportunities for professional growth, I accepted appointment as a sociology instructor in a state school in the Dallas–Fort Worth area. This school would later become part of the University of Texas System but at that time was just emerging from community college status and had a combined social science department in which I became the second female, the first in sociology. I was already conscious of a need to work toward my Ph.D. if I wanted a career in college teaching. In an effort to learn more about research, writing, and publishing, I volunteered to work in the research department of a nearby federal prison, where I had the opportunity to become part of a research project involving drug offenders. This work provided me with another mentor in the person of Dr. William Bates, who not only took leadership in authoring several research papers with me but also gave me the opportunity to present papers at professional meetings. In addition, he was responsible for the awakening and development of my political consciousness and for my acceptance into the doctoral program at Washington University in St. Louis, where I was awarded a graduate teaching assistantship.

Graduate School in the Turbulent 1960s

In the fall of 1967, I took a leave of absence from my teaching position in Texas and for two years became a full-time doctoral student. In the liberal environment of Washington University and the politicization of just about everything in the 1960s, much of my first semester was spent deflecting Texas stereotypes and the stigma of the Kennedy assassination. The war in Vietnam was in escalation, and the civil rights and antiwar movements were gaining momentum. Having dinner out on my first evening in St. Louis, a friend and I were warned that Stokely Carmichael would be in the city that evening and that we should get off the streets. The summer of 1967 became known as "the long hot summer," characterized by race riots numbering more than one hundred before year's end. For the latter part of the 1960s and into the 1970s, what was happening outside academe impacted all of higher education, especially sociology. Students were not passively sitting in classrooms learning the traditional canon. There was a continuous call for a more relevant education, and studies often took second place to teach-ins, protests, and even violent clashes with law enforcement as, for example, the Democratic convention in 1968, Kent State in 1970, and Washington University, where the ROTC building was leveled by arson. As in other schools, students at Washington University, particularly graduate students, were often more interested in the social issues of the day than their studies. We marched in support of civil rights for black people, against the Vietnam War, and against authority in general. Later we marched in support of poor people and to abolish the draft, wipe out poverty, support women's liberation, and save the earth. The 1960s presented a cornucopia of causes, all of which were within the subject matter of sociology, and we were convinced we could make a difference. It was a time when everything had moral and ethical implications and students assumed a morally superior posture vis-à-vis the establishment. Annual meetings of the American Sociological Association (ASA) were several times disrupted by calls for relevance and for the ASA to take a stand against the war. The discipline responded slowly but was changed forever, as were some departments and careers. Sociologists became more politically conscious and less wedded to a neutral, value-free science. Faculties making up the department at Washington University were far from value neutral but diverse in theoretical orientations, methodologies, and substantive interests. It seemed, however, that almost everyone in the department—students and faculty—were Marxists, but of different and often opposing camps, most notably theoretical versus activist.

As a graduate student, I was as conscious of external events as of the subject matter I needed to master to pass comprehensive exams. I spent an entire summer reading for exams and watching the news. The classics—Émile Durkheim, Max Weber, Karl Marx—were all dissected within a conflict paradigm or were treated only as "must knows." Even though the department at Washington University was considered liberal if not radical, our suggested reading bibliography comprised largely traditional works in sociology and included few works by black or female writers. Against the turbulent backdrop of the everyday many such readings were seen as irrelevant, although the graduate student subculture compensated with a consistent source of underground reading. In retrospect, the department was known for its personalities and internal conflicts as much as for its scholarly productivity or instruction. The faculty member who became my adviser and mentor was Helen Gouldner, for whom I worked as a graduate teaching assistant. She was the only tenured female in the department and somehow maintained neutrality in the midst of conflict. Although there were two Gouldners who held Ph.Ds., only Alvin was known as Dr. Gouldner; his ex-wife was known as Ms. Gouldner or Helen. She was peacemaker, confidante, informal adviser to all graduate students, and the glue of the department.

During my time at Washington University the sociology and anthropology programs were in the same department. Interdisciplinary research projects were common as were grants funding graduate students, for example, almost a million dollars to study the Pruitt Igoe housing project. Not infrequently, faculty or students made the news with publicity embarrassing to the university and its conservative supporters. For example, Laud Humphrey's 1970 dissertation research on male homosexuals made national headlines along with questions about the ethics of his methodology, a controversy with irrevocable impact on the discipline. Ultimately such publicity contributed to the department's being closed in 1991 and not reopened for more than twenty years. The demise of Washington University sociology has been analyzed from a variety of perspectives (see, for example, the entire 1989 winter issue of the *American Sociologist*), but for those of us who were there in the glory days, it is still a painful and very personal topic.

Lessons from the Community

Returning home to Texas, I began teaching again and collecting data for my dissertation, a qualitative study, by design time-consuming, of a black community in conflict. My exposure to qualitative research, specifically community studies, was largely through reading and the influence of Washington University faculty such as Lee Rainwater and Charles Valentine. Selection of a black community in Texas was determined by its being geographically near where I would be teaching, and it mirrored the racial conflict that was sweeping the country. However, white-on-black research came under fire at about the time I began my work, leading to reservations and warnings from my committee members that were mitigated only by Helen Gouldner. My committee included one black member whom I did not know because he joined the faculty as I was leaving residency. The committee member to provide me with the most substantive input was visiting professor and historian George Rawick. The person who guided me patiently through the dissertation process was Helen Gouldner, and the people who made it all possible were those in the community I studied. They influenced me then and have continued to influence me because of their commitment to the struggle for equality and because of personal and lasting relationships formed there. They accepted me, first with skepticism and suspicion, but when I kept showing up and when they discovered that I could be of use to them, I became a community participant rather than an observer.

During my graduate years, I was involved in various activities related to civil rights and the war, but it was my dissertation work that gave me the opportunity to apply much of what I had learned and to feel that I was relevant in working to alleviate a problem. It is not an overstatement to say that this research, later published as *Black Community Control*, was the best learning experience of my life. I emerged with some understanding of the reality of everyday life for black people and a heightened consciousness of white privilege. For example, I was surprised upon meeting a woman in my study community who had grown up in the same small Texas town as I had, but we did not know each other. I was a poor white girl from the wrong side of the tracks, yet I had never set foot in "colored town." I recalled and examined another experience, long repressed, involving the death of my father. He was an unskilled laborer earning forty dollars per month at the time of his passing. His funeral was held in our church, and as we exited, I observed two black men with whom my father had worked who had come to pay their respects to "Mr. Harry." They were dressed in their best, hats in hands, but standing at a distance. I recall asking my mother why Mr. Jim and Mr. Samuel did not come inside. I was silenced by a well-meaning aunt, but this experience was my first consciousness of the color inequality I had grown up taking for granted.

Passing on Sociology

I earned tenure at three schools: the University of Texas at Arlington, Trinity University in San Antonio, and Texas Woman's University (TWU). My six years at Trinity, where I was the only female in the department, were defined by my learning to balance teaching and research and to enrich and inform one with the other. In this private, selective liberal arts institution my students were a rather homogeneous group, and I felt it imperative to bring the "outside" inside the classroom. Volunteer work with a rape crisis center led to receipt of a major grant from the National Institute of Mental Health to study the impact of rape on survivors and to survey racial-ethnic variations in public attitudes about rape. This research, later published with Karen Holmes as *The Second Assault*, was a rich if sobering experience and was highly important in defining the dimensions of gender and race/ethnicity in both my research and teaching.

In search of a more diverse student body and drawn again to women's education, I left Trinity to take a position at TWU, where I spent the last twenty-two years of my professional life and where in addition to the usual activities associated with teaching I became involved in curriculum development, graduate student education, and administration. In contrast to earlier appointments, I joined a department with a female chair and where all tenured faculty were female. It was a student-centered environment and, even though a small department, offered master's and doctoral degrees. I added several new courses to the curriculum, including an undergraduate course on family violence, the first in the state, and a graduate-level class on the history of American sociology. A colleague and I developed an interdisciplinary, doctoral-level class (the scholarly career) that proved popular and useful across various majors for those interested in college teaching. The history of American sociology class attracted more students than expected, as they were apparently drawn to the opportunity to learn about unknown or unacknowledged sociologists, particularly those who were women or black, as well as about sociology's history of reform and activism. When I first began preparation for the class, the nearest thing to an appropriate text was Arthur Vidich and Stanford Lyman's 1985 *American Sociology*. While these authors gave some attention to the early identity of sociology with social problems, there was little mention of the important roles of either black or women sociologists in discipline building. I subsequently found several appropriate books on black sociologists and discovered the sociological side of W.E.B. Du Bois. Later, Mary Jo Deegan's *Jane Addams and the Men of the Chicago School* and Patricia Lengermann and Jill Niebrugge-Brantley's *The Women Founders* became available as texts, opening up new areas of research for students and new perspectives on the discipline, including the sociological work of American settlement houses in the progressive era. In fact, three doctoral dissertations originated from this class.

I found working with graduate students particularly rewarding and came to appreciate more fully the linearity of teaching in the generational flow of students and the substantive flow of sociology. Just as I adopted and modified the sociological visions of my mentors and passed these on to my students, they in turn were no doubt influenced by my sociological imagination and surely manifest modifications of this in their own work and professional lives. Of the doctoral dissertations that I directed over the years there are more than a dozen graduates that I am in touch with today as they continue to pass on sociology through teaching or serving as administrators, some in small liberal arts schools and some in large universities. One former student has waged a courageous legal battle with her university over freedom of speech issues; another has served several stints in overseas teaching; several serve as deans; others are practicing sociology in the public and private sectors, some in administration.

My first administrative assignment, not sought but accepted as a challenge, came at TWU, where for ten years I served as chair of a multidiscipline department: sociology, social work, criminal justice, and, for the last five years, women's studies. I experienced being chair with some ambivalence because the multitude of responsibilities often took priority over teaching, and research and writing were restricted to late nights and weekends. I found satisfaction, however, in being able to grow the doctoral program and in my ability to make a difference in some aspects of students' learning experiences and in the departmental culture. I consistently published my work but was never as productive a scholar as I would have been with a lighter teaching load or had I not taken the position as department chair, although I have no regret about my decisions and would not opt for a career redo.

On Being a Retiree

I retired with the long-term goal of writing a book, specifically to write a history of the early years of American sociology. Having recently accomplished this with the publication of *Settlement Sociology in the Progressive Years* (coauthored with Vicky MacLean), I have moved on to less ambitious tasks. However, I cannot write of retirement, as some do, in terms of hobbies, family, or new pursuits. Having always been a workaholic, I never cultivated hobbies or leisure-time activities and have now outlived most of my family. For me, the beauty of retirement is having time to read, travel, research, write some every day if I choose to, or spend the day on a mindless novel. I moved to a new geographic area where I have friends and an environment

conducive to writing and to teaching part time. I was also hopeful of securing a visiting scholar position for which, in retrospect, I am sure I did not
know how to market myself. Although I was interested in a title and not pay,
a position did not materialize even as offers for adjunct teaching were readily available. I have published consistently in retirement but have found it
challenging to get my work reviewed without an institutional affiliation. My
emeritus title has proven helpful as has an adjunct affiliation, perhaps sug-
gesting that I am still current. Although working as a retired, independent
scholar has presented obstacles, it also means freedom, and I have been able
to pursue areas long relegated to my "interest file." At the same time, I am
forced to find research I can do with nominal cost because the thing more
difficult to secure than interest in work performed by retirees is funding for
such work.

I have always been interested in the history of American sociology as I
knew it to intersect with early social problems and activism, and in retirement I have had the luxury and satisfaction of pursuing and continuing
research in this area. Years spent in this undertaking have been not only productive but fun as I learned to mine such diverse data resources as archival
collections and the Internet. I was fortunate to find a younger colleague who
shares my interest and was able to procure travel funds for archival "digs."
As we worked, we were continually amazed and delighted by the sociological
richness found in the meticulous records of such women as Jane Addams,
Julia Lathrop, Sophonisba Breckinridge, Grace and Edith Abbott, and Florence Kelley. Their works caused us to wonder whether they knew they were
making history and how we measure up to that history today. Additionally,
we examined and documented a long-ignored interlocking of the social gos-
pel and sociology as represented by the works of Robert Woods and Graham
Taylor and expanded on the early relationship between sociology and social
work. Our work builds on that of other feminist scholars and continues the
recovery of some of the lost or marginal history of settlement sociology. For a
discipline that has always exhibited some paranoia about its scientific legitimacy, a history inclusive of activism and religion propelled by women and
social gospelers is anathema for some. We have found publication outlets for
much of our work although are sometimes forced to rebut accusations that
the topic is not really sociology or that it is not relevant today. However, as
Ellsworth Fuhrman reminds us, "Every generation must come to terms with
the 'value' or 'purpose' of sociology. . . . The past can show us what others
have opted for but their actions do not dictate uniformly the choices of present actors."[1] For me, this quotation captures the elasticity and durability of

1. Ellsworth R. Fuhrman, "Images of the Discipline in Early American Sociology," *Journal of the
History of Sociology* 1, no. 1 (1978): 93.

sociology, generations past and for those yet to come. In retrospect, my life's work—no doubt influenced by my own life history and social location—is integrated by a common thread of social inequality that relates to race, class, and gender. Finding in the past valuable lessons for today, I continue my journey with sociology, the discipline passed on to me by my mentors and that I have pursued, nurtured, and passed on for almost six decades.

14

Sociology, Politics, and Policy

DAVID J. ARMOR

When I arrived at the University of California, Berkeley, in the fall of 1956, a career in sociology and public policy was not even a glimmer. At the time, I knew virtually nothing about these fields. In my small Victorville, California, high school, I excelled in math and science, so I was encouraged to study engineering. I was also a devout science-fiction fan, so I went to Berkeley to study aeronautical engineering and, I hoped, become involved in the exciting new space program—maybe even try for astronaut!

My Berkeley experiences took several turns, however, and I shifted away from engineering and a hard science career. After being introduced to sociology and getting involved in student politics, my interests turned to studies of human behavior and political activism. Eventually, these beginnings evolved into a career in public policy, both as a researcher and practitioner. My work in sociology has influenced each stage of this career.

Berkeley: Introduction to Sociology and Student Politics

Ironically, the engineering curriculum at Berkeley caused my switch from engineering to sociology. Responding to criticism about the narrowness of the engineering curriculum, the School of Engineering had adopted a comprehensive one-year social science course. The course was designed and taught by leading members of the Departments of Sociology and Political Science. I remember outstanding lectures and readings by Eugene Burdick

(*The Ugly American*), Seymour Martin Lipset (*Union Democracy*), and Lewis Feuer, to mention just a few who sparked my interest. This was not the only time Marty Lipset impacted my career.

By my sophomore year, I wanted to take more courses in the social sciences, especially philosophy and sociology. I had joined the University YMCA (Stiles Hall), which was home to a progressive student political movement that was advocating radical change in student government. We formed a political party called Slate that ran candidates for student government, advocating a more activist student council (chronicled in *Student* by David Horowitz). We wanted to support the new civil rights movement, make ROTC voluntary, allow free speech on campus, and convert the student store to a co-op.

I had virtually no intellectual background for these ideas, at least compared to most Slate members; my family was working class and apolitical. I was willing to delay my graduation if necessary to take more electives, but my engineering adviser said I could not change my program of studies. I wanted to take these courses now; studying more social science and philosophy would give me a better foundation for the political debates swirling around me.

Later that year, I caused a massive student government crisis when I disqualified the entire slate of Slate candidates for violation of election campaigning rules. I had become the director of the Election Committee, and my decision came after learning of illegal Slate campaign literature. Although I was a founding member of Slate, its campaign literature had clearly violated the rules, and my decision was upheld by the student Judicial Committee. There was an enormous political furor, with thousands of students demonstrating, so the student council threw out the election and called a new one. The controversy and publicity helped elect two Slate representatives to the student council, and it gave me immediate name recognition.

Since Slate expected me to run for student council in my junior year, at the end of my sophomore year I transferred from the School of Engineering to the College of Letters and Science, declaring majors in mathematics and sociology. Back home in Victorville I married my high school sweetheart, Marilyn Sells, and we set off for Berkeley and an incredible whirlwind of political activities.

I was elected to the student council, and later that year I was elected student body president—the only Slate candidate to win that office (1959–1960). There were many dramatic political events and controversies, most of which were generated by or supported by Slate: lunch counter sit-ins at Berkeley restaurants that still discriminated against black patrons; the Fred Moore hunger strike for voluntary ROTC; and the massive demonstrations against the House Un-American Activities Committee (HUAC) hearings in San Francisco. Marilyn, pregnant with our first child, Adrienne, was one of the marchers.

My first involvement in women's rights issues came when the student council adopted a Slate plank to integrate the men's rooting section in the football stadium. Naturally, Marilyn became the first woman in decades to sit in the middle of the (formerly) all-male rooting section. We were showered with frozen orange cups (called gremlins) that men liked to throw at one another, and many shouts of "roll 'em up" were directed at Marilyn—a tradition of lifting a man overhead and passing him up or down the rooting section. Although we got soaked with orange juice, Marilyn was never rolled up thanks to several Slate bodyguards.[1]

My experience in student government and politics initially led me to consider law school and possibly a political career. Two developments changed my direction. First, some members of Slate began backing issues and tactics that I would not support. Slate embodied a collage of ideologies ranging from Christian humanist (me) to democratic socialists to communist. Most supported peaceful civil disobedience as long as it was directed at laws or rules being challenged, like the civil rights movement. Some Slate members began breaking laws (i.e., damaging property) for dramatic effect, and some members supported these aggressive tactics and pro-communist causes such as Fair Play for Cuba.

Second, during my senior year I took a course on the theory of collective behavior taught by Neil Smelser, which was a major turning point. He arrived at Berkeley as I was starting my senior year, and my final paper used his value-added theory to explain the development of Slate and the student movement at Berkeley. Sociological theory could actually explain real-world experiences! The paper received an A+, and for the first time I gave serious thought to becoming a sociologist. Neil encouraged me to apply to Harvard to study under his mentor, Talcott Parsons.

During my fifth year at Berkeley, I was admitted to Harvard's Department of Social Relations, and I also received a Woodrow Wilson Fellowship, which was critical because my family could not afford the Harvard tuition. So I abandoned law school and a (possible) political career in favor of graduate studies and a (possible) academic career. As a Slate elder statesman, I attended meetings and other events but felt increasingly detached from a movement that was becoming more radicalized, especially after the San Francisco HUAC demonstrations. I met Tom Hayden that year, a founder of Students for a Democratic Society (SDS) who had come to Berkeley to learn more about Slate. As some were just joining the student movement, my interests turned to learning more about why this movement was taking place.

---

1. These guards were Dan Greenson, who became a San Francisco psychoanalyst, and Mike Myerson, who became a union activist.

Harvard: Sociology and Policy Analysis

I enjoyed being away from the crisis atmosphere of Berkeley student politics and immersing myself in the quiet academic environment at Harvard. I also enjoyed the interdisciplinary focus of the Department of Social Relations, taking courses in sociology, psychology, and anthropology from Talcott Parsons, George Homans, David McClelland, Gordon Allport, and Florence Kluckhohn. My dissertation was directed by Parsons, and while it led to my first book, *The American School Counselor*, in the end I found that sociological theory was not my primary interest.

Because of my math background, I gravitated toward quantitative methods and computer applications, stimulated by a statistics course from Fred Mosteller and a computer programming course by Arthur Couch. This was an important career development, because it led to many research projects that required quantitative and computer skills, eventually turning my interests to policy evaluation. I helped Couch develop one of the earliest computer packages for statistical analysis, Datatext, and my skills were in demand— very important because I needed the income to support my family. We had our second child, Daniel, during our second year at Harvard.

One of the most important events to influence my sociological perspective occurred as I was finishing my dissertation on the school counseling profession. I was asked by James Coleman to work on the massive national study of equality of educational opportunity (EEO) that had been commissioned by the Civil Rights Act of 1965, resulting in the controversial Coleman Report. I did survey design, analysis, and a write-up for school guidance counselors as a school resource.

The EEO team was astounded when it found no major differences in the distribution of school resources between majority white and majority black schools. Moreover, the relationships between test scores and school resources were small compared to the relationship between test scores and family background. Later, I contributed to a book by Fred Mosteller and Daniel "Pat" Moynihan that reported several reanalyses of the Coleman data. For the most part, the reanalyses upheld the major Coleman findings.

This was my first but not last experience where careful empirical research yielded findings contrary to widely accepted social science theories and explanations. Other experiences include my research in school busing and alcoholism.

After accepting an assistant professor position in social relations, I taught courses on multivariate data analysis, continued work on computer projects, and started my second major research project. Coleman had found that black students in predominantly white schools had higher test scores than those in predominantly black schools, thereby supporting the idea that school desegregation could help close the achievement gap. Since this was cross-sectional data, however, a rigorous causal connection was not possible. Accordingly, in 1967 I welcomed the opportunity to help with a longitudinal evaluation of the Boston Metco program. Metco was a voluntary busing program that allowed Boston black students to attend predominantly white schools in the suburbs. The study included a control group of children from the same families who attended Boston schools. The education psychologist Herb Walberg was also part of the study team and helped design the achievement testing component.

My study, "The Evidence on Busing," summarized the Metco busing findings and five other busing programs around the country. Contrary to social science theory at the time, these studies found that school desegregation was not raising black achievement, and moreover it had some negative effects on black racial attitudes. My study was very controversial, even though other early reviews of school busing by Nancy St. John, Harold Gerard and Norman Miller, and Walter Stephan had similar or at least mixed findings.

Before leaving Harvard, I consulted with the new National Institutes of Alcoholism and Alcohol Abuse (NIAAA) to design a monitoring system for its nationwide treatment center program; the system tracked outcomes for clients up to six months post-intake. This would lead to another major research project and also research findings that contradicted conventional theories of alcoholism.

Rand: Alcoholism, Military Manpower, and School Desegregation

After leaving Harvard as associate professor, I accepted a visiting professorship at UCLA for 1972–1973, and in the spring of 1973 I accepted a senior social scientist position at the Rand Corporation in Santa Monica. I started a research program in alcoholism studies, contributed to several military manpower studies, worked on several health and education projects, and continued my research on school desegregation—including expert witness work in several school desegregation cases.

The alcoholism work was supported by NIAAA, which gave Rand a grant to conduct a nationwide follow-up study that looked at eighteen-month outcomes. This study, *Alcoholism and Treatment*, was controversial because while some alcoholics were abstaining, some had returned to moderate drinking. NIAAA then funded a four-year follow-up study, which found relatively low rates of long-term abstention and even lower rates of stable non–problem drinking (*The Course of Alcoholism*). The results showed the very difficult challenges in treating alcoholism, even with the best methods known at the time. By the four-year mark only 13 percent were long-term abstainers; another 9 percent were stable non–problem drinkers. This study contradicted the conventional wisdom that abstention is the only successful outcome for alcoholics.

My military manpower research at Rand brought a sociological perspective to studies of the All Volunteer Force (AVF), which began in 1973. A long-standing Department of Defense (DoD) policy is that military forces represent the entire U.S. population, so the nation's defense does not fall on one sector of society. During the late 1970s, there was a dramatic increase in African American recruits, making DoD (especially the army) disproportionately black.[2] I was one of many social scientists who argued that higher military compensation was needed to attract a more representative cross section of the population. In addition, I led a study for the army showing that proficiency in a wide variety of army jobs was related to aptitude scores, and later I contributed to a large study, published by the National Academy of Sciences, which validated military enlistment standards in terms of hands-on job-performance tests. This was an important development in military sociology.

During my stay at Rand, publicity about my school busing study led to several requests to consult for school districts undergoing desegregation. In 1974 I was an expert witness for the Pasadena, California, school system, which was hoping to end a 1970 mandatory busing plan. Test scores showed that Pasadena black students had no gains after three years of desegregation, consistent with my 1972 study. Pasadena was also experiencing severe white flight, converting it from a majority white to a predominantly minority school district in just five years. I realized that the white-flight problem might be more critical than test scores, because it threatened the viability of desegregation itself.

After the Pasadena case, I consulted with the San Diego school board, which was designing a desegregation plan under a state court order. I conducted a parent opinion survey and put together case studies of white losses following either mandatory or voluntary desegregation plans, concluding that a voluntary desegregation plan relying on magnet schools and voluntary transfers would create more long-term desegregation than a mandatory busing plan. The school board adopted a voluntary desegregation plan that I helped design, and the court accepted the plan. Later, I published "White Flight and the Future of School Desegregation," demonstrating very large white enrollment losses after mandatory busing, replicating similar findings of separate studies by James Coleman, Reynolds Farley, and Christine Rossell.

Finally, in 1979 I consulted on desegregation issues for the Los Angeles school board, conducting a large survey of parents regarding their attitudes toward desegregation and their specific responses to a mandatory busing

---

2. This was due to an error in scoring the Armed Forces Qualifying Test (AFQT).

plan. The survey confirmed strong white opposition to being bused to a minority school some distance away but little opposition to minorities being bused into their children's current school. When a limited mandatory busing plan was implemented by a state court in 1978, white enrollment losses were similar to those estimated by the 1979 survey. Needless to say, the Los Angeles mandatory busing plan was very controversial, and it led to passage of California Proposition 1 by a 70 percent margin. Proposition 1 required that a state court had to find a violation of the Equal Protection Clause (that is, de jure segregation) before it could order a school desegregation plan.

Return to Politics: Congress and the Los Angeles Board of Education

Bobby Fiedler, a Democrat, was elected to the Los Angeles (L.A.) school board in 1977 on an antibusing ticket, and then she ran for Congress in 1980 as a Republican, largely because the Democratic Party supported mandatory busing. She defeated a long-time Democratic incumbent in a heavily Democratic district, again using an antibusing theme. In 1982, when I determined that my work at Rand had concluded, I resigned to run for Congress as a Republican in another heavily Democratic West L.A. district. I thought Congress would be a good place to pursue my sociological interests in education, voluntary school desegregation plans, and military manpower policies. I had some name recognition from my work for the L.A. school board, and I had the support of many local leaders, including Bobbi Fiedler, but I did not win.

Hoping to run for Congress again, I formed a social science research company with the late sociologist Howard Freeman, then a professor at UCLA. Fortuitously, after a couple of years, a West L.A. seat opened up on the L.A. board of education, which I won. A year later I received an offer to become the principal deputy assistant secretary of defense for force management and personnel, and rather than wait four more years to run for Congress, I accepted. This office oversees most of the manpower issues that I had worked on at Rand, so I thought I had the chance to influence military manpower policies, perhaps even more so than being a junior member of Congress.

Department of Defense: Women in the Military

In my new position, I was second in charge of a major DoD division, and when the assistant secretary returned to the private sector in 1987, I became the acting assistant secretary for a little over a year. The force management and personnel office was responsible for overseeing nearly all military personnel policies for the active force (except health), particularly the compensation package, recruiting policies, family policy, and the overseas school system. Most policy initiatives and reviews originated in the individual services, but they had to be approved by the assistant secretary before going to Secretary of Defense Caspar Weinberger for final approval. My background as a sociologist and policy analyst was very helpful in this regard.

Although I had many valuable experiences during my time at DoD, two were especially influenced by my sociological perspectives and research. One was being able to endorse and support the DoD Job Performance Measurement Program, which led to the first validation of aptitude standards using hands-on performance tests. This project was reviewed by two National Academy of Science committees and led to several major reports explaining and endorsing these efforts.

The other was serving as chair of the 1988 Task Force on Women in the Military, which was established by Secretary Weinberger in the wake of several major sexual assault incidents. The task force recommended a new policy called the "risk rule" that provided a uniform way to apply statutory combat restriction, which up to that time had been implemented in different ways by the four services. The task force also recommended an annual DoD-wide sexual harassment and assault survey, which up to this point had not been uniformly and regularly administered across all the services. Secretary Weinberger approved both of these recommendations.

Although the risk rule was less dramatic than the recent end of all combat restrictions, it did open tens of thousands of military jobs to women, particularly in the navy and Marine Corps. The sexual harassment and assault survey is still ongoing, and it has played an important role in tracking and evaluating the problem of sexual assault in the military. After retiring in 2011, I had the opportunity to work on the sexual assault issue again.

I left DoD in early 1990 after George H. W. Bush took office. I had hoped to find a position in the new administration, particularly in the Department of Education, but that did not happen. However, my wife, Marilyn, worked in the Bush campaign and had her own opportunity for government service. She became a deputy assistant to Attorney General Dick Thornburg, helping handle presidential appointments, among other duties. After Thornburg left to run for the Senate in Pennsylvania, she worked in that campaign and later finished working on public affairs as head of creative services in the Peace Corps.

After the end of the George H. W. Bush administration, as much as Marilyn and I had both enjoyed government service, we were ready to leave Washington politics. We bought a beautiful but run-down farm in rural Sperryville, Virginia, with the Hughes River running through it. After refurbishing the main farmhouse and several barns, Marilyn opened Sharp Rock B&B, and I planted a vineyard. The vineyard soon became a small winery, Sharp Rock Vineyards, and I took some time off my sociological career to become a vintner. That is one job, I admit, that did not benefit from my sociological perspective!

During the Sharp Rock days I still consulted on numerous education and desegregation cases, mostly as an expert witness, and I also wrote two books summarizing my sociological research on desegregation (*Forced Justice*) and factors affecting educational achievement (*Maximizing Intelligence*). We sold the farm in 2004, a few years after I had become a full-time professor at George Mason. Marilyn returned to her longtime artistic interests, becoming a resident watercolor artist in a Sperryville art gallery, River District Artists.

George Mason: Public Policy Analysis and Professor Emeritus

The next chapter of my professional career took place at George Mason University (GMU) and the School of Public Policy in Arlington and Fairfax, Virginia. I am grateful to Marty Lipset for opening the door for me at the Institute of Public Policy at GMU. He had accepted a chair there in 1992 after leaving the Stanford Hoover Institution. He introduced me to Dean Kingsley Haynes and recommended that I teach a course in multivariate statistics for the newly organized Ph.D. program in public policy. I started teaching the course in 1993 as a research professor, and I was also able to start a small research program looking at the effect of socioeconomic factors on academic achievement. When the institute became the School of Public Policy in 2000, I accepted an offer to become a full professor.

As at Harvard and Rand, I enjoyed the opportunity to be in an interdisciplinary program and to teach, write, and do research on a variety of applied policy issues. I taught graduate courses on multivariate statistics, research methods, culture and policy, and social policy, and I served as the Ph.D. program director from 2002 to 2005. I enjoyed the intellectual stimulation of colleagues from a wide diversity of fields, including Marty Lipset; political scientists Frank Fukuyama and Don Kash; and regional planning scientists Steve Fuller, Kingsley Haynes, and Roger Stough.

In 2010 I had back surgery, and although I returned to teach for the 2010–2011 academic year, I had finally lost the energy required for teaching research methods and statistics to very talented, young Ph.D. students from a wide variety of disciplines. I had not lost my interest in writing, consulting, and conducting research, so I knew that retirement would not mean just becoming a couch potato (although I do that some because I am a sports fan).

I admit that another factor in becoming emeritus was having more time at our second home on Cape Cod and enjoying our small boat for fishing and water sports. We spend every summer there, enjoying the company of good friends, our children, and of course our grandchildren. We sociologists know that grandchildren offer a second—and more relaxed—chance at parenting, especially for those of us whose parenting skills suffered when we were busy starting new careers.

After becoming professor emeritus in 2012, I continued my sociological activities by doing research, consulting, and writing in several areas. Topics include sexual assault in the military, the growth of poverty programs, and the academic benefits of universal preschool. Future topics include trends in minority enlistments in the U.S. military (following up a similar study published in 2010) and a major study on the impact of funding and other school resources on academic achievement.

I also continue working as an expert witness in school desegregation and educational adequacy cases. One of my most important contributions as a sociologist, I believe, was helping school districts undergoing desegregation. In earlier years, that meant designing school desegregation plans, especially those relying on voluntary methods like magnet schools. More recently, I helped school districts by evaluating the success of their desegregation plans and, if they met federal court standards, testifying about their eligibility for unitary status.

Looking back at my career in sociology and public policy, I am grateful for the contributions of many friends, colleagues, and teachers, but none more so than Neil Smelser, who led me to this field; Marty Lipset, who helped me return to an academic career at George Mason; and Dean Kingsley Haynes, who supported my professorship in public policy. Even more important has been the unwavering love, support, and wise counsel from Marilyn, the love of my life, during these many career changes and the inevitable family relocations.

15

The Last of Life for Which the First Was Made

Debra Kaufman

Biographical essays often assume a linearity and cohesiveness that real life rarely presents. What in retrospect we may describe as rational choices often simply reflect dumb luck or good or bad timing. This essay is unlike any other of my professional writings in that it requires no research, literature search, or statistical analysis. This is both liberating and limiting. The data need only be accurate to my own life, yet they must also ring true for others to have sociological meaning.

I write because I believe my story belongs to a group of men and women who over the past fifty years have seen enormous changes in the ways in which we think about and do sociology, let alone how we study and practice gender. My narrative is guided by my belief that our personal stories are always a part of what we study and how we teach sociology. While my story is told within the context of a particular cohort as we enter and engage in "retirement" (a most misleading term), it is also specific to my gender, class, race, ethnicity, and religion. And while the stories I choose to share are unique to me (a retread, an academic wife, a feminist, a Jew), I also hope they reflect where the particular and the universal meet, a phrase once coined by one of my favorite journalists who died several years ago, Ellen Willis. I share the following stories because I think they emphasize how the personal and the professional intersect throughout the life cycle and how wittingly or unwittingly they have prepared me for this stage of life.

Ann Arbor: The Reluctant Sociologist (1959–1963)

When I entered the academy, both as an undergraduate and later as an assistant professor, the study of, by, and for women in almost every discipline was a hotly contested issue. Women's studies programs, as a subject and political base for women, were nascent in the academy. The battles to bring women in focused on women not only as subjects of study in their own right but as writers, researchers, and students in the classroom. The prestigious presses and journals were male dominated, as were the subjects studied. I remember vividly the excitement so many of us felt when Joan Acker's "Women and Social Stratification: A Case of Intellectual Sexism" appeared in the *American Journal of Sociology* in January 1973 as part of a special issue aptly titled "Changing Women in a Changing Society." Even the cover of the journal changed from gray to red (or was it red to gray?).

Sociologists for Women in Society was in its earliest stages of development, and the journal *Gender and Society* did not exist. Although many of us were already writing and teaching about sex roles (as they were called then), these were inhospitable times for women's studies and feminist leanings. While I do not know if this is accurate, I was told that the librarians at Northeastern the year before I arrived did not order *Sex Roles: A Journal of Research* because any journal whose lead article was about menstruation could not be a serious academic journal.

I was a feminist sociologist long before I understood what that meant and before I later was to write and teach about feminist methodologies and theories. I had not one female professor at Michigan. I belonged to a cohort who was expected to marry even if it disrupted our studies and/or careers (think Matina Horner, fear of success, and the dire consequences for women who eschewed such roles).

In my junior year of college, Guy E. Swanson, then chair of sociology, invited me into his office. As I was a member of a very small honors sociology cohort, he fully expected me to apply to graduate school the next year. As typical of many women of the time, I had a serious boyfriend. He was applying to Rutgers for graduate work. Without missing a beat Swanson said, "Princeton and Columbia, those would be good schools for you." Soon after that visit I received a letter from Princeton inviting me to apply but also noting that I would be among the very few women ever to do so, there would be no housing or food accommodations for me, and there was no public transportation to and from campus.

A reference letter in my file (which I did not learn of until much later in my academic career) suggested that if there were a male applying for the same position who was as good or perhaps even a little less qualified, then he should receive the scholarship in my stead. Some thirty years later, as a member of Princeton's women's studies board of advisers, I told my story to an almost unbelieving crowd of faculty, students, and administrators.

As the course of true love is never straightforward, I broke up with the Rutgers boyfriend, married a University of Michigan graduate student, and remained in Ann Arbor. Because at the time it was not uncommon for women to put their husbands through graduate and/or professional training, I went to work. After two years as a research assistant at the Survey Research Center, where I honed my skills as a quantitative sociologist, I found that my husband and I were out of sync. I would come home after work, ready to play, he still hard at work on his dissertation. Later, his doctoral dissertation read, "And to my wife, without whose help I would have finished two years earlier."

If my marriage was going to survive, I needed to be similarly occupied as my husband. Because as an undergraduate I had been part of the senior honors seminar and was required to participate in all phases of that year's Detroit Area Study, I had already earned credit for a master's thesis at the University of Michigan. When we left Michigan two years later for Mike's first academic job at Cornell, I not only had a master's degree but also had completed almost all coursework for a Ph.D. in sociology. I never thought twice, at least at the time, about finishing my Ph.D.

Ithaca Daze: The Personal Had No Public (1966–1973)

Our years in Ithaca proved to be a testing ground for me and similarly for those of my cohort beginning families and professional training/careers. We were reared in the 1950s and entering adulthood in the 1960s. Despite my life as a radical undergraduate and graduate student, I was unprepared for the shift in our lives from our equality as graduate students to becoming an academic wife and within a year, a mother. Despite my active engagement in Planned Parenthood, La Leche League, and the National Childbirth Association (we brought the Lamaze method to the local gynecological teams), I did not expect the sense of dissatisfaction my new roles would bring.

I was the woman with the "no-name" problem. The birth of our first child only exacerbated my growing sense of disquiet. Years later, I realized that I had been in postpartum depression, a condition hardly recognized at the time (only one paragraph in the popular Dr. Spock book). How helpful the websites on this topic we have today would have been to me personally, to my marriage, and to my cohort then. Most of us felt conflict about combining parenting and professional life; postpartum depression only solidified such feelings. To resolve some of the conflict, I made a conscious decision to lower my academic expectations and give motherhood priority over my career. I never took a sabbatical leave away from home, applied for visiting professorships, or took advantage of any professional opportunities that might disrupt our children's schooling or home life when they were young.

Cornell was at the center of Ithaca's universe (although some at Ithaca College might contest that). From the mid-1960s on, students and many of the faculty were actively involved in the social justice issues of the time, symbolized for many in the takeover of the Willard Straight Student Union by black militants. As a faculty wife I felt once removed from this scene. I yearned to be a part, once again, of the public protest movement. My sense of marginality was so great that during my second pregnancy, I sought employment that would put me directly in the center of action.

I was hired by Harold Feldman, a bright, funny, and kind professor in the Human Development Family Studies Department in the School of Home Economics (soon to become the College of Human Ecology), who saved the sanity of many women and perhaps many a marriage by almost solely hiring wives of academicians, most of whom were unable to find academic employment in their fields of training within any department. At that time, nepotism rules extended even to spouses who were not in the same departments. Harold was no usual employer; he was flexible (encouraging one employee to bring her infant to work with her until she could find appropriate day care). He engaged in research critical to women's issues, especially women in poverty. He was instrumental in forming an interdisciplinary research group on poverty composed of family sociologists, social psychologists, and policy makers whose purpose was to research what was then, under Nixon, a plan to get women off welfare and into the labor market as quickly as possible.

Our data showed that Nixon's "Win" Program, while moving women off welfare, served as only a temporary solution since it prepared women for mostly dead-end, low-paying positions. With no day-care provisions the plan was unfair and had no long-term feasibility. This research experience was the beginning of my interest in the structure and function of the academy, policy making, social science research, and the place of each in women's lives.

I helped prepare and write the reports that were then delivered by Harold to the various Washington committees. It was clear, however, that without finishing my Ph.D., I would spend the rest of my academic life analyzing someone else's data. Dorothy Smith's apt words resonated clearly to me; I would be forever negotiating the real world for the men in my life. I applied to Cornell, was accepted, and went from an associate to a graduate research assistant.

Once a graduate student again (although a bit older than most) I was reinvigorated. I threw myself into the "other" revolution going on at Cornell, the one focused on creating a women's studies program (if not the first, certainly among the first in the country). We lobbied for more graduate and undergraduate courses related to women's lives.

During this time I met my longtime friend, colleague, and coauthor Barbara Richardson, a smart and fierce women's studies advocate. During our graduate days, we hatched the idea for the book we would eventually publish on achievement and women. The book was to be not only a critique of the psychological and sociological theories and methods used to measure achievement in the United States (think status-attainment studies at Harvard) but a close look at the ways in which women's everyday experiences, past and present, were shaped by and shaped our understanding of the meaning and measure of achievement in both the public and private spheres.

Our own everyday lives gave proof to the growing documentation that women's experiences were limited and defined by men's lives. We eschewed the fear-of-success explanations and preferred the structural and institutional set of gender arrangements, which put women at a disadvantage in the public sphere and often confined them to the private one. It was then that I was introduced to the nineteenth-century domestic feminists who used the only cultural tools at their disposal to argue for the vote (on moral grounds by "cleaning up" the world). I was to later use that body of literature when I wrote of fundamentalist Jewish women who used the same moral superiority arguments to defend and bolster their status in Jewish Orthodoxy.

As I began work on my own dissertation (a network analysis of the colleague/friend relationships among female and male academicians), I saw up close and personal the lives that academic women and men lived. How far I had come into the public sphere in my own right was made clear when I began one of my papers by introducing myself not by my married name but by my maiden one.

When my husband did not receive tenure at Cornell (his stellar teaching and his publications on women and African American writers did not help his case), he was recruited by State University of New York at Albany with the implicit promise that he would receive tenure after a three-year stint. Once again I left a campus without completing my dissertation to follow my husband. This time I was committed to becoming an academic in my own right.

Albany: We Hardly Knew You (1973–1976)

I applied to almost every school within commuting distance of Albany for any kind of academically connected job I could find. Jobs for "captive" academic wives were scarce. I was part of a reserve labor force that could be brought in and pushed out at will. Nepotism rules were unofficially in place even if husbands and wives did not share the same disciplines. In Ithaca I had met and admired Constance Cook (the only Republican for whom I have ever voted), a former lawyer who represented women within the academy and was now a state representative. She had formed a subcommittee on the status of women in the academy. When she asked me to testify as a sociologist on the plight of academic wives before the legislature in Albany, I readily agreed.

Fortunately, and quite unexpectedly, a less traditional academic route presented itself. I was hired to teach in an interdisciplinary, four-year residential college wherein seniors could complete their last year of high school and first year of college simultaneously (a Carnegie Mellon initiative) on the downtown campus of SUNY. We were predominately a left-wing faculty of fifteen (a mathematician, a philosopher, a political scientist, a historian, a psychologist, two physicists, several part-time faculty borrowed from other departments, and me). Simultaneously, I taught in the fledgling women's studies program in the uptown campus. There I learned from a most savvy set of colleagues how to negotiate with administrators, how to mentor other faculty and students, and how to build a feminist curriculum without mentioning the "f" word.

Those were a heady three years only to be wiped out in 1976 when New York State declared bankruptcy and the entire SUNY system went into retrenchment. Both my husband and I lost our jobs within three months of each other. He because he was in a department whose graduate division was shut down and I because SUNY reneged on its promise to take over the Carnegie Mellon Foundation program (although all of our syllabi were to reappear ten years later as a model for interdisciplinary work). Most severely hit were the last hired. Not unexpectedly, of the 10 percent of the SUNY system who were retrenched, 90 percent were women.

Because there were few openings in English departments across the country, unlike times past, my husband and I agreed that we would go wherever I could find a job. This time I was to leave a campus not only with dissertation in hand but with a book contract. I had five job offers and accepted what I thought would be the best fit for me: a place flexible enough to honor and reward my particular skills not only as a sociologist but also as an interdisciplinary women's studies scholar.

Northeastern: No Regrets (1976–2013)

In Michigan I was at the Harvard of the Midwest; at Cornell, the Harvard above the Cayuga; at Northeastern I was at Northeastern. Because Northeastern's upper administration was primarily oriented toward keeping the university solvent and because it was better known for its engineering, law, and business schools, the faculty, especially in the arts and sciences, enjoyed a professional autonomy no longer evident today almost anywhere in the country. Within the first two weeks of settling into my department (noteworthy at the time for its preponderance of women), I began to lay the foundations for a women's studies program. I literally went through all the university's course offerings and the entire faculty phone book, telephoning (before e-mail existed) anyone who taught anything that had women, family, or sex (biological or other) in the title. I found a congenial, talented, and very loose confederation of women (and a few sympathetic men) whose primary goal was to challenge pay inequities between men and women.

My earlier experiences at Cornell and Albany prepared me well. For both selfish and higher-minded reasons, I knew we needed to identify, strengthen, and develop a community of scholars/teachers and students not only in sociology and anthropology, or in our college, but also across the university. We needed visible advocates who would sit on tenure and curriculum committees, serve in the Senate, and become advisers and activists in support of women's and gender-oriented research and teaching. We pressured for new hires, and within five years our department had one of the largest women's and gender course offerings (and enrollments) at both the graduate and undergraduate levels, not only in our university but also in the city of Boston.

Simultaneously, I enjoyed the privilege of being a part of the growing women's contingency in the American Sociological Association, Eastern Sociological Society, Sociologists for Women in Society, and local study groups. These were exhilarating times, and many of the key figures in the field made themselves accessible to junior faculty in any number of ways. I am fairly certain that it was Cynthia Fuchs Epstein who nominated our book *Achievement and Women* for the C. Wright Mills Award (it received honorary mention), and I know she was the one to recommend that I write a chapter for Jo Freeman's *Women: A Feminist Perspective*, at that time the most widely read edited volume on women. In fact, I revised "Professional Women: How Real Are the Recent Gains?" for several editions. Each revision suggested that the gains professional women made were elusive. The data revealed that intra- and interprofessional stratification (as in the labor market in general) was as rigid, if not worse, for women by the time of the last edition as in the one I had written ten years earlier. The more things changed, the more they seemed to stay the same.

Once I was tenured, the necessary institutional structures for a women's study program were in place. I became its founding director and four years later, a full professor. I could now pursue subjects that had long interested me. Initially I thought my interest in Jewish studies, as both a woman and a Jew, would be just an extension of my work on gender. However, Jewish studies turned out to be more than the lure of yet another struggling interdisciplinary program for which I would soon become a director.

My husband had come from a secular Jewish home; I, from an Orthodox one. From the very beginning of our marriage he agreed that he would be supportive of what I wanted religiously for our family, but he would remain secular. While we kept a kosher home and our children were enrolled in a Jewish day school, my own identity, beliefs, and practices over the years had become more secular than sacred.

It was my feminist cousin who became deeply Orthodox (after going to Israel on an archeological dig in sympathy with the Palestinian cause) who aroused my curiosity about why women who had been involved in and/ or were inheritors of the radical movements of the 1960s would be attracted to fundamentalist religions. Baalot Teshuvah (as they are called in Hebrew) are secular Jewish women who have never practiced Orthodoxy but in their young adult years become Orthodox Jews. Since Orthodox Jews believe that all Jews, irrespective of their denomination or secularity, are "returning" to Jewish Orthodoxy, it was not surprising that the community believed my proposed research was a personal, not a professional, exploration (despite my very best professional presentation of self as researcher/academic) and openly welcomed me. Although I was no more religious at the end of the study than when I had begun, my research opened a second and unexpected turn in my career, religious studies.

Although never formally trained in the field, I found many soul mates among those marginalized within mainstream religious studies, especially gender and women's studies scholars. And to give Orthodoxy its due, earlier identity conflicts about my own practice as a Jew seemed to be resolved as I found myself practicing Judaism by studying it. The more involved I got in religious research, the more committed I became to my own identity as a secular Jew.

My book *Rachel's Daughters*, about the causes and issues implicit in the return to fundamentalist religion among Jewish women (some who contin- ued to call themselves feminists), resonated among other women who chose to join and/or to remain within fundamentalist and patriarchal traditions. Like Baalot Teshuva, many of them reject much of what they term "male" and "individualistic" values within the secular world, finding within their orthodoxies a moral order based on the feminine and the female. It was no surprise then that soon after my book's publication I was offered a one- semester visiting scholar appointment in Brigham Young University's (BYU) Sociology Department. It was a time when Mormon women were visibly struggling with their wish to remain within the religion, wanting the male authorities to recognize their claims for a female voice and vision. One of the first papers I delivered following my stay at BYU was titled "On Being Gentile: A Jewish Feminist Perspective."

Several years later I received a two-year leave as a Matthews Distin- guished University Professor from Northeastern that enabled me to do re- search on a project I was developing on post-Holocaust identity narratives among contemporary young Jews in the United States, England, and Israel (not necessarily children or grandchildren of Holocaust survivors). The data I collected while at Oxford University's Center for Hebrew and Jew- ish Studies were lost in transport back to the United States, but the Israeli data (collected while on a visiting appointment to Bar-Ilan) arrived intact.

My interest in twenty- to thirty-year-olds was twofold: there were virtually no identity data for that age group, and my children were within that age range. Indeed, my own children's often ambivalent relationship to Judaism (but never with their identities as Jews) provided the impetus to study post-Holocaust Jewish identities among contemporary young adults. I had now entered a new field of inquiry ripe for feminist analysis: Holocaust studies.

As guest editor of *Contemporary Jewry* in 1996, I invited several prominent academic women to join me in writing about women and Holocaust scholarship. My introductory essay, "The Holocaust and Sociological Inquiry: A Feminist Analysis," emphasized the paucity of sociological analysis and research on the Holocaust. I was to come under fire for that volume by the senior editor of *Commentary*. In an issue derogatively titled "Auschwitz and the Professors," he chastised me and others for engaging in Holocaust research to accrue academic advantage. Simultaneously, in an e-mail exchange with me, political sociologist Seymour Martin Lipset contended that the Holocaust was a particular event in history, not subject to sociological investigation. It is better suited, he wrote, to philosophical, historical, and religious analyses. Some years later I was proud to write for Judith Gerson and Diane Wolf's groundbreaking edited work *Sociology Confronts the Holocaust*.

In 2001, three Northeastern colleagues and I organized a conference to explore the ways in which claims related to the fate of Jews in the twentieth century have been made, struggled over, and fixed in the law, in historical canon, and in the popular imagination based on three trial contexts (Protocols of Zion, Eichmann/Nuremberg, Holocaust denial). We later edited a book further exploring the ways in which the racism and anti-Semitism embedded in Holocaust denial persist despite legal verdicts, historical renunciation, and "objective" reporting. My early training as a quantitative sociologist continues to give me both an appreciation and a wariness of abstract quantitative sociology. At the very end of my formal career at Northeastern I returned to my early interest in the methodological (never truly separated from the theoretical) issues and problems inherent in quantitative analyses, but this time among demographers who study contemporary Jewish identities. This resulted in another guest-edited work of *Contemporary Jewry*, in which I explore some of my favorite feminist themes: reflexivity, narrative, and voice in research.

Retirement: What's Next?

I live the sociology about which I read, write, and research. We all do. The personal and the professional are intimately and irrevocably intertwined across the life course. Retirement is no exception. Since at this stage of life our future is much shorter than our past, there is less time to ponder or delay. Choices about what's next are both limited and enhanced by forces within and out of our control. As I write this essay, almost three years into retirement, I find that I cannot type for more than twenty minutes at a time. My back problems limit how long I can sit in any one position (standing at a podium is only moderately better). On the upside, I can type faster than a speeding bullet. I have more doctors' appointments than ever. Each day I discover that I have pains in places I didn't even know existed. I view the world with a diminished clarity, but I am told that when my cataracts are removed, this will improve. And while resources may limit the number of meetings and conferences I can attend, having to choose conserves on energy, another increasingly limited resource.

Health and wealth at retirement may limit us, but they also encourage us to choose those projects that are time sensitive and that truly interest us. Although my ever-patient editor has been waiting for a book I contracted for over a decade ago, I am putting it aside yet again. Because I hope to see a woman in the White House, I am putting my energy into Hillary Clinton's campaign. I find one key to a happy retirement is focusing on what I can (and want) rather than what I cannot do.

After fifty-two years of marriage, my husband and I have decided that we are a stable twosome. We have entered retirement as equals, fully awaiting the call for the next project that takes our fancy. Who knows; maybe we will write a book together about Annie Templeton, the woman for whom the farmhouse we bought over forty years ago was built, and about the life and times of mountain women from 1880 to 1950 in rural and rugged New Hampshire. Or maybe I will develop a course on aging, ethnicity, gender, and identity, in a time when all such categories are being contested, for the Graduate Consortium in Women's Studies at MIT. I come to retirement with my interests intact and my commitments strong. Yet I truly do not know what is next. What I do know, as does Robert Browning's Rabbi Ben Ezra, is that the best may be yet to come, for it is the "last of life for which the first was made."

16

A Sociological Memoirist

FRED L. PINCUS

A s a sociologist and a memoirist, reflecting on my academic career has preoccupied me for years. Because I was trained as a mainstream sociologist, specializing in social psychology and race relations, my life seemed headed on a trajectory far different from what might be expected from my red diaper baby childhood. I had always rejected the activism of my working-class, communist parents, and a secure life as an academic looked pretty good.

Both my life and my scholarship veered sharply to the left shortly after I took my first academic job at the University of Maryland, Baltimore County (UMBC), in 1968 at the age of twenty-six. The tidal wave of social movements and political turmoil of the day swept me along.

Class and race inequalities in higher education replaced social psychology as a scholarly interest. Systems of racism supplanted my concerns with prejudice and discrimination. Marxism overwhelmed my theoretical eclecticism. Political activism competed with scholarship.

Soon it became impossible to separate sociology and politics. My research interest in community colleges, for example, emerged from my membership in the New University Conference (NUC), a national organization of radical graduate students and young faculty. NUC's Open Up the Schools program in the late 1960s argued that community colleges did more to perpetuate inequality than to provide avenues of upward mobility. I helped document that argument in my research for the next two decades, long after NUC had died.

Using memoir, I describe a few moments of my career that illustrate my conflicts involving race, scholarship, and activism.

Coming of Age (1970)

In addition to my antiwar activities, I worked with the Black Panther Party in Baltimore. Founded in 1966 in Oakland, California, the Panthers were best known for confronting issues of police brutality and for publishing materials with incendiary rhetoric like "Off the pigs" (i.e., the police). However, they also provided services like free health clinics and breakfast programs to the people in poor, black neighborhoods. Many people don't know that the Panthers were Marxists and were willing to work in coalitions with white groups that supported their programs.

In December 1969, the police had well-publicized gun battles with Black Panthers in Chicago and Los Angeles in which several Panthers were killed. In Baltimore, the police held a twenty-four-hour stakeout of the Panther office for no apparent reason. Then the local utility company announced that it was cutting off gas and electricity for nonpayment of bills. When the Panthers wouldn't let workers in to cut off the utilities, the company began digging up the street in front of the office.

In response to these provocations and to prevent any escalation, I helped found the Friends of the Panthers, a group of white radicals who were sympathetic to the political goals of the Panthers. Although I never felt totally comfortable with the Panthers' inflammatory rhetoric, I saw that they were a significant force in the black community.

After several meetings, the Friends decided to organize a Fight Repression Day on February 18, 1970. This would consist of forums held on ten college campuses around the city featuring the Panthers as speakers. I was one of the main organizers of this event and spent many hours trying to pull it together. At 1:00 A.M. on the day of the event, Robert, my contact at the Black Panthers, called me.

"We're not going to participate in any of the talks tomorrow," he said.

"What?" I said, feeling like three cups of coffee had been injected straight into my veins. "Why the hell not?"

"We have other priorities."

"But everything is set to go. You'll get exposure to several thousand college students and to the press."

"We have other things to do," said Robert. "We're also pissed that your organizing leaflet said that we had been infiltrated by the 'Red Squad' of the Baltimore pigs. It makes us look bad."

I tried to get him to change his mind, but no luck. I couldn't get back to sleep after hanging up the phone. *All that work, for nothing. I feel like an idiot. I'm pissed and embarrassed. The Panthers would have helped themselves by participating.* When I called my comrades around the city the next morning, they had the same reactions. We canceled the event, but the Friends of the Panthers never met again.

In April 1970, after a white policeman was killed in a black neighborhood, a judge banned the sale of the Black Panther newspaper for allegedly urging people to kill police officers. In addition, ten of the Panthers were arrested for a year-old murder. It seemed that more repression was to come. Although the Friends were no longer in existence, many former members and others in the Baltimore radical community (including me) decided to put our white bodies between the police and the Panthers. For a week, we kept a vigil in front of the beat-up row house that was the Panther office. We were voluntary human shields and held signs like "Save the Panthers" and "Off the pigs." Most of us were fairly certain that our white, privileged bodies were sufficient to prevent a police raid.

One night, there was a rumor that the police were going to attack, so about seventy-five of us gathered in front of the office. It was a comfortable spring night, and we milled around, drank coffee, and talked. Although the neighborhood had a reputation for drugs and violence, we felt safe, since we were there to protect the Panthers. The mood was mellow until someone yelled, "The pigs are coming!" The atmosphere got more serious.

I turned to a friend and asked, "What are we supposed to do?"

"What do you mean?" he replied.

"Do we lie down, sit down, keep marching, or what?"

He shrugged and said, "I don't know."

I asked the same question to several others and got the same response. I suddenly froze in terror with the realization that we were totally unprepared for what could be a life-threatening situation. To make matters worse, no one else seemed to share my concern. Was I crazy? Was I a coward? It got to be midnight, 1:00 A.M., 2:00 A.M., and still no one wanted to talk about it.

Fortunately for the Panthers and for us, the attack never came. By daylight, other people came and I left for my apartment, feeling both relieved and embarrassed. It was stupid of us to put ourselves in harm's way without a plan.

Although I didn't know it at the time, the FBI was monitoring the activities of the Friends. I learned this when I requested my files under the Freedom of Information Act in 1977. A March 1, 1971, report states:

He is a member of the Steering Committee of the "Friends of the Panthers." [True.] He assisted the Black Panther Party in fortifying its headquarters after a police raid in April 1970. [False.] Pincus is the prime sponsor of the radical element at UMBC. [Questionable.]

Later that spring I had begun to see myself as a Marxist, and I was an active opponent of the Vietnam War. Two speakers at UMBC helped everything fall into place for me.

Robert Bly came to campus to read his antiwar poetry. This was several years before Bly became identified with the men's consciousness movement. In front of several hundred students, he read one of his long, moving antiwar poems. At some point during or after the poem, he added the following:

> What are you going to do fifteen years from now when your kids ask
> you where you were during the great demonstration in Washington
> that is happening next week and you reply, "I didn't go. I had to study
> for a sociology exam"? What will you do when they spit in your face
> and the saliva slowly trickles down your cheek?

I felt like a small hand grenade exploded in my chest. I was weak, and my heart was pounding. How did he know that at the beginning of the semester, I had scheduled an exam for what turned out to be the day after the demonstration? It felt like Bly was talking directly to me. The exam paled in comparison to the killing in Vietnam. *Fuck the exam. Students should protest. I should protest.*

When I regained my composure, I realized that most of the students were not going to attend the protest for a variety of reasons, including my exam. I would administer the exam as scheduled but let the protesters make it up at a later date with no penalty. But Bly's words stuck with me.

A few days after Bly's talk, there was another antiwar event on campus, and one of my colleagues was the main speaker. After presenting a lot of the standard antiwar arguments, he said:

> The North Vietnamese and the National Liberation Front [i.e., Viet
> Cong] are not our enemies. They are fighting against American im-
> perialism and American capitalism. We are fighting against Ameri-
> can imperialism and American capitalism. The North Vietnamese
> and the NLF are our allies, not our enemies.

This crystallized everything for me. It wasn't just that the Vietnamese had a right to self-determination. Their fight against the American capitalist class was the same as ours—to let the working classes of both countries make decisions that influenced their collective and individual lives.

I was delighted about the intellectual and political clarity of these words but also frightened about some of the implications. I was an enemy of the state, just like the FBI said I was.

In spite of my politics and my participation in a student sit-in during that same period, I was granted tenure three years later. I was not promoted since I had published only two scholarly articles, one of which was my first community college article, in the *Insurgent Sociologist*. Fortunately, my department supported me—I was lucky.

Playing with the Big Boys

My critical scholarship on community colleges peaked in 1980 with an article in the *Harvard Education Review*. Several other articles in less prestigious journals followed, and I became recognized as one of a small number of national critics of community colleges.

In 1988, at the age of forty-four, I took an unpaid leave of absence from UMBC to become project director of an evaluation study of the Upper Division Scholarship Program, run by the College Board fifteen years earlier with funds from the Ford Foundation. The program gave scholarships to minority community college students who had transferred to four-year colleges. The evaluation study was run by the Academy for Educational Development (AED) with funds from the Ford Foundation. The College Board was also involved.

This job broke new ground for me. I would be a paid consultant for the first time. Also, I would be playing with the big boys—working with people from prestigious, mainstream organizations that weren't particularly friendly to Marxist analysis.

The first step was meeting with Sharon, the vice president of AED. I drove down to Washington and entered her posh office with a view of the nation's capitol building. After some small talk, we got to the business at hand. Everything was going fine until she asked me about my daily rate. I had no idea what she was talking about.

She smiled and said, "You haven't worked as a consultant before, have you?"

"No, this is the first time."

"Consultants get paid a certain amount of money per eight-hour day. Generally, consultants have a rate that they request. You would be a senior consultant, so I'm asking you what your rate is."

Cripes! Have I blown it already? I have no idea what I'm worth on a daily basis. I'm used to a steady salary that includes teaching, writing, and research. How can I quantify these things? She must think I'm really naive. What do I say?

"Sharon, I'll be honest. I'd like to talk to some people and get back to you about this."

"Fine," she said. "I'm sure we can agree on a rate."

We did agree, and on the first business day of January 1988 I showed up for work in New York City. Like the new assistant professor that I was twenty years earlier, I sported a suit and tie. My hair and beard, however, were longer, thinner, and grayer than they were when I first started teaching.

Over the first few weeks, I designed the study and showed it to Sharon. I expected her to say that it looked fine and we'd be off to the races. After reviewing my proposal, Sharon said, "This looks okay to me, but we'll have to run it by the folks at Ford and the College Board."

"Why do we have to do that?" I replied with a slightly annoyed tone. "You like it. I like it. Let's just start the research."

She looked at me, shook her head, and smiled. "This is not *your* research, even though you are project director. It's not even AED's research. We want to do more business with both Ford and the College Board, so we need them to sign off on the project before we proceed. I'm sure everything will be fine."

I was stunned but nodded my agreement. Previously, I had total control over everything I had ever written. It was *my* research based on *my* expertise. Suddenly, I had become a skilled research worker, doing *their* research. I wasn't like a factory worker controlled by an assembly line, but I had lost my autonomy as a professional.

The big meeting to discuss the research design took place on the elegant campus of the Education Testing Service (ETS) in Princeton, New Jersey, about an hour's train ride from New York. As the snow-covered suburbs of New Jersey flashed by, I tried to figure out how to negotiate my new role as a hired researcher.

The rolling lawns and beautiful buildings of the campus reminded me of the many elite colleges that I had visited over the years. As I was having drinks with the various representatives of all three organizations before the lunch meeting, the discussion turned to the SAT, the nation's most important college entrance exam, which was developed by ETS and owned by the College Board. At the time, the SAT was under intense criticism from within academia and in the press.

"People say the SAT is racist because blacks get such low scores," said one of the College Board representatives. "We can't help it that their reading and writing skills are so poor."

Wait a minute, I thought. *What the hell is he saying?*

"That's right," said another. "We're not racists. We're not saying that blacks are biologically inferior. They just come from an environment where learning isn't valued."

Are you serious? My back muscles tightened, but I tried to maintain a neutral expression on my face. *Bullshit!* I wanted to yell. *The SAT is definitely part of the problem, and better public relations won't change that. Tests like the SAT keep plenty of low-income students of color out of college. It's a cog in the system of institutional racism.*

As my mind raced and my emotions heated up, I caught myself. *Wait a minute. I am in one of the centers of power in the education industry. These are some of the decision makers that I criticize in my classes and in my writing. Maybe I can say something to change their mind. I rarely get a chance to be so close to powerful people. Maybe I can write something to expose them to the public.*

But I didn't say anything. *This isn't the time or place to challenge the College Board. I have to work with them on the research project, and I might embarrass my colleagues at AED. It probably won't do any good anyhow. Choose your battles! That's how I have survived in academia so far.*

After lunch, we met to discuss the research design in a conference room that put Sharon's plush office to shame. Previous research had shown that almost two-thirds of the community college students who transferred to four-year colleges eventually got their bachelor's degree, a very respectable number. My research would investigate why the Upper Division Scholarship Program was so successful. Since this had nothing to do with the SAT controversy, we were all on the same side and my proposal was approved with minor changes.

Over the next several months, the research itself went well. My research assistant and I conducted forty-eight interviews with former students who had entered their junior year in college thirteen to seventeen years earlier. We compared students who graduated with those who had dropped out and found that the more connected students were to their college, the more likely they were to graduate.

I was looking forward to using the material to write my first book, which would help me get promoted. But once again, we had to consult with Ford and the College Board, this time in the modest New York offices of AED. The Ford Foundation project officer spoke first: "I see a short report, popularly written, that begins with a list of policy recommendations. We don't need another scholarly book. We want people to read this thing."

My stomach muscles tightened and my mouth dropped. *My book! My promotion! What's happening?*

"That's great," said the College Board representative. "We'll pay to publish it and make it available to community colleges around the country at no charge."

"I agree," said my AED supervisor, and the three of them chatted happily for a few minutes while I silently pouted. The rich, chocolate cake I had enjoyed for dessert gurgled in my stomach. Finally, someone asked, "What do you think, Fred?"

As everyone turned to me, I felt my promotion slipping farther and farther away. *I don't control the product of my labor. I'm just a hired hand. Although I don't want to admit it, the project officer was right: a short report was more likely to be read and might even have some impact.*

"Sure," I replied. "Great idea." I even forced a small smile.

The next step was for us to develop a list of policy recommendations. The project officer then said, "Make sure that you make strong recommendations. Don't recommend things that the community colleges can say, 'We're already doing that.'"

This sounds good to me, I thought. *Maybe I won't get a promotion, but at least the research may have a positive impact.*

During the next few weeks, we came up with a list of recommendations about how community colleges could change their policies. The first and most important recommendation stated, "The transfer function should be the central role of community colleges." This was highly controversial, since most community colleges were emphasizing one- or two-year vocational programs that led to employment rather than programs that led to transferring to four-year colleges and bachelor's degrees.

I also insisted on a recommendation that the federal government promote a more egalitarian society with stronger civil rights enforcement. Although this wasn't a frontal assault on capitalism, it did challenge the racial and economic status quo.

At the next meeting, the project officer loved the transfer-as-the-central-role recommendation. "That will shake them up," she said. "However, we have to get rid of the talk about egalitarian society. We don't want to be seen as romantics."

I protested mildly but to no avail. No one else said anything. The discussion was over. We tweaked some of the other recommendations and ended the meeting. Although disappointed that the recommendations weren't stronger and more global, I felt like I could live with them and hold my head high. The transfer-as-central-role recommendation would be provocative.

Although the report was scheduled to be published in three months, the heads of the three participating organizations fussed over the wording of different recommendations. Finally, almost a year later, *Bridges to Opportunity: Are Community Colleges Meeting the Needs of Minority Students?* was unveiled at a press conference convened on October 30, 1989, at the AED main office in Washington, D.C. Since I was the lead researcher, I put on a suit and tie, trimmed my beard, and made my long hair look as neat as possible. I made some comments and answered questions, followed by the presidents of the College Board and AED. Articles about the book, several of which contained my picture, appeared in the major educational media and in the Associated Press. Letters to the editor followed.

Maybe all this work really will have an impact on education policy. I did okay playing with the big boys. Although we didn't challenge economic inequality directly, we did challenge the vocationalization of community colleges. My role as senior consultant had come to an end.

A year later, I decided to apply for promotion to associate professor—almost two decades after being granted tenure as an assistant professor. In two previous attempts at promotion, my department discounted some of my more political publications and concluded that I hadn't produced enough mainstream scholarship to warrant promotion. Several additional articles published in mainstream journals, the publication of *Bridges to Opportunity*, and my association with the Ford Foundation put me over the top.

I felt great being an associate professor—finally. In spite of my politics and activism, my scholarship was finally recognized by my colleagues and professional peers. It wasn't exactly like Frank Sinatra's "I Did it My Way," but it was close. The small raise in salary was like icing on the cake.

Memoir Writing in Retirement

A few years before retiring, I began writing a memoir. Since I didn't know the first thing about creative writing, I took a series of four memoir-writing classes and struggled to get away from the academic writing voice that I had used for decades. My classmates, however, always complained that my writing was too academic.

After retiring in 2012, I could devote more time to my memoir. My wife, Natalie Sokoloff, also a retired sociologist, and I began to develop a new life outside academia.

A few months after I retired, a colleague invited me to speak about my memoir in her class on the sociology of the life cycle. Students had read my childhood and college student chapters, and I was nervous about speaking. They asked me a wide range of questions, and I found myself talking less about sociological concepts and more about me. My colleague informed the class that my chapters were a good example of a methodology called autoethnography.

Huh? I thought. *What's that? I never heard of autoethnography. I'm writing a memoir.*

After class, she told me about a call for papers for a scholarly book on race and the life course and encouraged me to submit my chapters. I did and asked the editors if they were interested in memoir. After a few months, the editors expressed interest in publishing it, but there was a problem: it wasn't academic *enough*, they said.

I did a little reading about autoethnography, wondering if this would legitimate my memoir in the eyes of social scientists in general and the anthology editors in particular. This methodology is defined as connecting personal experiences to the larger social, political, and economic context. This opened up a whole new literature for me although I wasn't keen doing more academic reading. Maybe I could still be a sociologist and proceed with the memoir.

Most autoethnographical writing, it turns out, is very academic with jargon, footnotes, and references—the very thing I was trying to get away from. The Wikipedia entry on autoethnography, for example, was ten single-spaced pages with over forty references. *I don't want to enter a new academic field*, I said to myself. *I don't need more scholarly publications. I want to get a chapter of my memoir published as a memoir.*

After much negotiation with the editors, I agreed to add an academic conclusion to a slightly pared-down version of the memoir chapter. The editors' suggestions about revising the memoir section always violated my writer's voice. They suggested a passive verb to replace an active verb or deleted a few sentences that showed character development. Finally, I said, "You can do whatever you want to the conclusion, but keep your hands off the memoir."

The book's publication in 2014 was special because it was the first time any part of the memoir appeared in print. If they wanted to describe it as autoethnographical, so be it. I had a published memoir chapter.

A few months after the book came out, another publication opportunity arose. Mark Cuban, the owner of the Dallas Mavericks basketball team, caused controversy when he said that he would cross the street if he saw a young black man with a hoodie coming toward him late at night. Several decades earlier, I faced a similar situation and decided not to cross the street. I got mugged and had written about this experience in another memoir chapter. Although traumatized by the experience and wanting to avoid all young black men, I wrote, "I kept telling myself, over and over again, you were in the wrong place at the wrong time. Most young black men don't rob people. . . . Don't give in to the stereotypes."

Perfect for an op-ed piece, I thought. *I can combine memoir with some sociology.* I wrote a lead paragraph, cut and pasted the five hundred words from my memoir chapter, wrote a conclusion criticizing Cuban for perpetuating inaccurate stereotypes, and e-mailed it to the *Baltimore Sun*. The whole process took twenty minutes. Within twenty-four hours, the op-ed editor e-mailed me that it would be published a few days later.

My evolution continues during my fifth year of retirement. Some days, I'm a writer. I meet once a month with three other Baltimore memoir writers to share and comment on each other's work. None of them are academics.

Other days, when I teach noncredit courses on diversity to senior citizens, I'm still a sociologist. Although I can't ask my students to read anything, I don't have to read papers and exams. When I read about growing economic inequality in the morning newspaper I think, *I taught about that for years.*

Happily, I can be both a writer and a sociologist. I no longer have to worry about what is scholarly and what is literary. I'm retired.

17

Retiree

NATALIE J. SOKOLOFF

etiree, I thought.

It reminds me of the title of a Woody Guthrie song, "Deportee." Guthrie, of course, was singing about farmworkers from Mexico who were no longer needed to pick crops in the United States that year and who were being deported back to Mexico. They were no longer useful.

As a retiree, I felt like I was being deported from New York City to Baltimore, where my husband and son were living.

This was not the first time I felt I had to leave a place I loved. In the early 1960s, I looked at colleges far from Boston, the city of my birth. As the youngest of three children born during World War II to two parents trained as lawyers in the 1930s, I saw how frustrated my mother was because she never worked in the law after her children were born. My brother became a lawyer; my sister, a social psychologist who never worked at her profession when she had children. I knew I had to strike out on my own. I went to the University of Michigan and chose sociology as my undergraduate major because of an inkling that it fit my way of seeing the world, but without any certainty. I graduated in 1965, the very beginning of the campus teach-ins on the Vietnam War. It was my professors who made me aware of many of the injustices in the United States, connections to the Vietnam War, and U.S. imperialism.

After Michigan, I got my M.A. at Brown University and moved to New York City in 1967 to work at the New York State Division for Youth doing in-house program evaluation. It took me eight years to return to school for

my Ph.D., which I received from the City University of New York (CUNY) in
1979, when I was teaching at John Jay College of Criminal Justice.

I did not want to get married and have a family for a long time because
I feared repeating the pattern of my mother and sister. I decided to have
a child when I had published my second book. My father had died, and
I realized I wanted to leave more in this world than just books and other
publications. Combining education, sociology as a discipline (and where I
met my life's partner in 1970), teaching, and research; being an activist; and
becoming a mother were the best decisions of my life.

A Newly Minted Retiree: What I Was Leaving

I had no idea how hard it would be to become a *retiree* because, in part, retirement is really a process, not an event. And I had to take my time letting
the process play out. Retirement traditionally means giving up your job and
all its demanding requirements. But it also means relinquishing much of its
pleasures—expertise and daily contacts with students, colleagues, and many
of my longtime friends. For me retirement meant this but so much more. I
had to give up not only my job and my closest friends—outside as well as
inside academia—but my beloved New York City.

First, there were so many groups and activities at my own college that
I would miss. Over the past forty years at John Jay College, I was involved
with many students eager to learn, the Women's Center, the Gender Studies
Program, the Prisoner Reentry Institute, the new College in Prison Program,
and the Participatory Action Research Forum—as well as the CUNY Graduate Center where I got my Ph.D. and taught.

Moreover, I loved walking the streets of New York and experiencing the
cacophony of sounds, the sparkle of the lights, the ethnic aromas emanating
from pushcarts, the fascinating diverse sights, the free or low-cost activities,
and the ease of public transportation.

And, of course, the people—all kinds of people, speaking so many different languages from all over the world. Some wore turbans; some, full-length
burqas; some, disheveled clothes; some, long, flowing skirts with paisley
blouses; others, sparkly jeans; and still others wore gowns or tuxedos as they
headed for the opera. Even though New York is not the city of my birth, I
have always felt it is where I grew up. It has been home to me since 1967, and
I had been at John Jay College since 1972.

These multiple role losses occurred because I was retiring to Baltimore.
While it is not unusual for someone to move to a new city on retirement,
my married life was somewhat unique. My husband, Fred Pincus, like me a
sociologist, and I had a forty-year commuting relationship. He commuted
from New York City to the University of Maryland, Baltimore County, the
first twenty years; I commuted from Baltimore to New York City the second

twenty years. Our son now lives in Baltimore with his wife; thus, retirement where he lives was a no-brainer. And like so many people I know, Fred didn't enjoy the hustle and bustle of New York. I, however, loved it all and would miss it terribly.

I could be fearless in New York. One always had to know where it was safe to walk—especially at night; but I'd lived all over the city since I moved there in my early twenties. I smiled at people as we were crammed together on the subway. Usually they were caught off guard but often smiled back. I would help people who were lying on the street. Others told me not to, but at times I had to help. I couldn't just leave a vulnerable person on the street. When my son Josh was young, we usually gave away leftover food to a hungry person as we were walking back to our apartment from the pizza shop or the Chinese restaurant.

Walking along Broadway at any hour of the day or night I always felt safe. There were Asian fruit and vegetable markets and many restaurants open all night and all kinds of people on the streets. As Jane Jacobs argued in *The Death and Life of Great American Cities* in the early 1960s, continually crowded urban streets and public life make for greater diversity, accountability, and safety. I relished the safety as a young single woman, and I still do now as a senior.

And people have graciously reached out to me. I was the only white person on a train late one night going through Harlem when I first came to New York. I didn't even realize I was on the wrong train. An older African American woman came over and said, "I think you're on the wrong train. You should get off at 168th Street, cross over to the downtown side, and go back to 96th Street. Then make sure to find the train you need." How kind of her to notice I was out of place. People could be so helpful and caring in the Big Apple.

More recently, when I was going back to the apartment after my night class, I was walking along the island in the middle of Broadway at 61st Street to get to the uptown IRT train. I tripped on the base of a newly installed statue. My books and papers went flying. My arms shot out to protect me from the fall. I landed face down, breaking my glasses and unable to move my left arm. While some people clearly did not stop or want to get involved, others asked me what I needed. "Go down to the police station in the subway at 61st Street and get an officer to help me. I need an ambulance," I said.

One person collected my papers and books and stood guard over me while another ran down to get the police. Two officers came and stayed with me while we waited for the ambulance. Ironically, Roosevelt Hospital was only three or four streets away, but because of construction and so many emergency calls it took the ambulance well over an hour to reach me. Nevertheless, New Yorkers are often so helpful. Fortunately, I didn't break any bones; I just walked around with two big bruises around both eyes for a week.

Finally, I was diagnosed with thyroid cancer while I was still teaching and commuting. Learning about the cancer brought to light the reality for me that we never know how much longer we have in this world. Moreover, I'd been trying to decide just when I'd retire over the last three to four years. This all made me realize I had to ask some important questions: Do I want to continue commuting? Do I want to continue teaching full time? And grading papers? Do I want to put travel off? Can I afford to *not* pay attention to health issues that were emerging? After some anguished decision making, I decided the answer to all these questions was emphatically no.

All of this came tumbling down on me as I considered retirement in Baltimore. I had to deal with the question, "What do I want to do with the rest of my life?" Or, as we used to say, "What do I want to be when I grow up?" This was a serious question that took a lot of time and consideration. In my case, I decided to seek out a retirement counselor who works with people going through major life transitions. Part of my process was realizing the *grieving* I was going through given all the losses I was experiencing: job, college, colleagues, friends and neighbors, community activities and groups—and my beloved New York City. As we switch roles, we need space and time to grieve before we embark on developing new relationships in our changing lives.

Transitions: Finding My Place

I retired six years ago, on January 29, 2011. *I remember the official date as if it were yesterday.*

It has been a struggle to find my place in Baltimore. Since I commuted for the second twenty years of my forty-year teaching career at John Jay College, Baltimore is not new to me. But it has always been secondary in my life. Now it was to be my primary residence.

Local Activities in My New Retirement Community

I thought continuing some of my previous scholarly activities would be a good place to start. And it was. I taught doctoral classes at two University of Maryland campuses on women, crime, and justice and on domestic violence—two of my areas of specialization. But being an adjunct once a week was not very satisfying. Nor was guest speaking in different classes or at different conferences. These, of course, made me keep current in my areas of interest and made sure students, faculty, and community members were learning some of the most recent important information in these areas. But they did not create the close *social network* I was looking for.

I volunteered easily enough at different places over time. Since I retired I've helped out at an animal shelter—a great experience until a scared cat clawed me and I got very ill. That was the end of that volunteer activity. I also have helped out at a community center that caters to the nonmedical needs of people with cancer, where I have been a recipient of their services. I have also led a group at a wellness center for low-income women. I am on the board of directors of two wonderful organizations working with women in and coming out of prison. One helps women reintegrate back into Baltimore when they leave prison;[1] the other provides women (and men at one of Maryland's many men's prisons) college classes from a local elite college while in prison.[2]

When I retired, I began going to exercise, yoga, and Pilates classes each week and making sure I walked daily. Meditation, acupuncture, and massage have become a regular part of my life as well. I learned that I really *enjoy* taking care of myself. I usually exercise with a group of women at two different locations near my home. And most of the services are free or very low cost. Having a walking buddy is a big help. Mine is our gray-and-white fluff of a rescue dog, a twenty-two-pound miniature Schnauzer named Phineas. He is joyful and loving and fights me for my recliner chair; I always win, but he is allowed to jump up on my lap when I'm not eating.

But the question of developing a personal community is still one that I struggle with—not because people I work (or play) with or meet are unkind but because their lives are very busy, and they already have most of the connections they can keep up with.

I've done local collaborative research, which I've enjoyed: First, I researched domestic violence in immigrant communities in the Baltimore area. Since retiring, two articles from this research have been published in academic journals. Second, I did a study on how colleges in Maryland respond to applicants with criminal records and wrote a literature review on college education in prison and on reentry. So I have been using my sociological skills and feel good about that. I've participated in other important public issues by, for example, developing consciousness and policies (through a National Science Foundation grant headed by Beth Richie) to assist the all-but-forgotten women and girl immigrants who are caught at the Mexican-U.S. border and placed in detention centers in the United States and by taking part in community discussions on how the Black Lives Matter movement is relevant for women, too.

As my son says, "Mom, you've retired, but no one would ever know it. You're always so *busy*!"

---

1. This organization is Alternative Directions. See its website at http://www.alternativedirectionsinc.org/.

2. This organization is Advocates for Goucher Prison Education Partnership (GPEP). For more information, see https://donatenow.networkforgood.org/agpep and http://www.goucher.edu/academics/other-academic-offerings/goucher-prison-education-partnership.

In fact, he often wishes I'd slow down. I try to explain to him that I am energized and enlivened by this work, but I also can't do as much as I did when I was younger—or as much as I would like.

The Joys of International Travel and Exploration

Like lots of people, travel has been big on my list of must do's in retirement. The month I retired, January 2011, I decided I wanted to go to a relaxing, untrendy spa—with healthy, locally grown food, yoga, meditation, massage, pool classes, hikes, and sisterhood. I was so lucky. A friend had been to such a place, but I couldn't find anyone to go with me. So I went alone! Though not my favorite way to travel, I was learning new skills. The spa was in the Primavera Forests of Mexico. Rio Caliente is a Wellness-Thermal Springs Spa Retreat outside Guadalajara. For a week I reveled in daily massages, facials, nail polishing (mani/pedis to those in the know), easy hikes, yoga, and wonderful food and talks. I had to make a fire at night in my little one-room cottage. And I did it (of course, it was already set up for me in the fireplace). This would have been a yearly pilgrimage, but it closed the next year. I continue to look for a similar place.

I have taken several other big trips one to Vienna and another to the Galápagos. Each was fabulous in its own way. In Vienna, I was invited by the Austrian university system to participate in a program and spent a week as a tourist. As I walked the streets in the center of the city, I was spellbound by the amazing architecture, including the Romanesque and Gothic St. Stephens Church at the very center of Vienna—with its richly colored, mostly green and black with some yellow and red, glazed tile roof, with mosaics of double-headed eagles, and twenty-three bells. The musicians on each block playing every kind of music was so joyful an experience for me. I felt like I was walking through the rich, colorful slides of my art history class back in 1964 at the University of Michigan.

The gorgeous soprano voices of young boys singing once an hour for thirteen hours at St. Stephens Church every Sunday is an awe-inspiring experience. And I was so lucky to hear the Vienna Boys Choir at the Hofburg Palace in its small Imperial Chapel just fifteen minutes after I dropped off my suitcase at the hotel. Soloists from the Vienna Chorale Society and musicians from the Vienna Symphony Orchestra accompanied the Boys Choir. The music soared through the small, ornate, multistory chapel.

My trip to the Galápagos was a dream come true. I went with a college friend from forty-five years ago. We had just remet the year before for the first time. The Galápagos had all the amazing birds and fish and tortoises you could want to see: the blue-footed boobies had bright blue beaks and webbed feet; the males did intricate dances to attract the females when mating. And the males of the black frigatebirds hugely inflate their bright red throat pouches to attract the females in mating season. We saw both of these events up close on one island where blue-footed boobies and frigates honor their mating traditions.

We walked among the one hundred–year-old giant tortoises. Each type of tortoise is adapted to the terrain of the island on which it lives. Low-ground grazing tortoises are able to eat grass and seeds on the ground; but those tortoises living on an island with black lava rock as ground cover have shells that curve up near their necks so they can reach up to eat vegetation on the trees. Darwin documents all this—and we got to see some of these ancient creatures and hear about their fascinating histories.

The Unexpected Issues around Health and Illness

Retirement has given me the chance to travel and make visits to family and friends I had failed to do—or to the degree to which I would have liked—over all the years of working, mothering, and commuting. This became even more important when I retired, since issues of health and illness marched right in—just when I least expected it—and changed my life in an instant.

In fact, health issues came crashing down on me in more than one way. The most debilitating was falling on black ice three days before my seventieth birthday in the winter of 2014, breaking my pelvis in two places and my sacrum. I was in rehab for two weeks, had four weekly physical and occupational therapy visits at home for the next month, and three years later still have to go to physical therapy to deal with my injuries.

Wasn't rehab for elderly people? I'm not elderly, I thought.

My mother fell at eighty-seven years old. So I knew that it was commonly the elderly who fall as I did and break bones. She was in rehab for six weeks and survived another eight years. This was unusual, since falls are a major cause of death for elderly women. My doctor even told me I was the youngest patient of his with this injury. But my advanced stage of osteoporosis made me more vulnerable than other people. Most important, my mother was my role model. I knew if she could return to a state of relative health, then I should be able to do so, too.

I was on morphine for two months and hydrocodone for another month. I had to learn how to walk all over again. Being on medication was necessary for me to be able to do all my exercises as my bones healed. But it also meant I had to learn how to detox from megadoses of narcotics. My compassion for addicts was intensified as I realized that without such a supportive group of people to help me through detox, I would never have been able to get off the drugs. If this is true for me, what must it be like for all those people who are poor, are without resources, and/or do not have a supportive network?

And even though I no longer need heavy-duty drugs, I am in pain much of the time from my fall. Can you believe that a year later I still carried two pillows with me wherever I went so I could tolerate sitting better? It was a bit embarrassing, but two years later I finally don't need them.

New Opportunities: "She Never Stopped Trying"

My husband says that the epitaph on my gravestone will read, "She Never Stopped Trying."

What had been such a hard transition without my close friends and the institutional connections we all build up over a lifetime of work in our home communities has been getting easier. But it is important to realize that being a *retiree* in a new place where one doesn't have roots—with school, work, mothering when children are young, one's family of origin or that of one's partner's family—can be very challenging. As a wise man told me at a party when I was visiting Fred's relatives in Los Angeles, "It's not possible to make friends at seventy *in the same way* you can in your twenties and thirties. That's what *lifelong* friendship is about: it occurs over the course of your life."

And with some hard work, I have been making a new life for myself.

First, while I have had a hard time recuperating from my fall, I am lucky that I devoted so much of my retirement to taking care of my health *before* this injury. Since falling, I have worked my way back to some old (yoga and exercise) and have begun some new (Pilates pool therapy) classes. I have learned that I need to take care of my body on a regular basis. *This is not an option*. It is a requirement in my retirement status. And I know how lucky I am to have had a husband and son who were really so supportive and helpful in my recovery. Not everyone has this, which concerns me a lot.

And I do nice things for myself, like frequent massages and acupuncture. In addition, I have been participating in a weekly meditation group as well as different monthly reading groups: one on feminist novels, another on Buddhism, a third on compassion, and more recently on death and dying. I have been participating in several workshops for people in the second half of life—which covers issues of aging, meditation, writing, artistic activities, and so forth. Much to my amazement, I am enjoying it all. Moreover, Fred and I have been members of a Jewish Chavurah (a nonreligious cultural community) for a number of years where he was cofacilitator for many years.

Second, new joys have opened up to me. Most recently, I began taking memoir-writing classes. I decided that I wanted to write about falling and hurting myself—and I have never had such fun writing. I want to reach out to other aging women who break their pelvis, hip, or lower limbs so they can know what to expect and, most important, to know there is *hope* all along the way. Over forty years of doing research and teaching, I know well how to write as a social scientist. But I never knew I could *enjoy* writing. Learning how to write in a new way—a way that captures my feelings and creativity— is very exciting. I have known a number of people who have been writing their memoirs, including my husband. I now understand its deep appeal. While I only want to write a few articles on gender, health, and wellness at this point, it is more than enough for me. Also, as a senior, I am able to take courses from a potpourri of colleges in the Baltimore area. This is fun.

Through the college program in prison mentioned earlier, GPEP, on whose board I have been a member since its inception, I was fortunate to assist a gifted English teacher with an Inside-Out Prison Exchange class at the women's prison in Maryland.[3] *Outside* students are traditional college students who take classes behind prison walls with *Inside* students who are incarcerated in the prison. They learn as coequals in a small dynamic class—learning from and helping each other. I love this kind of teaching—passionate and challenging to all involved. Retiring gives me the opportunity to do this type of teaching in the future if I want.

And I have found that one can meet new people as a retiree, some of whom will become friends, others will be meaningful relationships, and others just pleasant connections. And sometimes you meet people in the funniest places—like a rabbi at Starbucks who was looking at a Power and Control Wheel, which helps people understand the underlying issues of domestic violence. So we talked—and I helped him with his sermon that week. He told me that many of the religious institutions in Baltimore (churches, temples, and mosques) educate their congregations about domestic violence during the month of October—Domestic Violence Awareness month. He asked me what would be the single most important message to get across to his congregation. I answered, "'Why did she stay?' is the wrong question," since most women leave, and they leave seven times before they can leave and be safe. He sent me his speech, in which that question was highlighted.

I also made a new friend from New Zealand, around my age, who takes care of her three young granddaughters so her daughter can work and study full time as a physician in the international Public Health School at Johns Hopkins University. I have been lucky to meet many courageous women I take exercise classes and volunteer with who are struggling through—with some conquering—their many stages of cancer. And through the classes I take I make new acquaintances all the time. They all inspire me.

I miss New York City, my close friends, and the excitement of the city. But I have become connected with all kinds of people and many kinds of activities in Baltimore. Moreover, I am lucky that I can see my son when he unexpectedly calls to go to lunch. I have the opportunity to investigate new possibilities; reach out to other people; begin new projects; work in feminist, antipoverty, and antiracist politics; and continue my participation in anti-prison and antiviolence work—for both women and men. I am feeling more and more grounded in my new home.

---

3. For more on the Inside-Out Prison Exchange Program, see http://www.insideoutcenter.org.

As I indicated in the beginning, retirement is a process; it is not an event. For many of us it takes time to come into our own as we blossom in our senior years. That's okay. I wouldn't have it any other way. It is a reminder of how important it is to cherish the people around us and maintain contacts from the past as we create a new future.

18

Spreading the Sociological Imagination to Lay Audiences

David R. Simon

Sociological Beginnings

I was born and raised in rural communities sixty miles west of Chicago: DeKalb and Sycamore, Illinois. I grew up in a Jewish family, but the towns themselves were over 90 percent Christian. At one point, I was the only Jew in my entire high school.

My father owned a children's toy and clothing store embarrassingly called the Simple Simon Juvenile Shop. The store was located on Sycamore's Main Street and contained a fourteen-foot sign over the entrance. I was perpetually called "Simple Simon" growing up. I was also bullied a good deal throughout my childhood by anti-Semitic working-class toughs.

I was forced to sing Christmas carols in school and to listen to New Testament readings by one of my teachers. These early life experiences created a deep sense of alienation and being on the outside looking in to the dominant culture.

In 1962, I entered the University of Illinois at Urbana-Champaign, majoring in political science and minoring in economics, psychology, and American history. My family had always had conversations about politics and loved President Kennedy. The only problem was that the dominant paradigm in political science at the time was pluralism, the notion that powerful interest groups tended to balance each other and compromise to obtain at least some of what they wanted. I found the notion boring and contrary to how the political system actually functioned.

Then in the fall semester of 1964 I took my first sociology class. One of the texts was David Riesman's *The Lonely Crowd*. The book had a profound effect on my worldview. At last I had encountered a reasonable explanation for the alienation from American culture I felt. Later I learned that Riesman's work was but a portion of the literature of mass society theory, especially the school interested in the decline of community and the rise of various types of alienation among the masses.

Having made the Dean's List my last four semesters at Illinois, I was awarded two fellowships to graduate school in political science, one by the University of Illinois and the other from the Patterson School of Diplomacy at the University of Kentucky. I accepted the one from Kentucky and wrote a master's thesis on Riesman's concept of other-directedness and its relationship to politics and foreign policy.

Then I undertook a four-year tour of duty in the U.S. Air Force. It was during this time that I learned firsthand how certain aspects of American political life appeared to function. While numerous draftees were fighting and dying in Vietnam, I remained in the States as a squadron administrative officer. My duties included sponsoring a beauty contest, the winner of which was termed "Miss Flame" in honor of the base's fire prevention program. I also wrote letters to the loved ones of airmen who had been killed in Vietnam and signed my name to numerous documents confirming that those who had just entered the squadron had indeed arrived, that those who were leaving the unit were indeed leaving, and that those who were accused of criminal activity were so accused. I also gave lectures on safe driving. In short, I felt I could have been replaced by a chimpanzee.

The entire military experience not only confirmed the alienation I felt but radicalized me against the Vietnam War and American politics. After my four-year tour of duty with an honorable discharge at the rank of captain, I was most anxious to reenter graduate school. I was accepted to Rutgers University in sociology and participated in demonstrations against the war. At Rutgers I read the works of C. Wright Mills, Hannah Arendt, Erich Fromm, Karl Marx, and other members of the Democratic school of mass society theorists. I learned that instead of being made up of numerous interest groups, real political power in America rested in the hands of a power elite.

I was also awarded teaching assistantships at Rutgers. One of the courses I taught involved culture and alienation. Following graduation from Rutgers in 1975, I took an assistant professor post in the Department of Political Science and Sociology at the University of North Florida in Jacksonville. Since I held graduate degrees in both disciplines, I was considered desirable for the post. A few years after my arrival a program in criminal justice was added. I taught courses in all three disciplines and remained in Jacksonville until

1986. Most of my teaching involved courses in deviance, political sociology, and American social character and alienation. I was awarded tenure and promotion in 1979.

Two important experiences stood out during my tenure there. First, I worked briefly with the Jacksonville Sheriff's Office (JSO) reviewing crime statistics. During one of my JSO visits I was given printouts on local crime statistics. I noticed that in the same closet where this information was housed were several boxes of files on the top shelf. I inquired about their content. I was informed that these contained the white-collar crime cases and were stored there until it was deemed appropriate to forward them to the district attorney's office. I was told that there were few prosecutors that handled white-collar crime cases, so the evidence was rarely forwarded to the courthouse until the statute of limitations had expired.

This was a firsthand lesson on the priority given the most costly and injurious type of crime. This was one of the inspirations for my writing *Elite Deviance*. The book was first published in 1981 and has gone through ten editions over thirty years.

A second experience involved a scandal a former student of mine and I discovered was taking place at a local U.S. Navy base. My former student was a female navy enlistee and had taken a deviance course with me two years earlier. One day in 1979 she came to visit me in my office.

She was applying to Officer's Candidate School and showed me a form she had been given to complete. The form concerned any previous affiliation with communist front organizations or the American Communist Party. The form was a leftover from the days of the House on Un-American Activities Committee hearings.

I immediately called the editor of the *Progressive* magazine and discussed the possibility of writing an article about the scandal that the form was still in use. He advised me to call the Naval Information Office at the Pentagon for its reaction, which I did. I was advised that the form had been banned for use six years previously.

Not only did the *Progressive* publish our cowritten piece on this topic; my former student and I went to a local television news station, and a lead story on the eleven o'clock news followed. This reportage spurred an official investigation on the naval base by the navy's inspector general's office.

This is one of the most rewarding sociological experiences I've ever had. I am a deep believer in muckraking sociology (now termed public sociology) and believe it is one of the ways we sociologists can have a real impact on public policy.

In 1983, I was awarded a postdoctoral fellowship in alcohol abuse and alcoholism research at the University of California, Berkeley's, Public Health School. My experience at Berkeley taught me that the overwhelming majority of studies of alcohol abuse involved people of lower- and working-class origins. Even when the military did a survey of abuse among its members, no one above the rank of colonel was interviewed. This, of course, is but one of the gaps in the study of elite deviance.

In 1993, I left the University of North Florida for a sociology and criminology post at San Diego State University (SDSU) at both its San Diego and Calexico campuses. The Calexico campus is on the Mexican border next door to Mexicali, Mexico.

Some of my students in Calexico were Border Patrol agents. Here I learned a good deal about the smuggling of drugs, arms, and illegal immigrants into the United States. Contrary to the view of the fence- and wall-builder approach to border security, much of the illegal trafficking on the border takes place in small airplanes landing in secluded locations. Some contraband is also smuggled in the trunks of vehicles, sometimes involving the bribery of Border Patrol agents.

After earning tenure and being promoted to full professor at SDSU, I accepted a post at San Jose State University in criminal justice in the late 1990s. Sadly, I developed a case of worsening bipolar disorder that affected my teaching and research, and I ended up taking disability retirement in 2002. I then retired to Jacksonville, Florida, the home of my children and grandchildren.

Postretirement Experiences

One discussion I had with my family doctor concerned my retirement. Retiring was a frightening proposition to him. He told me that a number of his colleagues had retired in the last few years with disastrous consequences. One had committed suicide, and another contracted Alzheimer's. Another had become severely depressed. He attributed these horrors to a lack of propinquity and colleagueship.

It then dawned on me how different my experiences in academia and retirement up to that point had been. I began thinking about my doctor's comments. Academia seems a different experience for many of the colleagues I had known. Large numbers of them long for lighter teaching loads, smaller classes, fewer meetings, and more time to do research. One poll taken at my last university revealed that most faculties resented the deans of their colleges. Many fellow colleagues are hundreds or thousands of miles away at other universities, and face-to-face interaction takes place largely at conferences. Often when one does befriend a local colleague, one or the other takes a post at another university (something I did at times in my career). Finally, I am in a field that is of little interest to over 90 percent of my sociological and criminological colleagues: elite deviance and white-collar crime. Indeed, most white-collar criminologists and sociologists do not approach the field from my paradigm.

In short, I do not much miss the everyday complaints I hear from regular faculty, but it took me awhile to conclude why. Following my doctor's visit, it hit me:

- There are no longer any bosses to obey, save perhaps the IRS.
- Tenure requirements are irrelevant.
- There are no deadlines to meet, save those that are self-imposed.
- One is free to ally oneself with the international, national, or local political or human rights causes of one's choosing.

Following my retirement I realized for my life to possess continued purpose and meaning, I would need to find nonacademic venues where there would be interest and utility in my sociological skills. One of my first stopping places was a radio talk show hosted by a former member of the Florida House of Representatives, Andy Johnson. For over a year I was a frequent guest on the program and even hosted it several times.

Jacksonville has a reputation for being a very conservative place, yet there are more registered Democrats than Republicans. One lesson made clear was that many of Andy's callers were neither conservative nor liberal. When they provided evidence for their positions, the dominant presentation was based on the ecological fallacy, that is, their personal experiences or those of someone they knew.

My strategy was to introduce the difference between private trouble and public issues and why there are many personal and societal consequences to attributing so many social problems to individuals. I discussed matters like our poisoned food supply, the consequences of having an African American president in a nation with a long history of racism, the Kennedy assassination, the stereotyping of various groups by the media, and the interrelationships between various types of crime.

The First Coast Free Thought Society

The First Coast Free Thought Society (FCFTS) is a 501(c)(3) (i.e., not allowed to make political campaign contributions) organization made up of nonreligious free thinkers (i.e., people whose approach to problems is based on scientific evidence and secular humanism). I have given nine talks to this group since 2003 on a wide variety of sociological subjects (e.g., scandals within the major religions, the Kennedy assassination, alienation in mass society, crime myths, and the HBO documentary *Questioning Darwin*).

Conclusion

What I have learned from these and other experiences is that we sociologists do not have to end up like my doctor's colleagues. Aside from radio talk shows and the FCFTS, I have been an adviser to the Southern Christian Leadership Conference regarding the Florida State Racketeering in Corrupt Organization statutes and local fraud cases. A friend of mine, Dr. Steven Morewitz, has initiated a field termed "forensic sociology." In this field, people use their sociological skills by testifying in court. Contrary to my doctor's fears, I have discovered new realms of topics and activities in which to form interests and the freedom to pursue them in retirement.

19

Networking across Stages of a Career

Elizabeth Higginbotham

In May 2011, while talking with a colleague, I mentioned my plans to retire within a few years. He remarked that only a minority of African American faculty get to retire on their own terms. While I often thought about my struggles in the field, his comment pushed me to place my privileged experience in perspective. Indeed, I watched some people of color leave graduate programs; some who completed their doctorates did not get tenure at their first jobs. In the face of the racism in research universities, I knew people who had left the academy altogether, while some found life more comfortable in teaching institutions. As a Black woman from the working class, I, too, have stumbled over many obstacles. To cite the line from Langston Hughes's poem "Mother to Son," "Life for me ain't been no crystal stair."

I attribute some of my success to being a sociologist with the skills to analyze academic settings just as I would analyze any social organization or institution. My racial and class background also connects me to a history of accomplishing goals by working with others. Networking with others and collaborating on projects have been central to my individual mobility. As an outsider, I saw social inequality differently from the structural functionalism in texts in the 1960s. Being able to test that thinking with people from the

Acknowledgment: In addition to Peter Stein and Rosalyn Benjamin Darling and the anonymous reviewers, I thank the following friends for their comments: Margaret Andersen, Maxine Baca Zinn, Brenda Berrian, Bonnie Thornton Dill, Beverly Harris-Schenz, Emma Lapsansky-Werner, Carole Marks, Yvonne Newsome, Jennifer Pierce, Rafia Zafir, and Ruth E. Zambrana.

same cloth was essential to challenging the canon I confronted—one that excluded people like me. Once I completed my degree, I wanted to teach others, particularly members of marginal groups, that connecting with fellow travelers could help them face the challenges of surviving as outsiders in the academy.

I went to college in the 1960s; we were deep into the Cold War with the USSR, and the launch of the first Russian spacecraft *Sputnik* spurred the United States into a historic expansion of higher education. New campuses sprouted up around the nation, many in cities. Students like me could commute to college and enter a wide range of professional and managerial jobs. When I finished high school in 1966, the City University of New York was tuition free; attending college meant paying a student fee of fifty-seven dollars and, of course, having the grades to gain admission. Like many of my friends, I worked part time to pay for living expenses. Thus, I was part of a group of New Yorkers from the working class who not only entered the academy but also changed the nature of many fields. We crossed numerous barriers, including those of social class, race, and gender, but my journey would have been harder had I not been part of an important cohort of colleagues and friends who provided essential support for me to face the challenges of the academy. As I retire, these networks will continue to sustain me.

Early Experiences

Born in 1948 into a Negro family (the terminology of that day), I grew up in New York City. My mother, born in 1925, had graduated from high school; my father, born in 1905, was literate but never discussed his formal schooling. However, both parents read widely and encouraged their five children to read. My father had been a Pullman porter, where he was a union member; he continued union involvement later as a bartender and hotel waiter. He was also a member of the National Association for the Advancement of Colored People (NAACP); thus, I had a model of political involvement. My mother stayed at home with five children, but she also kept us busy with trips to museums and parks. Both parents expected that all of their children would finish high school. My mother had attended integrated public schools in Pittsburgh, and she wanted that experience for her children. Because of this goal, my parents moved the family out of Harlem, where the local school was unacceptable to them. My father tended bar in a jazz club called Snooky's in Greenwich Village, so they found an apartment closer to his workplace.

In 1953, we moved to St. Mark's Place on the Lower East Side of Manhattan, a significant change for us, because this new community was very racially and ethnically mixed. We were, though, in the minority as Black people. We had two Jewish men as neighbors who befriended the family, babysat for the children, and became lifelong friends. They taught me to play chess and had conversations that spoke of expanding opportunities. Family and friends visited our home; many were involved in the arts and in music. Over time, my neighborhood became the East Village, but in the 1950s, it housed working-class people in four- and five-story walk-up buildings surrounded by family-run stores and small artisan shops that were characteristic of the city at the time.

Public schooling shaped my life until graduate school, starting with the morning kindergarten class at Public School 122 in 1953. The school was integrated, with the racial composition varying over time but consistently working class. Among this student body, I was one of many "others": there were children of immigrants, a few second-generation Americans, and an expanding Puerto Rican population. As a Negro family we were perceived as more American than most because both of my parents spoke English. Many other parents spoke with accents or had their children translate for them. My mother was comfortable talking with teachers, an advantage that helped me navigate the school environment. I was at ease with racial and ethnic diversity, but at the time I did not realize the lack of class diversity in my school.

Much of my success comes from the support and encouragement of family and the New York public school system. In 1960, we moved to the Upper West Side. Joan of Arc Junior High School was racially integrated but had more class diversity than did my elementary school. I met children who had their own bedrooms, something unknown from my old neighborhood of one-bedroom apartments. My high school, Julia Richman, was all girls and provided solid academic preparation for college and rich cultural exposure. I was lucky, like many in my cohort, to attend these schools when they worked or at least enabled many working-class people to achieve their goals. I graduated in 1966 with much cultural and human capital since the schools exposed my classmates and me to many of the riches of New York City.

Higher Education

I spent my freshman year of college at the Borough of Manhattan Community College (BMCC), which at the time was on a couple floors in an office building in Midtown Manhattan. There was a dress code, since we could not look like college students in that environment. The following year I transferred to the City College of New York (CCNY). Going to a real campus was a challenge; it meant changing classes and walking across campus, but it also offered me the freedom to dress more comfortably. My initial occupational goal was to be a New York City high school history teacher. I had taken advance placement American history at Julia Richman and the world civilization series at CCNY. Then in the spring of 1968, sociology caught my attention when I took a course on minority groups with Professor Arnold Birenbaum. The discipline provided me with a language and understanding for many of my observations. Much of my upbringing had involved moving from place to place among various social groups, and I had to navigate these different worlds to survive. When I realized I could make a living using my skills in "reading" organizations, institutions, and groups, I was ready to declare a major. However, when declaring a major in sociology at CCNY, you had to select a career goal. I had not gotten that far, but Professor Birenbaum, my adviser, wrote on the form next to career goal: graduate school. I was too embarrassed to ask him what that was, so later I asked friends and learned about schooling possible after a bachelor's degree. Looking back, I can see how lucky I was that Dr. Birenbaum and other faculty members recognized my potential and reached out to me by inviting me to lunch and interacting in ways that helped me develop confidence in myself. Many professors at CCNY were the first generation in their own families to secure higher education; perhaps they knew more about what I would face than I did.

In college, I worked part time, both on and off campus, but did not realize how moving between various workplaces, working with children from different social-class backgrounds, and having experiences with diverse people would later help me theorize about race and class. Working to support myself made the college years hard; I studied at night, did not always make deadlines, and often could not afford to eat out, so I was hungry during many days. But I was committed to finishing school. My college education, which took four and a half years, was unproblematic in many ways because I was getting an education with people of varied backgrounds, but we were all city kids. Other Black students and I, as we were called by then, were a minority on the campus of CCNY, but I did not feel like a token standing in for my racial group.

The token experience begins with the move to Boston and my entrance into Brandeis University in the fall of 1971. While sitting in a seminar room, as my classmates and I introduced ourselves, it was clear that I was not getting an education alongside city kids anymore. Now I was out in the suburb of Waltham, Massachusetts, with White people who had grown up in homogeneous communities—small towns, college towns, and suburbs. Although I built significant relationships in graduate school, I worked very hard to be seen and heard. I think many in my cohort accepted the racially biased scholarship at the time and likely put me in that unique category of being "exceptional for my race." However, I had a good support group, mostly other women of color from the working class, who helped sustain me. We all drew strength from each other and came to see our status as graduate students through the lens of race, social class, and gender.

After my years of juggling work and study, Brandeis offered the opportunity to be a full-time student for the first time since high school. It was a privilege and I think essential for my adjustment. In my second year, I began teaching part time at the University of Massachusetts at Boston, and that experience sealed my commitment to getting a doctorate. Initially I was intimidated, but over the year I took delight in crafting courses that provided opportunities for students to learn from each other and to engage with the material. Much of the competition and verbal jockeying that happened in graduate seminars at Brandeis were troubling and not inspiring for me. However, once I knew that I would enjoy college teaching, I was committed and determined also to conduct research examining the inequalities that I knew others like myself faced.

In fall of 1975, when I was a participant in the first seminar on women at Brandeis University, I began my long journey of exploring race and gender. Few in the seminar could appreciate my goals; research on Black women was not valued because their own behaviors were seen as the source of their problems. However, in that seminar I began an investigation of the intersection of race, class, and gender by interviewing twenty-nine Black women who were college seniors in 1976. I learned from this small study and planned for a dissertation that involved sending questionnaires to Black women who had graduated from predominantly White colleges in the late 1960s to examine their socialization, their family's strategies for negotiating racism in housing and schools, their experiences in high school and college, and their current family and occupational circumstances. As I worked on my dissertation, I connected with other graduate students on the East Coast researching Black women. Bonnie Thornton Dill was at New York University writing her dissertation from interviews with Black women who worked as domestics while raising families; Cheryl Townsend Gilkes was at Northeastern University examining the paths to public service of Black women community activists; and Regina Arnold, at Bryn Mawr, was looking at the early childhood experiences of Black women caught up in the criminal justice system. We critiqued each other's work but also organized panels for professional meetings and expanded appreciation of how looking at gender and race could inform scholarship. Although our dissertation committee members were supportive of our work and taught us about methods and theory, they knew little about Black women, and, in fact, the literature about Black women was sparse and problematic.

My first full-time job was at the University of Pittsburgh, where I went as an ABD (all but dissertation) in the fall of 1977. I had two years to finish my degree, which I did with the determination and careful attention to planning that had sustained me as a student. Again, I built a supportive community of people in and outside my department. They consisted of a few people of color on the campus, faculty and graduate students of working-class backgrounds, and women of various class backgrounds. We were all marginal in the academy. In the 1970s, universities admitted or hired "us" but were clueless about the exclusionary practices and policies we faced as well as the everyday microaggressions. We were present but invisible, as many colleagues resented our hiring and never personally engaged in conversations with us. Even with prestigious degrees, we still had to prove our legitimacy as scholars, often with colleagues and students who questioned our authority. We might not have understood the issues in each other's fields, but we provided support as we faced sexism and racism that were generally unacknowledged by others. Challenging the isolation we faced in individual departments, we could reframe our problems from personal to institutional.

As soon as I finished my dissertation in 1979, I started to read the emerging literature on women of color. Along with Bonnie Thornton Dill and Cheryl Townsend Gilkes, I joined with Evelyn Nakano Glenn, who studied Japanese American women in domestic service, and Ruth Zambrana, who researched health and well-being among Latinas, to examine the intersections of race and gender. Our goal was to compare the dimensions of inequality in the lives of different women of color to generate theory. Our efforts were facilitated by a grant from the Ford Foundation; we read books and articles and had meetings where we pushed each other's thinking and supported ideas that were clearly outside the canon.

When we secured the Ford Grant in 1980, I was on a Ford Foundation Postdoctoral Fellowship and back in New York at Columbia University, where I welcomed opportunities to engage with other sociologists. Clara Rodriguez and I organized a group that met at Fordham University to read new race scholarship. I pulled together a women's group to read the new feminist scholarship. By now I could identify the ways that "the women's experiences" they were theorizing about were limited to White women. These lifestyles were built on racial and class privileges. The missing stories about women of color were critical to expanding theories. In the history of the United States, Black, Latina, and Asian women were not protected by private patriarchy. As members of colonized groups, they were thrown into the labor market because their earnings were essential to family survival. Feminist theories at this time actually rendered class and racial privileges as invisible, because no one was asking: How did these isolated, White nuclear families in the suburbs get there in the first place? Families of color were unable to move to the suburbs that expanded in the 1950s and 1960s because they were deeded as White spaces. Discrimination in housing was blatant along with racial biases in access to mortgages. Unlike White people, only a minority of Black people inherited wealth and houses. It was more common for my cohort of first-generation college graduates to supplement their parents' income. We could also see that for most in the Black and Latino communities, discrimination in employment limited work options, so only a few had the resources to secure housing and other symbols of the middle-class lifestyle White feminists critiqued. When I challenged these theories, I was often told that I needed to read more to fully understand the role of sexism. Fortunately, my peers and I were based in New York City, which provided many exchanges with colleagues and a variety of venues to test ideas and expand the intersectional analysis.

Institution Building

My move from New York City to Memphis State University in 1983 was very significant because it allowed my colleagues and me to initiate a stage of institution building. I worked with Bonnie Thornton Dill and Lynn Weber to expand the funding for the Center for Research on Women that was established in 1982. Aware of our marginalization, we knew that collaboration was essential for survival. We held a Summer Institute in 1983, where our Ford-funded working group shared our findings. I recruited more women scholars of color to serve as faculty, which expanded their own networks and ended their academic isolation. We publicized the institute to graduate students and faculty. It was a great offering because women and men gathered to listen to us, to share their research plans, and to receive support to move forward. Afterward many attendees kept in touch with one another to provide continued support and even to collaborate on projects. The programming that we did at the center was grounded in our experiences as graduate students, and we wanted to enable other scholars to form networks that would enhance their own research.

Afterward we secured funding to both do intersectional research and disseminate groundbreaking scholarship on the campus in the city of Memphis and over time nationally. Long before the Internet, we built a research clearinghouse on women of color and southern women. We held national workshops and institutes to share this new scholarship with wide audiences. We often traveled to campuses for faculty workshops on integrating race and gender into the curriculum. Faculty often did not appreciate the value of our work and resented our acclaim. I went up for the same promotion twice, because the first time, my chair in her letter misrepresented a reviewed article in *Signs: Journal of Women in Culture and Society* as an editorial in a women's magazine. At least I could recognize her racism and sexism. The following year my bid for promotion was successful. Our greatest accomplishment at the center was training and mentoring many men and women from diverse backgrounds who worked with us as they completed their master's degrees in our sociology program. Many pursued doctoral degrees at other institutions, where their experiences at the center helped them negotiate the next educational stage and make contributions to the discipline.

My years in Memphis were personally rewarding; I was close with center colleagues, and our professional and personal lives were connected. Plans and discussions continued over meals, and colleagues' children grew up listening to talks about center business. We were encouraged by other scholars, and the work we were doing on intersectionality both in research and curricula development moved us from the margins to the center. As a consequence, we were recruited by more prestigious institutions: Bonnie went to the Department of Women's Studies at the University of Maryland in 1991, Lynn left to head the Women's and Gender Studies department at the University of South Carolina in 1996, and I was the last of the trio to leave in 1998 for the University of Delaware. In 2012, the Center for Research on Women at the University of Memphis celebrated its thirty years in operation; while its present focus differs from that of its past, it continues to engage in research and socialize future scholars.

Rethinking Career

The move to the University of Delaware in 1998 brought me a different set of challenges along with opportunities. In Memphis, people often talked about race, but I had spent enough time in suburbs to know that the topic was often taboo there. While there are many first-generation students at the University of Delaware, the cultural tone of the campus largely reflected the lives of students raised in more privileged homes. The campus differed from the commuter schools where I had much of my experience. In relocating, I had to create space for discussions of race and class, which meant developing new courses and collaborating with faculty who taught social inequality classes.

Unlike my University of Memphis classes, where students of all colors talked about race, I initially found the White students at the University of Delaware to be very quiet. On the evaluations, some students commented that they were quiet because they were listening to the students of color, voices they had not heard in other classes. To build a community among the students, I incorporated letters of introduction so that students could share their backgrounds at the beginning of class. The assignment was effective for enhancing participation among most students.

Teaching classes on race, gender, and poverty at the University of Delaware meant acquainting some students with inequality for the first time. Living in the city of Wilmington, I saw economic diversity on a regular basis, but most of the suburban-raised students were not familiar with poverty. The location of the Food Bank of Delaware in Newark provided a firsthand look at how a nonprofit organization responded to one manifestation of poverty. A visit was incorporated into our class schedule, so students learned information from people on the front line, and they volunteered their time. Documentary films were also great in taking students to locations where they had not been before. Over the semester, students not only learned a structural approach to poverty but also became more comfortable talking about inequality, and some even thought about ways of working to end poverty.

At the University of Delaware, I no longer divided my time between being a professor and an administrator. As a full-time professor, I turned my attention to big writing projects. I revised my dissertation into a book and published it. Then I worked with Margaret Andersen on anthologies for teaching race and ethnicity. I continued to do research on professional Black women by interviewing Black women attorneys, an occupational group that expanded in the 1970s but still faced patterns of segregation. This scholarship continues to keep me connected to an expanding group of scholars addressing new questions about racial oppression.

When I lived in Memphis, I was a five-minute drive from the campus. On my arrival in Delaware, I found myself involved in a forty-minute commute, so I made connections in Wilmington. I joined the Wilmington Trail Club to walk with people and to see the beauty of the region. The members were of a wide age range, including retirees. This was my first time to interact on a regular basis with people who had ended their work careers, so these retirees from DuPont, the public schools, and other venues became role models of how to remain involved. Not only did they hike, but they volunteered for Habitat for Humanity and other civic projects. I had been on nonprofit boards in Memphis, but in 2007 I began a formal involvement with the Delaware Humanities Forum as a member of the council that promotes humanities programming. Previously I had attended events, but my role on the council pushed me to think about how I could craft ways to share ideas in the academy with the wider community. The work with the forum expanded my networks to civic-minded people who had careers in nonprofits and in the corporate world.

Another important connection I made was with the Center for the History of Business, Technology, and Society at the Hagley Library and Museum. I was initially drawn to the center's public talks and a seminar series because of my interest in work. I found many colleagues there who are investigating important questions in history but also thinking about the major shifts we are experiencing with technology and globalization. The center has become an intellectual home for me as I have become involved in its activities.

I officially retired from the University of Delaware in September 2015 and entered a new life stage. I did not have many role models in my own family. To prepare myself, in 2010, I traveled to Philadelphia to hear Sara Lawrence-Lightfoot talk about her book, *The Third Chapter: Passion, Risk, and Adventure in the 25 Years after 50*, which reports on interviews with people who had made the transition, some taking on new challenges and others returning to earlier passions. Reading the book, I was excited about new possibilities as I thought about the work it took to sustain an academic career as an outsider.

In different institutions, I can see enhanced diversity in the student body, but there remains a paucity of faculty of color, which means that service and advising demands fall on a small number. Our viewpoints, not only on institutional matters but on scholarship, are continually questioned. The climate has changed a little, but not significantly. Lawrence-Lightfoot's book confirmed a feeling that it was okay to leave this struggle for others to continue. I am proud of my accomplishments and of my career spent working with others. We, no doubt, expanded the field of sociology to be more inclusive and facilitated more scholars' joining the ranks of academe. However, the ordeal has been burdensome, because institutions are slow to change. In shaping my retirement, I know that I have a rich network of colleagues and friends. My community connections mean that I will not be lost without a university affiliation. In fact, retirement means more time for reflection and writing, including writing for a broader audience. I am aware that not every Black woman in the academy has this privilege, so I plan to use my time wisely. My next chapter is evolving, but I know that I want to spend time with good friends, continue to do creative work, and be involved in the struggle for social justice.

20

The Impact of Sociology on One Man's Life

Henry Fischer

It was *in dubious battle* during *the winter of our discontent* when it began. Reading John Steinbeck in my eleventh-grade history class revealed my life's work. I did not know its academic name yet; I did know its content. My quest: identify, explain, and change the social structure responsible for creating the oppressive human problems Steinbeck inserted into my consciousness.

History was my first major in college. I soon learned my high school experience with Steinbeck was not to be replicated in undergraduate school. On to psychology. This insightful, extremely interesting field soon became one of my minors rather than a major. Social psychology was a helpful starting point but lacked the big-picture, social-structural frame I was seeking.

Serendipity led to an introduction to sociology class. Finally, I was home. This was it. The academic name for what I sought was sociology. Frame of reference, culture, norms, roles, values, status, power elites, social structure, social conflict, socialization, social movements, oppression, capitalism, socialism, primary and secondary societies all combined to begin to provide a unique set of lenses through which to view the world. The sociological perspective! Thank you, Émile Durkheim, Max Weber, Karl Marx, and all the many theorists who followed. I was amazed how the so-called sociological perspective enabled me to increasingly understand so much about myself, my family, my community, and the culture of my birth. I could see in my mind's eye the social structure creating and expanding, as well as controlling and limiting, human thoughts and aspirations. For the first time in my life, I could understand. I could identify social problems, sociologically understand the forces behind their creation and perpetuation. There was clarity in viewing potential pathways to change social structure, thereby, perhaps reducing the misery social problems wrought on so many. Watching the civil rights movement in the 1950s–1960s suggested a process through which power relationships could be altered. Martin Luther King Jr.'s work in leading marches, such as those in Selma, demonstrated the brilliance of the nonviolent demonstration as a strategy for social, societal change. I was invigorated with the sociological tools at hand.

Growing Up

I was an only child the first eight years of life. This enabled me to be the sole beneficiary of all my parents' verbal and physical abuse. Please understand I valued my parent's efforts to house, feed, and clothe me. I also benefited from their socialization: "Get an education, get ahead, and become more successful than we are." These were the benefits of living in the Fischer household. The costs, however, were great. Ages zero to eighteen were fraught with a daily onslaught of emotional explosions resulting in a posttraumatic stress disorder (PTSD)–type experience.

As I learned more sociology, I increasingly understood the family dynamic of my youth—and its impact on me. I also came to understand that I was not alone. My experience was common, unfortunately, akin to that of many others. What I was learning helped me come to terms with my formative years and launched me on a path to attempt to make a difference. Teach others. Lessen their pain. Teach others. Help them break the chain. Avoid repeating the abuse. Spare future generations. Teach others. Seek to change the silence, the roles, and the acceptance of the unacceptable.

My undergraduate education was very good; my graduate school experience was absolutely fantastic. The depth of knowledge gained in pursuit of a master's and doctorate was, to me, akin to water for a thirsty desert nomad. Perhaps my greatest, most thorough learning experiences, however, came during my thirty years of teaching. As we know, teaching others is the best way for one to learn for himself or herself. Conducting research, sharing the findings of your work and that of others, and applying theory in pursuit of understanding combine to bring great clarity to the teacher.

Life Experience and the Academy

My childhood experiences, in combination with others along the road of life, provided me with material to share with my students. I took a personal risk in doing so. I soon learned, from my students, how relating the larger societal issues down to the individual, personal level is what excited them about sociology. We all have experiences to draw from, and we each do not have to experience every social problem to effectively teach. We are all impacted by the social structures in which we live; therefore, we all do have stories to share. Taking the risk with our personal stories is worth it. Students quickly grasp the power sociology has in their lives.

Let's consider a few of my own examples. I experienced child abuse and observed spouse abuse in my family of orientation. Teaching concepts such as domination, roles, socialization, patriarchy, unearned privilege, and so forth became much easier and longer lasting in the minds of students when I peppered classroom discussion with my own life experiences. Students often related their own experiences, as well, through journaling, office hours, or classroom discussion. It was often a cathartic experience for the student. Many sought therapy as a result of confronting their own reality. Without exception, I would later learn of their gratitude for the improvement they experienced in their personal lives. Nothing motivates like being able to see the power of insight afforded by sociological concepts in one's own life.

I was sexually abused by a friend of the family. The first time was on my tenth birthday. The abuse continued for several years. Why has our society historically ignored or hid from such problems? Several relatives suffered from various mental illnesses, along with the stigma. My mother attempted suicide. It was never discussed again after she came home from the hospital. Why do we have this attitude in our society? Several male relatives suffered alcoholism. Others developed drug addictions or eating disorders. Are these personal failings or a genetic problem or a dysfunctional adaptation to a social structure that fails to meet our needs? A grandfather sexually abused one of his grandchildren while another grandfather allegedly beat his wife to death after she gave birth to their eleventh child. He was not charged. It was the 1930s. The children all went to orphanages, including my mother. Patriarchy? What is it about our culture that enables such things?

One of my daughters is a lesbian, meaning she has suffered many times the discrimination and threats our society visits on the stigmatized. And it continues even now during an era of increased enlightenment and after a Supreme Court ruling that expands marriage to all. A critical mass for social change was reached rather quickly in her lifetime, yet too many continue to equate human sexuality as meaning only heterosexuality.

My parents came from lower-class families. They bought a house, purchased a car, and obtained one of the first televisions in our neighborhood. They hoped their children would experience upward mobility. After World War II, economic changes in the United States enabled working-class families to advance financially. Their children benefited with increased educational opportunity. My siblings and I did experience upward mobility. I have seen how coming from the working-class environment does not prepare one as well as middle-class socialization does for entering life in middle-class institutions. Socialization helped tremendously, as did a society believing, at least during the 1950s–1960s, in education. Student loans were created to help many of my generation gain an otherwise largely unattainable education (yes, I paid back my loans, with pleasure—it was more affordable then).

During my entire life, at least since age seventeen, I have suffered from major depressive disorder (MDD). Even with the education I was fortunate enough to have gained, I behaved too much like a member of this society. I did not agree to take medication until I was in my fifties. Worse, I did not agree to individual therapy, the other half of the recommended duo, until I was retired and in my late sixties. Had I sought treatment sooner, my struggles would have been less painful throughout my life. The quest continues. Sociology has improved my life economically, emotionally, and intellectually.

The previous paragraphs contain a few examples of social problems that are prevalent in our society. Having experienced them firsthand seemed like a curse. Don't get me wrong; it was. Yet at the same time, these very same experiences provided at least two great advantages. First, I could better understand myself, my life, and my world by turning the sociological microscope inward. And second, they enhanced my teaching.

Every time I watch the evening news, read a newspaper, or visit another culture, a sociological perspective always filters my perceptions and feelings. I remember when my oldest daughter, who was then in high school, was watching a news program with me one evening. I believe the piece was reporting on economic development taking place in a so-called Third World nation. Several U.S. corporations were described as leading the way to provide jobs and a better way of life for the villagers. I turned to my daughter and asked her what she thought. Her answer suggested she believed everything as presented. It was good for the country we were helping. I asked her if she ever thought about the story behind the story. What else might be motivating these corporations, who were, after all, seeking to create more wealth for themselves and their stockholders? I asked if she wondered what the company might be getting from this nation they were "helping," such as raw materials at a bargain price, low wages paid to the workers, and no environmental standards. My daughter told me years later that her critical-thinking skills began to develop with our conversation that evening. Sociology was at work. The Cold War, September 11, 2001, the several Gulf wars, and other events on the world stage have all provided the *opportunity* for sociology to be at work in the minds of all.

Identify, Explain, and Change

Remember my quest—for me sociology was the means through which to effect change and thereby reduce human misery. If we could identify problems and the variables that contribute to their creation and perpetuation, then we may be able to apply sociology in an effort to identify appropriate individual, group, and societal changes. The outcome: reduce human misery and increase social justice. Idealism and another utopian model? Perhaps. A young man has dreams, ambitions, goals, and a desire to do something meaningful, to make a difference.

I never viewed teaching as something that got in the way of my research. I loved to teach. My experience was extremely gratifying. Students were very gracious in their laudatory evaluations. Personal communications from former students continue to be very kind. My teaching approach was to make sociology clear, easily understood, and applicable to daily life and world issues. I believed drawing on my own personal experiences and being fearless in sharing them would work. And work it did, beyond my wildest expectations. Regardless of major, students learned and applied sociology. I still hear from them. When I meet them by chance, they can still quote me and apply the concepts, the theories. Quite a few went on to graduate school, and several are now colleagues in the discipline.

Over the course of my career I ended up teaching ten different graduate and undergraduate courses, including theory, research methods, and social statistics (for which I published a book). I was quite fortunate to have decided in graduate school that I would not align myself with one or the other of warring camps, such as Marxists versus non-Marxists, statistical analysis versus ethnographic studies. I wanted to learn all of the theories and all of the research and analysis methods. It did not make sense to me to limit myself to research projects that would conform to my theoretical and methodological expertise in the singular. I thought it was more reasonable to select research questions and then determine the method(s) appropriate and the various theoretical paradigms that would be most applicable. My courses reflected this attitude. I believe my students were the better for it.

Have you heard of the Social-Structural Theoretical Model (SSM)? I suspect not. I told my students they might hear of the SSM only from me, but they would hear its contents from any sociologist. I combined every sociological theory and concept into what I call the SSM. And I required students to apply it in every situation to more completely understand what they were investigating. The social construction of reality, basic sociology concepts, symbolic interaction, structural functionalism, conflict theory, postmodernism, the various middle-range theories, and so forth explain various parts of the whole. I trust that I am not alone in this trend. Each of my other courses was, of course, well grounded in theory—the SSM. When applied to personal experiences of both teacher and student, it does *not* bore; it enthuses.

Research Focus

The seeds of my research focus on the organizational and behavioral response to disasters were sown in graduate school. In other words, how do individuals, families, communities, and societies respond to disasters? What variables have an impact on whether the response and recovery are effective or not? Are the challenges we face in disaster those we expected? What myths govern our response, and how can they be overcome? How are the myths perpetuated? How should social structure be changed to effect the desired outcome?

A book (in three editions); a disaster scale for assessing catastrophic, major, and manageable disasters; a couple dozen journal articles; and several dozen professional papers later, I decided I had done everything I could toward my goal of understanding and changing social structure. In particular, I had sought to help move disaster planners from myth-based mitigation and response policies to an implementation of plans that address actual human needs. My grant-supported research (e.g., National Science Foundation funds) conducted throughout the world, such as Hurricane Katrina and the Christmas Day tsunami in South Asia, resulted in many speaking engagements. I was fortunate and enjoyed the opportunities.

One particular opportunity was very satisfying at the time. I was asked to write a white paper that was to be the basis for training activities the federal government was developing in the post-9/11 years. I was asked to serve on a panel and make a presentation to an audience that included undersecretaries from various departments, such as defense and state. The paper was essentially a review of the literature on organizational and behavioral response to disaster. It contrasted what had become known as the "disaster mythology" with the very different responses researchers found to commonly occur. The implications were clearly outlined, detailing which organizational and individual needs were being overlooked and the attention being paid to what was not necessary. For example, many fear looting, panic, and price gouging will occur and must be dealt with by law enforcement. These events rarely occur in a disaster, yet lives are risked when people refuse to evacuate to protect their property and avoid being swept away in panic.

I was making progress influencing political leaders (as well as major national news outlets, such as CNN). For decades mass media contributed to myth perpetuation. They inadvertently fostered the tradition of using valuable resources in the early hours of responding to disasters, often including activities that were unnecessary while not completing those that were vital to saving lives. Reporters were often found to believe in the mythology as well. My academic institution invited Robert Hager, formerly of NBC News, to campus and honored him with an award for his accuracy in disaster news reporting. This was both a tribute to Bob and a signal to other reporters.

I believe my speaking and consulting activities inadvertently contributed to Secretary Mike Brown of the Federal Emergency Management Agency (FEMA) during Hurricane Katrina commenting that "we didn't think they would loot." He had been severely criticized for not being more pro-active in getting food, water, diapers, and so forth into the Superdome in New Orleans, which was a major evacuation site. The inhabitants were largely left to fend for themselves. Since they quickly ran out of everything needed to support life, they were becoming angry, and some took what was needed from local closed stores. The lack of an effective local, state, or federal response to help the evacuees created the conditions for looting (or more accurately, appropriating necessary supplies to support life in an emergency—an ethical undertaking). President G. W. Bush said, "Brownie, you are doing a heck of a job here." Secretary Brown was, in fact, failing. He lacked a background in emergency management and apparently suffered from exposure to summarized research findings on disaster behavior, without the caveats. So close, yet so far away with respect to my goal of making changes.

Sociology of Disaster, Online Courses, M.S. in Emergency Management

Once again, my earlier life experiences provided fodder for research and teaching. I lived through Hurricane Hazel's impact on my childhood home, a flash flood in New Mexico where I had to climb a tree to save my life, our voluntary evacuation during the meltdown at Three Mile Island, and others. I was able to draw from these personal experiences to compare and contrast them with what disaster researchers and theorists found. My research interest led to creating a new course, sociology of disaster, which I eventually offered online along with several other courses, drawing students from my campus and as far away as South Korea. I was one of the first to experiment with online teaching. Like any approach, it has its advantages and disadvantages. I worked with several other faculty members to create the Center for Disaster Research and Education (CDRE) and was named its first director. We collaborated with student research assistants as we worked on our projects. We eventually created a totally online M.S. in disaster and emergency response. Words cannot describe how gratifying it was to work with students as junior colleagues. They accompanied us to various post-disaster sites throughout the United States and the world. We collaborated on conducting research, presenting papers, and coauthoring articles.

How gratifying it was to teach the sociology courses I wanted to teach, to be rewarded by students for doing so, and to feel that I changed lives. It was also gratifying to be doing the kind of research I wanted to be doing and have the necessary university and grant support.

Yet I also felt frustration. My original motivation for pursuing sociology (facilitating social change) seemed increasingly unattainable. Societal social structure, elite power and interests, and the socialization that worked against the best interests of those imprinted with it all combine to so effectively perpetuate Steinbeck's social problems. If we don't first become a toxic virus that destroys the species, then perhaps in time we will create the petri dish from which such a goal is more attainable in at least some aspects of the human condition. Of course, natural science informs that we have already entered the sixth extinction. A sobering thought; it reminds us of our limitations as humans. While we apparently created the conditions to effect this extinction, we seem to lack the ability, or the will, to avert it.

Retirement

I decided to retire when I realized I had dealt with one too many disasters involving death, injury, and destruction. I wrote all I had to say on the subject. I had made contributions. Now I wanted to do something else. Brainstorming resulted in a list of possible articles and books within sociology and beyond. I always loved being outdoors. Interest in wildlife was always great. For a change of pace, I began a study of dragonflies in general, and the ebony jewelwing in particular. After learning a fair amount through a literature review and field observations, I managed to publish an article on the mating behavior of the ebony jewelwing. The editors were gracious. I enjoyed being able to apply my training in one field to work in another.

I now write letters of recommendation for jobs and promotion. Two former students invited me to write the foreword to their first book. It was delightful to do for my students what my mentors had done for me.

Being a secular humanist, I find religious practices and beliefs of interest. I am currently working on a book addressing issues such as contradictions in religious writings and violence perpetuated by religious institutions, as well as an application of the SSM. Free thinkers might enjoy the finished product; practitioners within various flocks will not.

I am considering placing a version of my ten sociology courses online, providing free access to anyone teaching or any student taking these courses. I am currently uncertain whether to proceed, as a great deal of work is required and I would have to create it in a way that would not involve my regular input—a great departure from my online norm.

Losing one's identity and reference group is much more difficult than I anticipated. Dr. Fischer isn't really Dr. Fischer anymore. Mentoring is gone.

My wife is not as impressed with me as my students were. The American Sociological Association (ASA) Opportunities in Retirement Network (ORN) is a welcome development. Since becoming involved, I have reconnected with many former colleagues and students. Renewed involvement with the ASA and colleagues via ORN will certainly help with these retirement issues. We hope that our skills and experience will be useful in making new contributions to the discipline and its practitioners.

Closing Remarks

I now realize since beginning an undergraduate major in sociology, I live, breathe, and think sociology practically twenty-four hours a day. Why? I am sure I am not alone in this. Yes? I will answer for the benefit of readers who may not yet be sociologists. I can't imagine living life and thinking about the world around me without looking through the lenses that sociology provides for the many aha moments that result.

As a kid, I had hoped to be a scientist and perhaps write a book as well as travel during my future career. Growing up in a working-class family did not imbue me with certainty that these were attainable goals. I offer thanks to a family that encouraged me to learn, to a public education system that did a very good job educating me, and to a society that created the guaranteed student loan program making it possible for this blue-collar kid to go to college. I also thank a wonderful graduate school program and stipend, which made it possible for me to go on to graduate school; my graduate school mentors par excellence; and my publishers and colleagues. Most of all, I thank my students, who made it all worth it. Finally, I thank my wife and children for being my support and partners in my endeavors. Pinch me. It all came true. I did not wear a white lab coat, but I was a social scientist teaching and researching, publishing, traveling, and presenting the findings. Wow. Thank you, sociology!

Conclusion

Peter J. Stein

W hen Roz Darling asked me what I thought of a book of retirement stories written by retired sociologists, I was interested, and as we spoke, I could not help first thinking of my own life story.

I was born in Prague to a Jewish father and a Catholic mother just before World War II broke out, before my homeland, Czechoslovakia, had been invaded by Nazi Germany. My father's entire family was murdered in concentration camps in Poland and Belarus while he managed to survive Terezin in Czechoslovakia. The Nazis controlled the schools during the war, and I was frightened by German soldiers on the streets and photos of Adolf Hitler and Nazi flags in my classroom. My father returned in May 1945, and after an almost two-year wait (there was a small quota for all Eastern Europeans), we finally received an American visa. In 1948, eleven months after the communist coup, we were allowed to immigrate to the United States; we landed in New York Harbor the day Truman upset Dewey for the presidency.

Educated in public schools and at the City College of New York, which was then tuition free, I later found myself at Princeton for graduate work. From there it was a rich teaching career, a marriage to a lovely woman, one son, and now a grandson—for me, the epitome, in some ways, of my life. And fifty years after beginning my career in sociology, I find myself still teaching; now it is about the Holocaust in Europe and genocides around the world—something I knew from my parents' experience. I have joined the ranks of survivors who speak at schools and colleges as I try to explain the unexplainable.

The essays in this book fill me with pride for the accomplishments of the sociologists who have shared their professional and academic lives and the impact they made on the advancement of our discipline, their impressive research and publications, and the positive influence they had on their students' lives. The authors have used a life-course perspective in focusing on their experiences of growing up, schooling and careers in sociology, and retirement. It is clear that all experienced dramatic social change in their personal and professional lives and changes in the ways they think about and "do" sociology. Their essays suggest that lives, including retirement, can be understood only in the context of each author's social class, race, gender, and ethnicity/religion. These lives document how the personal and the professional intersect throughout the life course. I explore the following questions: How and why did these men and women become sociologists? What persons, circumstances, and turning points influenced their lives and careers? How did social class, race, gender, and religious affiliation influence personal and professional lives? What are their experiences of retirement?

Becoming Sociologists: Serendipity, Mentoring, Social Class, and Race

The essays indicate that our personal stories are strongly linked to what we study, what we write about, and how we teach sociology. Since fewer people grow up wanting to become sociologists than doctors, lawyers, entrepreneurs, or entertainers, how do some become sociologists? As noted in the Introduction, in his 2015 presentation at the American Sociological Association meetings in Chicago, Earl Babbie described his career as that of an "accidental sociologist." Twenty years earlier in 1995, Beth Hess, in a book about women in sociology, titled her chapter "An Accidental Sociologist," writing, "I am an accidental sociologist, an unintended consequence of chance events."[1]

Many authors write about encounters, often with a mentor or significant other, that led to an event that sooner or later led to a career in sociology. From a life-course perspective, these critical incidents are what Anselm Strauss called "turning points," incidents that modify one's self-understanding, a recognition that one is not the same as one used to be.[2] Michael Shanahan and Ross Macmillan observe that turning points can be

---

1. Beth H. Hess, "An Accidental Sociologist," in *Individual Voices, Collective Visions: Fifty Years of Women in Sociology*, ed. Ann Goetting and Sarah Fenstermaker (Philadelphia: Temple University Press, 1995), 37.
2. Anselm L. Strauss, *Qualitative Analysis for Social Scientists* (Cambridge: Cambridge University Press, 1987), 166.

abrupt or can turn lives around more gradually, producing change in both internal and external aspects of the life course.[3]

Many of the authors speak of mentors who shaped their future as sociologists. The importance of mentoring cannot be overstated. Most of the authors write about important teachers who helped and guided them as undergraduate and graduate students and in their own careers becoming mentors to their students in turn. For example, Edward Tiryakian notes that he was influenced by "a young instructor, Harold Garfinkel, whose courses were exciting ventures into what he later termed 'ethnomethodology.'"

The original mentors for the twenty authors and two editors represent a veritable who's who in American sociology over the past sixty to seventy years. They include Gordon Allport, Sarah Frances Anders, Jessie Bernard, Leonard Broom, Rose Coser, Arlene Kaplan Daniels, Cynthia Fuchs Epstein, Erving Goffman, Helen Gouldner, George Homans, Alex Inkeles, Suzanne Keller, Florence Kluckhohn, Seymour Martin Lipset, Wilbert Moore, Talcott Parsons, Peter Rossi, Tamotsu Shibutani, Neil Smelser, Pitirim Sorokin, Mel Tumin, and others.

In his essay, Bob Perrucci notes that both predictable transitions and discontinuities are shaped by unexpected events. There can be "gain by indirection," a positive outcome that was not pursued intentionally. For Perrucci, joining the marines led to receiving the Korean GI Bill benefits, which in turn allowed him to enter college. When he was ready to quit college, a chance encounter convinced him to stay and eventually to graduate.

For many the defining moment was their first sociology course. Joyce Williams, in her introductory class in sociology, knew it was to be her field of study. Hank Fischer found that serendipity led him to an introductory sociology class where he felt at home and later offered a path where he could make a difference by teaching others.

As a young assistant professor, Glen Elder found a "shelf of monographs on longitudinal studies" in the University of North Carolina library, which turned out to be a very important turning point for his research and publishing career.

A number of authors experienced feeling different, like outsiders in their communities. Some of these differences were dramatic; others were more subtle. Janet Giele identifies such differences in her study of how six men and women, all from one county in Ohio, became sociologists. She finds four common threads in their lives—families that were unconventional in some way within the community; families embedded in a thick community of informal connections, friendships, and social ties—a "friendly world"; individuals who were academic achievers exploring "questions that were

---

3. Michael J. Shanahan and Ross Macmillan, *Biography and the Sociological Imagination: Contexts and Contingencies* (New York: W. W. Norton, 2008).

personally important"; and individuals who occupied a somewhat marginal position with respect to community norms.

Among our authors there was considerable variation in social-class location. Many grew up in an economically solid, professional middle class and enjoyed the privileges of comfortable affluence; others had working-class parents or were raised by one parent. Wendell Bell was raised by a young mother who emphasized the values of hard work and early employment. Williams spent her formative years in rural Texas living on the "wrong side of the tracks" without indoor plumbing or electricity and from an early age worked at part-time jobs. She became the first person in her family to graduate from high school and to earn a B.A. and eventually a Ph.D.

Elizabeth Higginbotham grew up in a black urban working-class family that could not afford to send her to college. She had to find work to support herself, often experiencing hunger. Fortunately for her (in 1966) and for me (in 1955) and my coeditor (in 1965), the City College of New York (CCNY) was tuition free for high school graduates with a high average and satisfactory New York State Regents exams. My family would have been pressed to pay for my undergraduate education, but a four-year free ride supplemented with a scholarship made it feasible. Ironically I was on the faculty of Lehman College in 1976 when the CCNY Board of Higher Education imposed tuition.

Gender Differences across the Life Course

As reported in many studies, and as Roz Darling notes in the Introduction, there were major differences in the life-course experiences of men and women. Most of the women growing up in the 1950s and 1960s were socialized into traditional gender-role expectations—marrying early, bearing children, postponing career development while husbands pursued their professional training, and then moving with husbands to their new posts. Undergraduate and graduate courses reflected traditional sociology and included few works by black or women writers. As a sociology major at the University of Michigan, Debby Kaufman never had a woman instructor. When I studied sociology at Princeton, there were no female professors until the department hired Suzanne Keller; in 1968 she became the first woman in Princeton's 221-year history to receive tenure.

Elinore Lurie writes about the influence of geographic location on women's opportunities. In the Northeast there were many colleges and universities and more job opportunities; when she returned to the San Francisco Bay area, there were fewer academic jobs. Women experienced pressure to complete their families, but balancing child care, dissertation work, and further employment became difficult. There was little institutional support, and good child care was expensive and tough to find. As my research with Ellen

Galinsky shows, many professional women put together a "patchwork" of child care that periodically unraveled.[4] Most corporate and academic workplace cultures were unsupportive of addressing issues of work-family balance, and professional women learned not to talk about children at work.

Giele's chapter discusses two women, Giele and Joan Huber, who had professional and personal aspirations that were at odds with the expectations that women become well-educated homemakers and caregivers. Giele notes that "the principal struggle of my early adulthood was to reconcile my strong desire for independence and achievement with the desire to be a wife and mother." For Huber, her early marriage and the birth of two children, combined with her husband's career moves, delayed her graduate education until she was close to forty. Such tensions are echoed in virtually all the experiences of the women in *Journeys in Sociology*. In the Introduction, Roz notes that she identified with Debby Kaufman and Elinore Lurie, whose careers, like hers, took a backseat to those of their husbands. Kaufman's husband was hired by the English Department at Cornell, and she moved as an ABD (all but dissertation), prioritizing being a mother and an academic wife over her career. Tongue planted firmly in cheek, she writes, "I never took a sabbatical leave away from home."

It is clear that the women and men in these pages have, over the past fifty years, seen dramatic changes in how they thought about and did sociology, including how gender is studied and practiced. There is agreement that working conditions for women in academia and in sociology have improved with more opportunities, less overt sexism, and support for greater egalitarianism among employed spouses. One major change was achieved through organizing and action around race, ethnicity, inequality, and gender. For example, Lurie writes that in the early 1970s a Bay Area chapter of Sociologists for Women in Society (SWS) formed with research and paper presentations by members. It was also a place to socialize and share information. Nationally SWS advocated for better academic positions for women and battled against sexual harassment and overt sex discrimination.

Outsiders: Experiencing Anticommunism, Anti-Semitism, and Racism

Some authors had to cope with being political, social, and racial outsiders. Peter Hall was a "red diaper baby—an announced and attributed, hidden

---

4. Ellen Galinsky and Peter J. Stein, "Balancing Careers and Families: Research Findings and Institutional Responses," in *Marriage, Family, and Scientific Careers*, ed. Marsha Lakes Matyas, Lisa Baker, and Rae Goodell (Washington, DC: American Association for the Advancement of Science, 1990), 16.

and revealed, identity." He learned that what his parents did was dangerous, radical, and un-American—a heavy stigma for a teenager who was harassed for being a "commie kid." These early experiences shaped his sense of marginality and a drive to be critical and focus on inequality.

Fred Pincus writes about rebelling against the rigid communist orthodoxy of his parents and developing his own politics. Later, when he saw his FBI files, he found his name as an "enemy of the state" based on meetings attended, newspaper interviews, and his support of the Black Panthers in Baltimore. Others experienced anti-Semitism while growing up. Arthur Shostak's family lived in a section of Brooklyn that had only two Jewish families. His parents had to cope with the anti-Semitism in the neighborhood and in American culture in the 1930s: for example, the radio broadcasts of Father Charles Coughlin, whose weekly vitriolic anti-Semitism reached some ten million people; and the German American Bund pro-Nazi rally in Madison Square Garden. Shostak writes that this anxiety and marginality were central to his childhood and influenced his current writing in *Stealth Altruism*, stories of care of and by Jews in Nazi-occupied Europe. David Simon grew up in a rural area west of Chicago where he had to face anti-Semitism, endure teasing by gentile schoolmates, and be forced to sing Christmas carols in school and listen to New Testament readings by his teacher. These were powerful experiences of alienation and being treated as an outsider.

Elizabeth Higginbotham writes about the racism she experienced as both a student and faculty member. In a predominantly white graduate school she was one of a few African Americans, a token. Her important research on African American women was marginalized because she was studying a marginalized group whose members were blamed for their problems. A misunderstanding and misrepresentation of her work by colleagues revealed a racism and sexism that cost a deserved promotion.

Higginbotham and other academic women of color formed their own support system in a structure similar to SWS. They read each other's work and organized sessions for professional meetings to explore the intersection of class, race, and gender. They shared encounters of blatant and subtle racism, exclusionary practices and policies, and everyday microaggressions. In the process they collectively overcame the academic isolation they felt individually.

Early Work Experiences

For some, exposure to social inequality became an important predisposing factor to a career in sociology. Early work experiences led to an understanding of how people's lives are shaped by injustices of race, class, gender, and power. As a young man, Wendell Bell held jobs that demanded hard physical labor—working in a vineyard alongside an immigrant from India, a Sikh who wore a turban in very hot California; picking peaches with Mexican coworkers who helped him complete his work quota; and laboring on a bull gang with many Italian American workers hauling 100- to 150-pound sacks. Bell learned about their heartbreaking lives through stories that also revealed their shared common humanity. And as a young man, he also discovered that some coworkers were already burned out and defeated.

For Tuck Green, it was a high school summer job in a landscaping nursery that introduced him to the reality of social class. He was the only white worker doing low-paid work in a setting where higher-paid white workers were pitted against lower-paid black and Latino workers. This often resulted in racist comments by the white workers to get the hourlies to work faster. The experience made Green sympathetic to the plight of minority workers and aware of his own privilege as a white person. Similarly, Bob Perrucci learned a lot about ethnicity and street culture while immersed in a working-class Italian neighborhood in Queens, New York. He also learned about gambling, betting on horses, working with black people, and unions and the challenges of working class life.

Political and Social Activism

Sociologists became politically active in graduate schools throughout the country early in their careers and have maintained their activism into retirement. Berkeley was one such place—the decade of the heady 1960s was a breeding ground for activism. For example, David Armor participated in lunch counter sit-ins at local restaurants that would not serve black patrons and in hunger strikes and massive demonstrations against the House Un-American Activities Committee (HUAC) hearings in San Francisco. Gary Marx was active in many Berkeley-based political activities, including the Congress of Racial Equality, the free speech movement, and meetings with local Black Panther leaders. Tom Scheff tried his hand at unionizing a radiation lab on and off the Berkeley campus, movements that interested the FBI, which photographed his activities and interviewed coworkers and teachers.

Kaufman writes about developing women's studies programs at Cornell and Northeastern University, lobbying for undergraduate and graduate programs reflecting women's lives, challenging gendered pay inequity, and being very active in SWS. Corinne Kirchner's activism spanned several social movements of the 1970s and 1980s—civil rights, feminism, and the disability rights movement—and she saw the strong parallels between the causes and goals of these movements. Natalie Sokoloff focused her activism on educating women coming into and out of prison and helping those who suffered from domestic violence.

During her graduate years, Joyce Williams was involved in civil rights and the antiwar movement and continued her activism throughout her career. As an academic, she developed courses and wrote about unacknowledged sociologists, especially women and black sociologists, as well as sociology's history of activism. Tuck Green got involved in civil rights work and traveled south to register voters until beaten up by the police in rural Tennessee. As a young assistant professor, Fred Pincus was involved with a white group in Baltimore who organized to support local Black Panthers. As a young assistant professor at Rutgers, Douglass College, I helped organize teach-ins to protest the Vietnam War. A few years later I supported student demonstrations to save free tuition at Lehman College of CUNY.

Teaching Styles

Many who attended graduate school in the 1950s, 1960s, and 1970s received little or no training in how to teach undergraduates. There seemed to be an assumption that anyone capable of getting a Ph.D. was able to teach. Sociologists seeking success were told that research and publishing were the major goals to be pursued and the way to craft a career. Teaching, especially of undergraduates, was something that had to be done, part of the job, but one's focus should be on scholarship. Seasoned scholars sought to do as little teaching as possible to maximize time to pursue research and use grants to "buy out courses." The prestige of universities and teaching loads were inversely related—the higher the institution's prestige, the lower the teaching load.

Yet a number of our authors spent considerable time developing teaching styles that worked for their students and themselves. Hank Fischer states that he never viewed teaching as something that "got in the way of my research. I loved to teach." His teaching experiences were gratifying, and his goals were to make sociology easily understood, clear and "applicable to daily life and world issues." A number of his students went on to graduate school and are now colleagues in the discipline.

Some developed teaching styles beyond the traditional lecture. For example, Tom Scheff, during his first teaching job at Wisconsin, changed the seating so that students formed a circle and sat on the floor to see each other while he facilitated discussions. Later at Santa Barbara he became more of a coach and resource, making students responsible for part of the traditional teaching role. Classes became livelier and even exhilarating.

As a young assistant professor at Douglass College I experimented with new teaching styles, moving away from assigned seats to using circular seating to facilitate interaction. As with Scheff's experience, my students enjoyed the dialogue, sharing insights, community, and occasional humor. A problem occurred when a senior colleague would not evaluate such an unorthodox teaching style and asked me to prepare a conventional lecture so I could be properly observed.

Tuck Green became very active in developing his teaching to "kick the lecture habit." He was dissatisfied with the "sage-on-the-stage" model of teaching and experimented to get students more actively involved and applying what they learned to their lives and wider social structures. When he arrived at University of Wisconsin–Whitewater, he was challenged to get students to participate in class, so he devised a teaching method that got students to do the readings and discuss them critically.

These teaching innovations reflect research that emphasizes different ways of learning, including how knowledge can be applied. Green became active in and helped develop the ASA Section on Teaching and Learning, later becoming a deputy editor of *Teaching Sociology*. Our field has changed dramatically—now the ASA presents an annual award for Distinguished Contributions to Teaching. Fittingly, the 2009 recipient was Carla B. Howery, not only a staunch promoter of teaching sociology but also dedicated to the professional development of new and experienced faculty.

Retirement

In one of the few sociological books about retirement, *The Experience of Retirement*, Robert Weiss explores three major approaches to defining retirement—the economic, the psychological, and the sociological. The economic focuses on when people actually retire and how they deal with expenses and savings, investments, and available retirement support. He notes that people usually enter retirement uncertain of how well their finances will hold up. The psychological approach focuses on whether the person has established a retirement identity, which, however, may change as a person moves in and out of the labor force. He concludes that all retirees face two basic sociological challenges—how to manage the threat of marginality stemming from retirement and how to utilize its promise of freedom.[5] How we deal with these twin challenges strongly influences the quality of life in retirement.

But, as is clear from the essays in this book, social class, gender, race, religion, and health must be included to fully understand the relative freedom of one's life course and retirement. All of the authors have retired—some recently; others have been retired for ten, fifteen, even twenty years. Gerontologists advocate an active aging, and our authors have indeed led very active retirements of research, writing, and publishing articles and books; consulting and advising; teaching and volunteering. Giele's mainly retired sociologists continue to go to the office, do research, produce numerous publications, and enjoy the freedom that allows them to avoid unrewarding

---

5. Robert S. Weiss, *The Experience of Retirement* (Ithaca, NY: Cornell University Press, 2005).

duties and instead focus on what they most love to do. Similarly Bob Perrucci continues to go to his office daily to work with students and colleagues on research projects and papers for publication.

Many use their sociological skills in volunteer activities and social and political causes. Many have traveled, developed new interests, stayed connected, and enjoyed life. Some retirees move to be closer to family members or enjoy milder weather, and some move for economic reasons. For example, Art Shostak and his wife, longtime East Coasters, moved to a gateless, self-governing retirement community in Northern California. The move allowed them to be closer to three adult sons and four grandchildren living on the West Coast, to escape the extremes of Philadelphia weather, and to get involved in California's progressive social policies.

With the loss of a regular paycheck, the cost of participating in professional programs becomes an issue for many retired sociologists—lower membership rates and reduced fees for retirees set by the ASA help, but travel, hotel accommodations, and meals are costly. And there may be less energy to participate in meetings and fewer recognizable faces in attendance. However, retirees are freer to skip conferences and choose destinations more carefully.

Some have opted for phased retirement. For example, Wendell Bell chose to work at Yale about one-quarter of the time for four years and then to fully retire at age seventy. For another decade, he worked on the development of futures studies and at age eighty-eight wrote a memoir, *Memories of the Future*. Others have found phased retirement a useful way to decrease their institutional commitment, but they miss previous privileges—enjoying full departmental status and influence, having respect from colleagues, being part of what's happening—and thus feel that they have lost their voice and vote on departmental business, are left out of the loop, and are moving in the direction of being an outsider. And some sociologists definitely miss the classroom contact—Edward Tiryakian writes that "the hardest adjustment has been not teaching my regular departmental courses."

Most had plans for retirement, but some plans did not materialize as imagined, and some authors did not anticipate how difficult the transition would be. For example, during her first decade after retirement, Ellie Lurie and her husband wound up providing intensive informal support—caregiving and care management—for their parents. Williams's goal was completing a book on the early years of sociology, but funding research became more problematic, and she found it difficult to get work reviewed without a current institutional affiliation. She admits that, as a workaholic, she had little time to develop hobbies or leisure-time activities.

Many have had to cope with health issues that surfaced close to or in retirement, such as back problems, strokes, fatigue, falls and fractures, heart attacks, and various cancers. For most, there are more frequent doctor's appointments, an increasing regime of pills, and the discovery of pains in some unusual spots. At least five authors have been dealing with cancer. For example, Peter Hall writes movingly that the watershed moment of his retirement arrived in 2011 when he was diagnosed with duodenal cancer. He fully believed that he would survive, but life changed dramatically for him and his very supportive wife. For Kirchner, after suffering a stroke, many important functions such as getting around New York City—her home—socializing with friends, relatives, or students; writing and reading books and journals; and needing to use a computer became more difficult and took longer to accomplish.

People's experiences of retirement vary considerably. Some make the decision to retire with little hesitation, whereas others experience considerable angst. Natalie Sokoloff writes that she did not expect the experience of retirement to be so difficult and had to allow time to let the process play out. She experienced "multiple role losses" stemming from job loss, loss of institutional connections, and a move from a city that had been part of her cultural life to one she did not know as well.

Tom Scheff notes that a major advantage is that retirees have much more time free of professional duties. Importantly, retirement helped him phase out of departmental, campus, and disciplinary politics. He began to feel like a "different, liberated, more energetic person," realizing how much tension he had previously experienced. Other authors had similar feelings. But there are also costs attached to retirement. Because his university kept changing its early retirement program, Scheff took a hefty hit on his postretirement income by accepting an earlier offer. However, Santa Barbara allowed him to keep his office, parking, and other privileges. Perrucci's university was not so cooperative. He notes that a major problem is that one becomes a nonperson in the university community. Retirees are generally excluded from departmental and college e-mail lists and, more important, are not asked to serve on or advise ad hoc committees, which could benefit from retirees' knowledge and experience.

It is clear from these essays and the discussions at an earlier American Sociological Association Opportunities in Retirement Network (ASA-ORN) meeting in New York City that many colleges and universities do not support continued participation by retirees. Some retirees make side deals with their ex-employers, but most are on their own. This seems to be a structural issue, because, as Perrucci reports, "most universities don't have codified procedures for dealing with their retired members and making use of their skills and experience." Moreover, they do not develop procedures and policies for retired members that would utilize their skills and experience. This is similar to the inaction of many public and private organizations. Along with others, I studied succession planning among Fortune 500 corporations and among state and municipal governments, finding a woeful lack of planning for the retirement of employees at many levels and the loss of valuable information ("lost knowledge") among organizations.

More optimistically, Perrucci notes that "the current effort by ASA to reach out to retirees is a great example of how to draw on their knowledge and experiences." Fischer also writes that ASA-ORN is a welcome development through which he's reconnected with former colleagues and students. We hope that future ORN activities—and this book—continue to contribute to better and more meaningful experiences during the retirement phase of our colleagues' journeys in sociology.

Contributors

David J. Armor is professor emeritus of public policy in the School of Policy, Government, and International Affairs at George Mason University. He was research professor there from 1992 to 1999 and professor of public policy from 2000 to 2011. He taught graduate courses in multivariate statistics, social theory and policy, and program evaluation and served as director of the Ph.D. program in public policy between 2002 and 2005. Armor received a B.A. in mathematics and sociology from the University of California, Berkeley, in 1961 and a Ph.D. in sociology from Harvard University in 1966. He was an assistant professor and associate professor of sociology at Harvard from 1965 to 1972 and a visiting professor of sociology at the University of California, Los Angeles, in 1972–1973. He joined the Rand Corporation as a senior social scientist in 1973, where he conducted research in education, alcoholism, and military manpower until 1982, when he left to run for the U.S. Congress. In 1985 he was elected to the Los Angeles Board of Education. Armor subsequently served in the Department of Defense as principal deputy and acting assistant secretary of defense for force management and personnel from 1986 to 1989. He has conducted research and written widely on numerous public policy topics, including education, school desegregation, academic achievement, alcoholism, and military manpower. Selected publications include "The Evidence on Busing," *Alcoholism and*

Treatment, Forced Justice: School Desegregation and the Law, Maximizing Achievement, "Manpower Quality in the All-Volunteer Force," "Can NCLB Close Achievement Gaps?," and "Restoring a True Safety Net." Armor married his high school sweetheart, Marilyn Sells, in 1958; she is a watercolor artist with a studio at River District Arts in Sperryville, Virginia. Between 1995 and 2003, they established and operated Sharp Rock Vineyards, with a winery and bed and breakfast, near Sperryville. They have two children, Adrienne and Daniel, and four grandchildren, Tyler, Ashlee, Zackry, and Keelee. They divide their time between homes in Jeffersonton, Virginia, and Cape Cod, Massachusetts. David Armor can be contacted at darmor@gmu.edu.

 **Wendell Bell** holds a Ph.D. from the University of California, Los Angeles, and is professor emeritus of sociology and a fellow of the Koerner Center at Yale University. He joined the Yale faculty in 1963; served as chair of the Department of Sociology; helped found the Program (now Department) of African American Studies; headed the Comparative Sociology Training Program, which required students to do research abroad; and was a senior research scientist in the Center for Comparative Research from 2000 to 2005. Before coming to Yale, he served on the faculties of Stanford University, Northwestern University, and UCLA. He was a fellow at the Center for Advanced Study in the Behavioral Sciences at Stanford University in 1963–1964 and a visiting fellow at the Institute of Advanced Studies at the Australian National University in 1985. During World War II he served as a naval aviator. His early research was on the social areas of American cities. Later he studied political and social change in the new states of the Caribbean and served as president of the Caribbean Studies Association from 1979 to 1980. For the last four decades, Bell has worked mostly on the sociology of the future. He is the author or co-author of more than 250 articles, chapters, and book reviews plus ten books, including *Social Area Analysis, Jamaican Leaders, The Democratic Revolution in the West Indies,* and the two-volume *Foundations of Futures Studies* (which the Association of Professional Futurists selected in 2008 as being among the ten most important futures books of all time). His latest book is a memoir, *Memories of the Future.* In 2011 the British journal *Futures* devoted a special issue to his work. In 2005 the World Futures Studies Federation awarded Bell a Lifetime Achievement Award in recognition of his contributions to futures studies. And in 2014 the Futures Research Committee of the International Sociological Association recognized his contributions to a forward-looking sociology with an Inaugural Lifetime Achievement Award. Wendell Bell can be contacted at wendell.bell@yale.edu.

Rosalyn Benjamin Darling was born in New York City in 1946 and received her Ph.D. in sociology from the University of Connecticut in 1978. She began her teaching career at Central Connecticut State University. After moving to Pennsylvania in 1977, she founded and served for fifteen years as the executive director of Beginnings, an agency in Johnstown that provided services to families of young children with disabilities. In that capacity, she founded and was the first president of the Early Intervention Providers Association of Pennsylvania. She also served on the boards of several national disability organizations and the Commission on Applied and Clinical Sociology. From 1994 until her retirement in 2008, she was a professor of sociology at Indiana University of Pennsylvania (IUP), where she was also the coordinator of the master's and doctoral programs. She is currently professor emerita at IUP and a visiting scholar at the University of North Carolina at Chapel Hill. A medical sociologist and symbolic interactionist, Darling is the author of ten books and numerous articles and chapters, mostly on the sociology of disability. Her first book was *Families against Society*, and her most recent book, *Disability and Identity*, written after her retirement, was selected as a *Choice* best academic book of the year. She lives in Pittsboro, North Carolina, with her husband, Jon, and has two sons and three grandchildren. Among her many other activities in retirement, she started and continues to organize PORCH Fearrington, which collects more than a ton of food every month for the local food pantry, and Chatham Voices for Justice, a progressive grassroots organization. Roz Darling can be contacted at rdarling@iup.edu.

Glen H. Elder Jr., Howard W. Odum Distinguished Research Professor of Sociology at the University of North Carolina at Chapel Hill, is a prominent figure in the development of life-course theory, methods, and research. He studies individuals and groups of people through interviews and other measurements across different times in their lives with the objective of investigating how changing environments influenced them. Over his career he has served on the faculties of the University of California, Berkeley; Cornell; and the University of North Carolina at Chapel Hill. His website provides additional details about his work: http://elder.web.unc. Glen Elder can be contacted at glen_elder@unc.edu.

Henry Fischer is professor emeritus at the Department of Sociology and Anthropology and director of the Center for Disaster Research and Education (CDRE) at Millersville University of Pennsylvania. Thirty years of experience conducting research into behavioral and organizational response to disaster has resulted in the production of a body of work that includes the following: designing and teaching ten graduate and undergraduate courses; mentoring students who are now colleagues in the discipline; presentation of more than three dozen papers at professional conferences; publication of two dozen scholarly journal articles, three books, and two monographs; consulting for Research Planning, Inc./Department of Defense and for the Office of Emergency Management/Justice Department on TOPOFF 2 (a national exercise to combat terrorism); and appearances on CNN and MSNBC to discuss high-consequence-event issues. Professional memberships have been held in the International Sociological Association, International Research Committee on Disasters (IRCD), European Sociological Association, American Sociological Association, and International Association of Emergency Managers. Service positions have included editor of IRCD's official newsletter, *Unscheduled Events*; editor of IRCD's online journal of reviews, *Contemporary Disaster Review*; and webmaster for the online version of *International Journal of Mass Emergencies and Disasters*. He created a multidisciplinary minor in environmental hazards and emergency management, an online master's degree in emergency management, and the CDRE, all of which involved eighteen faculty from across the university as well as many student research assistants. Funding sources included the Federal Emergency Management Agency, Pennsylvania Emergency Management Agency, Natural Hazards Center (University of Colorado), and National Science Foundation. Hank Fischer can be contacted at hankfischer@msn.com.

Janet Zollinger Giele holds an A.B. from Earlham College and a Ph.D. from Harvard University. She is professor emerita of sociology, social policy, and women's studies at Brandeis University. She was the founding director of the Family and Children's Policy Center in the Heller School for Social Policy and Management and acting dean of the Heller School. In the 1960s she taught at Wellesley College and in the 1970s was a Bunting Fellow at Radcliffe and principal consultant to the Ford Foundation Task Force on Women. She has received grants and fellowships from the National Science Foundation, National Institute on Aging, Lilly Endowment, Rockefeller Foundation, and Ford Foundation.

In 2000 she was honored by Radcliffe with the Graduate Society Medal. The author or editor of ten books, her special areas of interest are women's changing roles, methods of life-course research, and sociology of the family and family policy. Since 1976, when she joined the faculty of the Heller School, she has directed over thirty doctoral dissertations and is currently writing a guidebook on doctoral research and the earmarks of a good dissertation. Outside the academy, she is active in her local church (as warden and choir member) and town affairs (as Town Meeting member; founding president of Wellesley Neighbors, a "village" for midlife and retired adults) and as a leader in creating the first Neighborhood Conservation District in Wellesley. Janet Giele can be contacted at giele1@brandeis.edu.

Charles S. (Tuck) Green III passed away in 2016. He was born in New York City in 1937 and raised in Princeton, New Jersey. He held an undergraduate degree from the University of Virginia and master's and Ph.D. degrees in organizational behavior from the New York State School of Industrial and Labor Relations at Cornell. He spent four years as an applied sociologist in state mental hospitals in the late 1960s. His academic career was spent at the University of Virginia and the University of Wisconsin–Whitewater, from which he retired in 2002. His interests included the sociology of the arts, the sociology of teaching and learning, applied sociology, complex organizations, and social movements and collective behavior.

Peter Mandel Hall is affiliate professor of sociology at Colorado State University (CSU) and professor emeritus of sociology and education at the University of Missouri. He received his Ph.D. from the University of Minnesota in 1963 and has also taught at University of Iowa; University of California, Santa Barbara; and York University (Canada). Hall is a charter member of the Society for the Study of Symbolic Interaction and received its George Herbert Mead Award for career contributions in 1994. He is currently a coeditor of the *Sociological Quarterly*. He is working now on time, space, and the environment with a focus on energy and spatial inequality. His past work has been on metapower, social organization, inequality, and the policy process. Hall is currently affiliated with the School of Global Environmental Sustainability and the Center for Research on Disaster and Risk Analysis at CSU and the Millennium Alliance for Humanity and the Biosphere at Stanford University. Peter Hall can be contacted at Peter.Hall@colostate.edu.

Elizabeth Higginbotham holds a Ph.D. and is professor emerita at the University of Delaware, where she had worked as a professor of sociology with affiliations with women's studies and Black American studies since 1998. She spent much of her career at the University of Memphis in the Department of Sociology and at the Center for Research on Women, where, in addition to research and teaching, she organized curriculum transformation workshops in the 1980s and 1990s. Along with Bonnie Thornton Dill and Lynn Weber, Higginbotham was awarded the American Sociological Association (ASA) Jessie Bernard Award and the ASA Distinguished Contributions to Teaching Award in 1993. She is author of *Too Much to Ask: Black Women in the Era of Integration*; coauthor with Margaret Andersen of *Race and Ethnicity in Society: The Changing Landscape*; and coeditor with Mary Romero of *Women and Work: Exploring Race, Ethnicity, and Class*. Higginbotham is widely recognized as a major scholar of intersection of race, class, and gender. Elizabeth Higginbotham can be contacted at ehiggin@udel.edu.

Debra Kaufman is a professor emerita and Matthews Distinguished University Professor at Northeastern University. She was the founding director of the Women's, Gender and Sexuality Studies Program and one of the founding directors of the Jewish Studies Program. Her award-nominated books include *Rachel's Daughters* and *Achievement and Women* (coauthored with Barbara Richardson; C. Wright Mills Award, honorable mention). Her other publications that relate to her current work on gender, Jewish identity, and post-Holocaust narratives include the article "Demographic Storytelling" in *Contemporary Jewry*; the edited volume *From the Protocols of Zion to the Holocaust Denial Trials: Challenging the Media, the Law and the Academy*; and a special edition of *Contemporary Jewry* titled "Women, Scholarship and the Holocaust." She is currently working on a manuscript tentatively titled "Post-Holocaust Jewish Identity Narratives: What Do We Talk about When We Talk about the Holocaust?" She has been a visiting scholar at the Center for Hebrew and Jewish Studies, Oxford University; the Murray Research Center at Radcliffe College; and the Wellesley Center for Women at Wellesley College and has been a guest lecturer at universities around the world, including Frei University in Germany, where she conducted a seminar on post-Holocaust narratives among young adults in the United States and Israel. Debby Kaufman can be contacted at debrarkaufman@gmail.com.

 **Corinne Kirchner** received her B.A. in sociology from Barnard College in 1957 and a Ph.D. from Columbia University in 1987. Much of her career was spent conducting social research, largely at Columbia University: first at the Bureau of Applied Social Research, then at the Ford Foundation, and then back to Columbia at the School of Public Health, where she joined the Sociomedical Sciences Department. She taught there as an adjunct lecturer, both before and after she moved to the American Foundation for the Blind (AFB) as director of social research for thirty years. AFB has created the Corinne Kirchner Research Award to encourage more social research in the blindness and low-vision field. After retiring from AFB, she began to focus on sociolinguistics. While in the AFB role, she became active in the Society for Disability Studies, serving on its board and as president, then as coeditor of the *Disability Studies Quarterly*. She has also been active in the American Sociological Association, American Association for Public Opinion Research, and American Public Health Association. She has two daughters, born before she graduated from college; they have excelled in their respective careers and have made Corinne a grandmother six times and, recently, a great-grandmother. Corinne Kirchner can be contacted at ck12@cumc.columbia.edu.

 **Elinore E. Lurie** received her Ph.D. in sociology from Columbia University in 1970. She specialized in gerontology and in research on services to the elderly throughout her career. Lurie taught and conducted research at the University of California, San Francisco, in mental health, aging, community-based services, and new professional roles for nurses. She also conducted evaluation research in community-based settings, such as agencies that serve the elderly, and has published in these areas. She has also been active as a volunteer in both national professional organizations and local agencies in the field of aging. She lives with her husband in San Francisco, California. Elinore Lurie can be contacted at elinore.lurie@gmail.com.

 Gary T. Marx is professor emeritus at Massachusetts Institute of Technology. He received his Ph.D. from the University of California, Berkeley, and has also taught there, at Harvard, and at the University of Colorado. He has written books and articles for academic and popular sources dealing with race and ethnicity, collective behavior and social movements, law and society, and surveillance studies, most recently in *Windows into the Soul: Surveillance and Society in an Age of High Technology*. Additional information and articles are available at www.garymarx.net. Gary Marx can be contacted at gtmarx@mit.edu.

 **Robert Perrucci** is professor emeritus of sociology at Purdue University. He joined the faculty in 1962, was promoted to full professor in 1967, and served as department head from 1978 to 1987. He was research director for three years of the study of the engineering profession sponsored by the National Science Foundation (NSF) and conducted by the American Society for Engineering Education. He was a Simon senior research fellow at the University of Manchester, England, in 1969. He has received major research grants from the NSF, National Institute of Mental Health, and Sloan Foundation. He is author or editor of nineteen books and more than ninety book chapters and research articles in leading journals, including five in the *American Sociological Review*, on topics related to work and occupations, complex organizations, and the impact of the global economy on workers, communities, and structures of inequality. He has served as editor of *Social Problems*, the *American Sociologist*, and *Contemporary Sociology* and associate editor of the *American Sociological Review*. He has held elected positions as president of the Society for the Study of Social Problems and the North Central Sociological Association and chair of the Organizations and Occupations Section of the American Sociological Association. Two of his books have received the Scholarly Achievement Award from the North Central Sociological Association, and he has received Distinguished Alumnus Awards from the State University of New York at Cortland and Purdue University. In 2005, he received the Lee Founders Lifetime Achievement Award from the Society for the Study of Social Problems, and in 2008, the J. Milton Yinger Award for a Lifetime Distinguished Career from the North Central Sociological Association. Bob Perrucci can be contacted at perruccr@purdue.edu.

 **Fred L. Pincus** is professor emeritus of sociology at the University of Maryland, Baltimore County. He received a bachelor's degree in psychology from University of California, Los Angeles (UCLA), in 1964. He received his Ph.D. is sociology from UCLA in 1969 and spent his entire academic career at the University of Maryland, Baltimore County. He has published three books—*Race and Ethnic Conflict: Contending Views on Prejudice Discrimination and Ethnoviolence*, coedited with Howard J. Ehrlich; *Reverse Discrimination: Dismantling the Myth*; and *Understanding Diversity: An Introduction to Class, Race, Gender, Sexual Orientation and Disability*—and a research monograph, *Bridges to Opportunity: Are Community Colleges Meeting the Needs of Minority Students?* In addition to writing dozens of scholarly articles, he was on the editorial committee of *New China* magazine, published

by the U.S.–China People's Friendship Association; wrote many articles for the *Guardian*, the major U.S. radical weekly newspaper in the 1960s, 1970s, and 1980s; and served as a member of the board of directors of Research Associates Foundation, which gives mini-grants to activist groups in the Baltimore area. He lives in Baltimore with his wife, Natalie J. Sokoloff, and is writing a memoir. Fred Pincus can be contacted at pincus@umbc.edu.

 **Thomas Scheff** is professor emeritus at the University of California, Santa Barbara, and author of many books and articles. His principal interests are emotions, causes of destructive conflict, and more integration of disciplines. He believes that the current division into separate fiefdoms is a disaster. His book *Emotions, the Social Bond and Human Reality: Part/Whole Analysis* is an approach to integrating the social sciences, particularly sociology and psychology, and ending separation from the humanities. As in the physical sciences, advances and practical applications both depend increasingly on integration. His most recent book concerns the emotions implied in pop-song lyrics: *What's Love Got to Do with It?* Tom Scheff can be contacted at scheftj@cox.net.

 **Arthur Shostak** was born in 1937 and raised in Brooklyn, New York. He earned a B.S. in industrial and labor relations at Cornell University in 1958 and a Ph.D. in sociology at Princeton in 1961. After teaching in the Wharton School of the University of Pennsylvania from 1961 through 1967, he joined the sociology faculty at Drexel University, from which he retired in 2003. He also taught as an adjunct professor from 1975 to 2000 at the AFL-CIO Meany Center for Labor Studies. He was awarded grants by the National Science Foundation, Social Science Research Council, Wilson Foundation, and others. He introduced courses in futuristics, race and ethnic relations, social implications of twentieth-century technology, and urban sociology. He headed the Pennsylvania Sociological Society, the American Sociological Association (ASA) Section on Sociological Practice, and was active in the Clinical Sociological Society, Eastern Sociological Society, and the Society for the Study of Social Problems. He authored, edited, or coedited thirty-four books, including an ASA teacher's guide to utopian literature, the first-ever study of men in abortion clinic waiting rooms, and several books dealing with blue-collar life and labor innovations. In 2002 he was awarded the ASA Annual Distinguished Award in Sociological Practice and also a Drexel Lifetime Achievement Award. In retirement he has written three books, two urging the use of futuristics in K–12 schooling and a

third exploring the forbidden sharing of care by Jewish victims throughout the Holocaust. His more than 165 articles range widely, and he continues to add to them. He lives with his wife, Lynn Seng, in a retirement community (Oakmont) outside Santa Rosa, California, and enjoys spending time with four sons and their four children. Art Shostak can be contacted at arthurshostak@gmail.com.

 **David R. Simon** earned a B.A. in political science from the University of Illinois in 1966, an M.A. in diplomacy from the University of Kentucky's Patterson School of Diplomacy in 1967, and a Ph.D. in sociology from Rutgers University in 1975. He was awarded a postdoctoral fellowship in alcohol abuse in 1983–1984 from the University of California, Berkeley, School of Public Health. Simon is the author of nine books, including *Elite Deviance*. He is also the author of some fifty-six refereed articles, book chapters, and book reviews. He has published articles in a number of periodicals, including the *Los Angeles Times* and the *Progressive* magazine. He has taught at a number of institutions, including Rutgers University, UC Berkeley, the University of North Florida, San Diego State University, and San Jose State University. David Simon can be contacted at simondrdrs@gmail.com.

 **Natalie J. Sokoloff** is professor emerita of sociology and has worked at John Jay College of Criminal Justice and the Graduate Center of the City University of New York for four decades. She taught courses on women, crime, and justice; race, class, and gender intersectionalities; imprisonment and empowerment; and domestic violence. Of the seven books and more than fifty articles she published, two of the most critically acclaimed are *The Criminal Justice System and Women: Offenders, Prisoners, Victims, and Workers*, coauthored with Barbara Raffel Price, and *Domestic Violence at the Margins: Race, Class, Gender, and Culture*. She is on the board of directors of Alternative Directions, Inc., a prisoner reentry program for women in Maryland, as well as the Goucher College Prisoner Education Program at the Maryland Correctional Institution for Women and the Jessup Correctional Institution for Men. Sokoloff has been honored with the Outstanding Teaching Award at John Jay College and was awarded two distinctions from the American Society of Criminology's Division on Women and Crime: the Distinguished Scholar and Lifetime Achievement Awards. Natalie Sokoloff can be contacted at nsokoloff@jjay.cuny.edu.

Peter J. Stein was born in Prague, Czechoslovakia. He came with his parents to the United States three years after the end of World War II and nine months after the communist coup d'état. He attended public schools, graduated from the City College of New York, and received his Ph.D. in sociology from Princeton University in 1969. He is professor emeritus at William Paterson University, where he served as professor, director of graduate studies, and codirector of the Genocide and Holocaust Studies Center. Until his retirement, Stein was a senior researcher at the University of North Carolina Institute on Aging in Chapel Hill, focusing on older workers and age discrimination. He served on several American Sociological Association and Society for the Study of Social Problems committees and was vice president of Eastern Sociological Society. With Beth Hess and Liz Markson, he authored six editions of *Sociology*; with Markson he authored *Social Gerontology: Issues and Prospects* and other books and articles about work-family issues, singlehood, marriage, aging, older workers, and caregiving. Stein was a keynoter, speaking about the economics of aging at the North Carolina Governor's Conference on Aging, and he edited *Report of the Forum on North Carolina's Aging Workforce*. For the past eight years he has been presenting talks and workshops at schools and colleges about genocide and has served as a scholar for the North Carolina Council on the Holocaust. He is currently working on a memoir of his childhood. Stein, with his wife, Michele, has been active in North Carolina's Special Olympics, Moral Monday protests, and local organizations that feed the homeless. They make frequent trips to Washington, D.C., to visit their son and his wife and to enjoy grandson Jackson. Peter Stein can be contacted at steinpeterj@gmail.com.

Edward A. Tiryakian holds a Ph.D. from Harvard and is professor emeritus of sociology at Duke University. Before a long career at Duke, he taught at Princeton and Harvard. Past president of the American Society for the Study of Religion and of the International Association of French-Speaking Sociologists, he has written extensively on the sociology of religion, sociological theory, and the history of sociology. He is active in several sections of the American Sociological Association, and his current research is on the sociology of genocide and modernity. Ed Tiryakian can be contacted at durkhm@soc.duke.edu.

 **Joyce E. Williams** grew up in the Central Texas area and until retirement lived and worked in Texas. She earned a B.A. from Mary Hardin-Baylor College, an M.A. from Southern Methodist University, and a Ph.D. from Washington University, St. Louis, all in sociology. She taught at Mary Hardin-Baylor, Arlington State College, Trinity University, and Texas Woman's University, where she also served ten years as department chair before retiring in 2003. Her areas of specialization include race/ethnic group relations, inequality, and, more recently, the history of American sociology. In addition to journal articles, she is the author of four books: *Black Community Control, The Second Assault, Lest We Forget,* and *Settlement Sociology in the Progressive Years.* Joyce Williams can be contacted at je25williams@msn.com.

Index

Acker, Joan, 152
Activism 3, 4, 137, 139, 141, 161, 162, 169, 212–213
Addams, Jane, 139
Adolescence, 10, 20, 42, 44, 59, 120
African Americans, 4, 155, 173, 185, 187, 211. *See also* Blacks
Aging: active, 214; as a lifelong process, 45; sociology of, 2; study of, 79–80, 82, 83, 84, 85; teaching on, 94, 95, 96, 160; workshops on, 178
Alcoholism, 145–146, 183, 199
Alienation, 24, 182, 185, 211
Allport, Gordon W., 21, 23, 50, 144, 208
Altruism, 27, 116, 211
American Association of University Professors (AAUP), 64, 114
American imperialism, 164, 171
American Journal of Sociology, 104, 152
American Psychological Association, 83
The American School Counselor (Armor), 144
American Society on Aging, 86
American Sociological Association (ASA): Medical Sociology Section of, 86; meetings of, 23, 25, 26, 44, 97, 114, 135, 207; membership in, 85, 157, 215; officers in, 51, 54; Opportunities in Retirement Network (ORN), 1, 2, 3, 37, 117, 205, 216, 217; Sociological Practice Section of, 83; and support groups, 87; Teaching and Learning Section of, 106–107, 214
American Sociological Review (*ASR*), 36, 37, 55, 56, 104
American Sociologist, 37, 129, 135
American Sociology (Vidich and Lyman), 137
Americans with Disabilities Act (ADA), 92–93, 96
Anders, Sarah Frances, 132, 133, 208
Annual Review of Sociology, 43
Anti-Semitism, 112, 159, 210, 211
Aoki, Richard, 123, 126
Applied sociology, 78, 107, 201
Arendt, Hannah, 182
Arnold, Regina, 191
Association Internationale des Sociologues de Langue Française (AISLF), 25, 26
Association of Black Sociologists (ABS), 84
Autoethnography, 169, 170

Babbie, Earl, 3, 207
Balandier, Georges, 25
Baltzel, E. Digby, 117